DECONSTRUCTING THE HIGH LINE

DECONSTRUCTING THE HIGH LINE

Postindustrial Urbanism and the Rise of the Elevated Park

EDITED BY CHRISTOPH LINDNER
AND BRIAN ROSA

RUTGERS UNIVERSITY PRESS
New Brunswick, Camden, and Newark, New Jersey, and London

Library of Congress Cataloging-in-Publication Data
Names: Lindner, Christoph, 1971– editor of compilation. | Rosa, Brian, 1982– editor of compilation.
Title: Deconstructing the High Line : postindustrial urbanism and the rise of the elevated park / edited by Christoph Lindner and Brian Rosa.
Description: New Brunswick, New Jersey : Rutgers University Press, [2017] | Includes bibliographical references and index.
Identifiers: LCCN 2016032169| ISBN 9780813576466 (hardcover : alk. paper) | ISBN 9780813576459 (pbk.) | ISBN 9780813576473 (e-book : epub) | ISBN 9780813576480 (e-book : web pdf)
Subjects: LCSH: High Line (New York, N.Y. : Park) | Urban parks—New York (State)—New York. | Land use—New York (State)—New York. | City planning—New York (State)—New York. | Railroads, Elevated—Remodeling for other use.
Classification: LCC F128.65.H54 D43 2016 | DDC 307.1/21609747—dc23
LC record available at https://lccn.loc.gov/2016032169

A British Cataloging-in-Publication record for this book is available from the British Library.

∞ The paper used in this publication meets the requirements of the American National Standard for Information Sciences—Permanence of Paper for Printed Library Materials, ANSI Z39.48–1992.

www.rutgersuniversitypress.org

Manufactured in the United States of America

CONTENTS

FIGURES AND TABLES

FIGURES

TABLES

HIGH LINE TIMELINE

1934 Inauguration of the elevated West Side Line, built to replace a mid-nineteenth-century street-level railway and to separate the railway from surface-level traffic.

1960 As a result of decentralization and the increasing market dominance of trucking over freight railways, Saint John's Park Terminal is sold by New York Central Railroad, and the southernmost section of the viaduct is dismantled by the city.

1976 The West Side Line viaduct is bought by the federal government's Consolidated Rail Corporation (Conrail).

1980 Rail service ceases on the West Side Line viaduct.

1983 Conrail begins efforts to divest from the High Line.

Congress passes the National Trails System Act, which leads to the conversion of disused railway rights-of-way to recreational "rails-to-trails" projects.

Architect Steven Holl proposes to construct housing and public space atop the viaduct.

1989 Chelsea Property Owners, a consortium of landowners, files an application with the Interstate Commerce Commission requesting an adverse abandonment order, which would require Conrail to demolish the viaduct and allow them to develop on land beneath the viaduct.

1991 Rockrose Development Corporation demolishes the southern portion of the viaduct to build 265 housing units, leaving the viaduct in its current form, ending on Gansevoort Street in the Meatpacking District.

1993 Promenade Plantée is completed in Paris, a linear park built above a disused viaduct that served as an inspiration for the creation of the High Line.

1999 CSX Transportation acquires Conrail and works with the Regional Planning Association to strategize on the future use of the viaduct.

Friends of the High Line (FHL) is founded by Joshua David and Robert Hammond after meeting at a community hearing in Chelsea on the future of the former West Side Line viaduct. The designation of the structure as the "High Line" came from a local nickname for the viaduct dating back to the 1980s.

2001 Photographer Joel Sternfeld completes a visual survey of the landscape atop the High Line, published as a book titled *Walking the High Line*, which was used to generate support and funding for the FHL.

2002–2003 FHL conducts a study to examine the feasibility of converting the viaduct into an elevated linear park and opens a design competition for imagining the future of the structure.

2004 As a result of the design competition, FHL and the City of New York select the landscape architecture firm James Corner Field Operations, the architecture and design studio Diller Scofidio + Renfro, and the garden designer Piet Oudolf.

City of New York commits $50 million to establish the High Line park.

2005 City of New York assumes ownership of the High Line viaduct from CSX.

City approves zoning for the Special West Chelsea District (an area bound by 10th and 11th Avenues from West 30th Street to West 16th Street) to release height restrictions, encourage residential and commercial development, and facilitate the reuse of the High Line.

Federal Surface Transportation Board issues a certificate of interim trail use, allowing the city to remove most of the line from the national railway system.

2006 Groundbreaking begins on the first, southernmost section of the park from Gansevoort Street to West 20th Street.

2009 Phase 1 completed and opened to the public.

2011 Phase 2, from West 20th Street to West 30th Street in West Chelsea, is completed and opened to the public.

CSX Transportation agrees in principle to donate the northernmost section of the viaduct, from 30th to 34th Streets, to the city. Related Companies, owner of the development rights to the West Side Rail Yards, agrees not to tear down the 10th Avenue spur of the elevated railway.

2012 Groundbreaking begins on Hudson Yards, a $20 billion, twenty-eight-acre mixed-use redevelopment project at the northern tip of the High Line jointly funded by the City of New York, the State of New York, and the Metropolitan Transit Authority, partially over the West Side Rail Yard, to stimulate further development along the Hudson River.

2014 Phase 3 of the High Line, from West 30th Street to Hudson Yards at West 34th Street, is completed and opened to the public.

2015 New home of the Whitney Museum of American Art, designed by Renzo Piano, is constructed at the southern tip of the High Line at Gansevoort Street in the Meatpacking District.

Extension of the 7 Subway Line to Hudson Yards opens at 34th Street and 11th Avenue.

2016 10 Hudson Yards, the first tower completed in the Hudson Yards development, opens in May. The tower is built directly over the High Line, with the pedestrian promenade running through its base.

2017 Projected construction of the Spur, an extension from Phase 3 of the High Line into Hudson Yards.

DECONSTRUCTING THE HIGH LINE

INTRODUCTION

From Elevated Railway to Urban Park

BRIAN ROSA AND CHRISTOPH LINDNER

An innovative public promenade created atop a disused elevated railway in Manhattan, the High Line is recognized worldwide as being among the most iconic urban landmarks and public spaces of the early twenty-first century. It has stimulated public interest in landscape design while simultaneously reintegrating an industrial relic into the everyday life of New York City. As many critics and journalists have noted, through its elevation from the street below, the High Line provides a unique experience of being at once in, and separate from, the city (see chapter 6, by Christoph Lindner). Its architectural and horticultural design, arts commissions, and cultural programming further offer unique, immersive experiences while encouraging an appreciation of the historic urban landscape in a zone restricted exclusively to pedestrians. The park offers views onto former industrial districts and the waterfront, dramatizes the creative reappropriation of disused infrastructure, and revives the nostalgic, faded pastime of the urban promenade.

Since opening in 2009, with second and third branches completed in 2012 and 2014, this unique greenway has attracted unprecedented numbers of visitors and has stimulated investment and property development in

Manhattan's West Side. The High Line is widely celebrated as a monument to neighborhood activism, an innovative example of the adaptive reuse of urban infrastructure, and cutting-edge ecological design. Accordingly, the park has inspired a proliferation of similar initiatives to redesign infrastructural and postindustrial landscapes in cities throughout the world.

Apart from a handful of newspaper and magazine articles and some recent scholarly publications, a select few of which are republished in this volume, the vast majority of initial commentary on the High Line has been celebratory in tone, treating the park as an unmitigated success in terms of producing new public space, raising surrounding property values, and increasing property tax revenue for the city (Levere 2014). Indeed, the High Line has stimulated public interest in urban design and landscape architecture in a remarkable way, leading to claims that it is "America's most original urban park" owing to its "revolutionary landscape, romantically post-industrial and progressive in its embrace of emerging ecologies" (LaFarge 2014: 21). For the most part, the High Line has been treated as a quintessential "win-win" scenario: a new public open space creating—through the perseverance of neighborhood activists, philanthropists, and the administration of Mayor Michael Bloomberg—a new way of experiencing the city and providing newly accessible green space, as well as stimulating revitalization in a district that was seen by some as run-down, reincorporating a disused structure into the urban fabric in the process. The transformative effects of the High Line are undeniable.

However, as the impact of the High Line has become clearer in recent years, including a proliferation of high-end signature architecture projects lining its corridors, some journalists, bloggers, and scholars have become increasingly critical of the ways that the elevated park has impacted its surroundings (Cataldi et al. 2011; Duany and Talen 2013; Littke et al. 2015; Millington 2015; Rothenberg and Lang 2015). The blogger writing under the pseudonym Jeremiah Moss, for example, published a high-profile rebuke of the High Line in a 2012 opinion editorial in the *New York Times.* Calling the High Line "Disney World on the Hudson," Moss lamented that it had become "a tourist-clogged catwalk and a catalyst for some of the most rapid gentrification in the city's history," and that it was part of "the Bloomberg administration's creation of a new, upscale, corporatized stretch along the West Side. . . . Gone entirely will be regular New Yorkers, the people who used to call the neighborhood home. But then the High Line was never really about them" (Moss 2012). Beyond being elevated above and separate

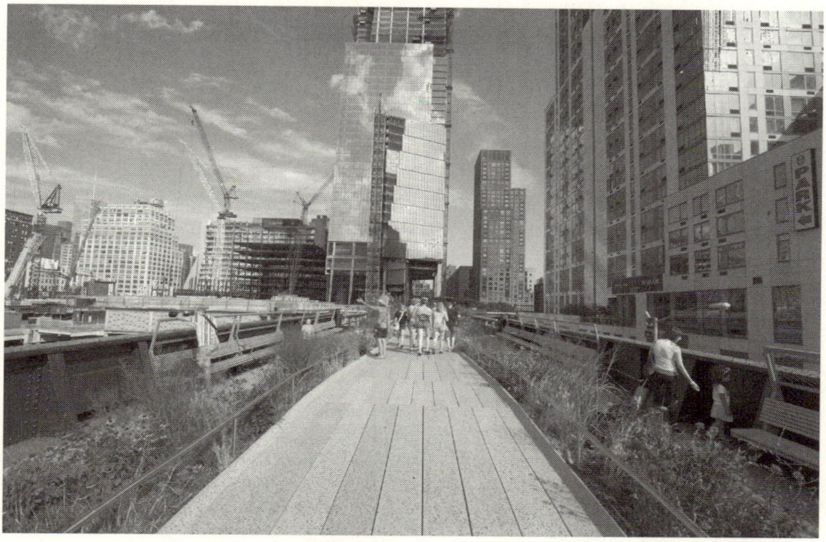

FIGURE I.1. Tourists, cranes, and high-rises under construction, 2015. Photograph by Brian Rosa.

from the everyday life of the city, the High Line is increasingly imagined by "regular New Yorkers" as being aloof. When Mayor Bill de Blasio, Bloomberg's successor, declined to attend the inauguration of the third section of the High Line in 2014 and acknowledged that he had never visited the park, he reinforced speculations that he was positioning himself as a champion of struggling parks in the outer boroughs, rather than the highly funded, showcase park that had come to symbolize the mayoralty of his predecessor (Grynbaum 2014). Questions of uneven funding for parks and emerging issues of equity are addressed in chapter 5, by Julian Brash.

To date, these critiques have largely existed in isolation, and at a distance, from larger conversations about broader trends in contemporary urbanism. It is time that the High Line and its implications within larger processes of urban transformation—whether social, ecological, economic, or cultural—be explored critically by scholars and urban practitioners. It makes little sense to consider the successes and failures of the High Line as a new type of urban public space without acknowledging its relationship to larger processes of entrepreneurial, neoliberal, and culture-led urban restructuring, trends that are often associated with making urban spaces increasingly unequal and exclusionary (Brash 2011; Brenner and Theodore 2002; Hackworth 2007; Kaminer et al. 2011; Peck and Tickell 2002).

In this regard, the High Line needs to be understood as being deeply site-specific, while at the same time indicative of larger processes of urban change and new trends in the revalorization of urban infrastructure through landscape architecture. With one of the main theoretical trends in contemporary landscape design being "landscape urbanism" (Waldheim 2006), an attempt to scale up landscape design and to engage with postindustrial and infrastructural spaces, the High Line serves as the most high-profile exemplar of broader contemporary trends in design approaches to rationalizing and programming the residual spaces of infrastructure in cities worldwide (Allen 1999; Hauck et al. 2011; Rosa 2014, 2016).

Further, it is our view, as well as the overall position of this book, that the celebratory responses that the High Line so often attracts benefit from being counterbalanced with a more critical perspective—one that gives greater attention to the more troubling, and sometimes unanticipated, processes that the park aids and instigates. The theoretical approach of critical urban theory informs this endeavor. Rather than focusing on normative questions of best practice, technocratic concerns of economic efficiency or rationality, or the inevitability of growth-oriented urban entrepreneurialism, "critical urban theory emphasizes the politically and ideologically mediated, socially contested and therefore malleable character of urban space—that is, its continuous (re)construction as a site, medium, and outcome of historically specific relations of social power" (Brenner 2009: 198). From this perspective, any understanding of the value and significance of the High Line would therefore be incomplete without a careful examination of its impact on its immediate surroundings and New York City as a whole, the ways in which it has influenced other urban design initiatives throughout the world, and what it reveals about contemporary processes of urban redevelopment. Seeking to address precisely these issues, this interdisciplinary volume brings together scholars from across the fields of architecture, urban planning and design, geography, sociology, and cultural studies to critically interrogate the aesthetic, ecological, symbolic, and social impacts of the High Line. In so doing, the book also considers the High Line's relation to public space, creative practice, neoliberal modes of urban renewal, and policy-led gentrification.

A SHORT HISTORY OF THE HIGH LINE

To help provide more context for the discussions that follow, we wish to offer here a brief history of the creation of the High Line. Many details and key points are, of course, further developed, analyzed, and supplemented by the individual chapters within this volume. It is also important to mention that there are various sources available that delineate the major events of the site's transformation (David and Hammond 2011; Design Trust for Public Space and Friends of the High Line 2002; LaFarge 2014; Washburn 2013), and a selective timeline relevant to this volume's main concerns can be found in the front matter. For the sake of brevity, and to avoid repeating what is readily available elsewhere, we focus here on essential background for understanding not only the transformation of this former elevated railway but also this volume's various critiques of that transformation.

The physical structure that would later become known as the High Line is a steel railway viaduct that snakes through the West Side of Manhattan. Built on top of landfill, the landscape and industry west of Tenth Avenue in Manhattan has long been dominated by the railway, which was built at-grade along Tenth Avenue in 1847. The viaduct was constructed between 1929 and 1934 as part of Robert Moses's West Side Improvement project,

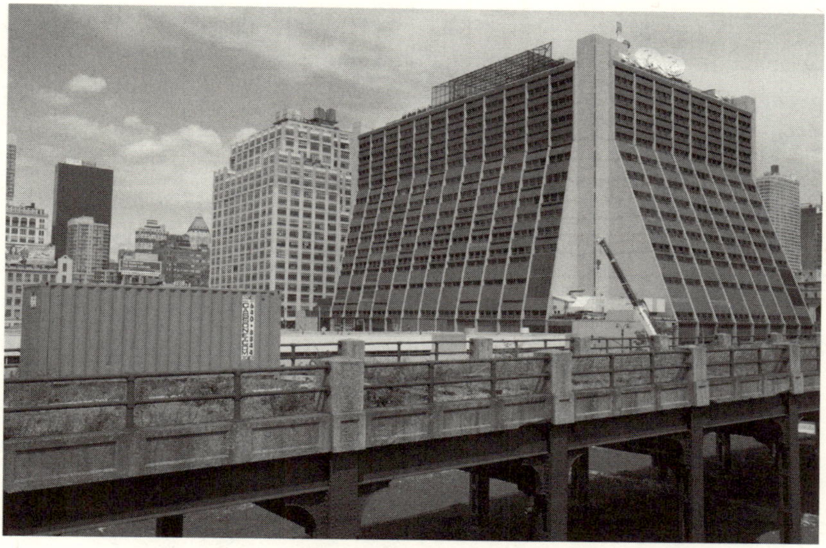

FIGURE I.2. Section 3 in 2011, before construction began. Photograph by Brian Rosa.

which intended to relieve street-level congestion and safety hazards by lifting the railway twenty feet overhead, carrying primarily food products from the waterfront to warehouses, factories, and slaughterhouses. In its original form the railway ran from Saint John's Park Terminal to 34th Street. As one of the latest elevated railways (or "els") constructed in New York City, and responding to a general public distaste for the appearance, noise, and dereliction associated with els and their corridors (Brooks 1997; Cheape 1980; Dennis 2008), the High Line was constructed in the middle of the block, in order to minimize its visual presence in the city. In this sense, it was unique compared with the majority of other earlier els within Manhattan, which were constructed primarily above the north–south avenues. At the points where the High Line viaduct was visible at street crossings, it was adorned with art deco detailing, while elsewhere its aesthetic was more purely utilitarian. It was also integrated into many of the refrigerated warehouses and food processing centers of the Meatpacking District, reflecting the functionalism and aesthetics of architectural modernism.

Despite the massive public outlay of funds and spatial intervention in the city, within only two decades this massive infrastructural modernization project was already starting to become obsolete for the needs of the food processing industry. With the development of the interstate highway system in the 1950s and 1960s, industry was encouraged and able to decentralize from congested urban districts. By 1960, rail traffic to St. John's Park Terminal was shut down, resulting in the southernmost end of the railway between Bank Street and the terminal being closed and quickly dismantled. Twenty years later, the railway was closed entirely and left in a state of disuse, and the structure was again truncated in 1991, when the five-block section between Bank Street and Gansevoort Street was dismantled by the Rockrose Development Corporation to make way for housing development. According to the president of Rockrose, "The day [the viaduct] was removed, it was like lifting a weight off the West Village" (Dunlap 1999). The High Line now terminated abruptly in the Meatpacking District at Gansevoort Market, while still extending northward to 34th Street near the Javits Convention Center.

Although disused and apparently abandoned in the 1980s, in legal terms the High Line nonetheless continued to constitute a railway easement and could therefore have been restored for use as a railway at some point. The viaduct was sold by New York Central Railroad to Penn Central Railroad in 1968 and was then acquired in 1976 by the federal government's Consolidated Rail Corporation (Conrail), which had assumed control of a number of failing railways in the Midwest and Northeast. By the 1980s, Conrail was seeking to divest from the structure completely. The first proposed reuse of the structure was not for a linear park but for its restoration as a rail line. Spearheaded by the West Side Rail Line Development Foundation's (WSRLDF) founder, Chelsea resident Peter Obletz, this initiative would continue through the mid-1980s. Obletz's group came close to being able to purchase the structure, which might have been used to expand Amtrak's service, but in 1986 the Interstate Commerce Commission (ICC) ruled that the WSRLDF did not have the appropriate resources to run and maintain railway infrastructure (David and Hammond 2011: x).

While various groups sought alternative uses for the High Line structure, including forms of mass transit as well as more far-fetched proposals such as housing, a powerful coalition was emerging who actively sought the demolition of the viaduct. The Chelsea Property Owners (CPO), a cadre of property investors and developers who owned land beneath and along the viaduct, were pushing the ICC as early as 1989 to issue an order requiring Conrail to abandon and demolish the structure. For more than a decade, the CPO continued to pursue the demolition of the el through various legal channels and public campaigns. CPO represented landowners whose properties would be prime for development if the High Line were demolished—a process many of them anticipated in purchasing cheap land for temporary use as parking and storage, waiting to realize its value when the structure was removed. Though the group won a 1992 court order to demolish the structure, the members could not arrive at an arrangement about how the costs of the demolition would be distributed, leading to a standstill.

The CSX Corporation, which had assumed control under the privatization of Conrail, inherited the viaduct in 1999. Considering the options of restoring the structure to active use or releasing its hold on the site, CSX commissioned the Regional Planning Association (RPA) to conduct a feasibility study for the reuse of the viaduct, with the RPA suggesting restoration of the structure for light rail usage or converting it into an elevated greenway. At this point there was a great deal of interest in housing development on the West Side, and the planning establishment and the Giuliani administration were firmly behind the push to have the viaduct dismantled. Joseph Rose, commissioner of the New York City Department of City Planning, was quoted in 1999 as saying, "that platform has no right to be there except for transportation, and that use is long gone. . . . This has become the Vietnam of old railway trestles" (cited in Design Trust for Public Space n.d.).

It was in 1999 when two Manhattan residents, Joshua David of Chelsea and Robert Hammond of the West Village, met at a community board hearing addressing the High Line viaduct. This is often considered to be the genesis of the High Line's transformation. Both men were interested in saving the structure from demolition, although they were initially unsure of what it should or could become. Together they cofounded Friends of the High Line (FHL), a nonprofit organization that became the driving force behind preserving the railway and, later, behind creating the High Line park. David and Hammond embarked on a savvy campaign to raise awareness of the structure and solicit ideas for its reuse. Though this was not the first proposal for the repurposing of the High Line, they were able to catalyze interest among the economic and cultural elite of the city and influence the mayoral debate, eliciting the support of all six mayoral candidates for the viaduct's reuse.

Backed by wealthy patrons and leaders of the fashion and art world in the vicinity of the High Line, FHL was quick to organize a team to produce a variety of studies, panel discussions, and campaigns promoting the reuse of the site. Among the most influential documents for realizing the park as it currently exists was *Reclaiming the High Line*, a comprehensive feasibility study produced by the Design Trust for Public Space and FHL in 2002. The main results of the study, which attracted support from incoming Mayor Bloomberg, were that reuse outweighed demolition and that any reuse should be focused on pedestrian rather than railway usage. The justification for this strategy is telling. It emphasized the commercial activity that could be stimulated by the new park and that property values adjacent to the High Line would greatly increase because of their proximity to the new open space.

These claims were further articulated by Bloomberg in his foreword to the design study, where, echoing the rhetoric of green renewal surrounding Paris's Promenade Plantée and its redevelopment of the Vincennes railway in the early 1990s (Heathcott 2013), he argues for a direct link between parks and the revitalization of neighborhoods: "New York City would be unlivable without its parks, trees, and open spaces. They provide aesthetic relief, enhance our health, add to our enjoyment, and increase our property values. Where parks have been revitalized, the neighborhoods have blossomed with new life. Where public open spaces have been renovated, the surrounding areas have become cleaner and more secure" (Bloomberg 2002: 4). Bloomberg's quotation reveals much about the approach to public space provision and planning that would guide his time in office. As Julian Brash reveals in *Bloomberg's New York* (2011), it was an approach that promoted environmental sustainability within a market logic, emphasized urban entrepreneurialism, aligned with the property and banking sectors, and branded New York as a world-leading city of luxury.

The 2002 design study reveals with great clarity the motivation and justifications behind the creation of the park. Arguments focused on economic development were central in the early phases of the process, framed as offering a symbolic boost to the recovery of New York City in the wake of the attacks on the World Trade Center the previous year: "It is clear that all new construction in Manhattan, of private buildings and public spaces alike, has a vital role to play in our city's recovery. Any brick put down or any tree planted must recharge the urban economy; it must attract *new* businesses, residents, and visitors by creating appealing, healthful, safe work and home environments; it must spark financial activity, raise property values, and generate tax revenues. . . . Preserving open land and creating new public spaces boosts property values and generates higher property tax revenues" (Design Trust for Public Space and Friends of the High Line 2002: 15, emphasis in original). This guiding document offers insight into the strategic alliance building between FHL, resistant property owners, and the city government. To coax owners into believing that their properties could be worth more if the viaduct remained, FHL worked with city planners to rezone the area for new residential and commercial development so that oppositional property owners would be able to monetize their unused property rights, resulting in what came to be known as the "West Chelsea rezoning."

In the planning process that led to the creation of the Special West Chelsea District, concerns over the potential impacts of the High Line were apparent, and a number of players found themselves in conflict. According to David, "You had a group fighting to keep buildings as low as possible, and a group pushing for more affordable housing. There was a smaller group pushing for retention of manufacturing space, not just for the galleries, but also to support a continued manufacturing sector. . . . The reality was [that] moving the development rights away from the High Line sites was going to mean that some buildings were going to be taller. And in order for the economics of the development right transfers to work, there had to be a major chunk of market-rate housing in the formula, which was not what the affordable housing group wanted to hear" (David and Hammond 2011: 65). Hammond and David went along with the rezoning, while David expressed some misgivings on what effect the High Line would have. Aside from being concerned that too much residential development would displace the art galleries from West Chelsea, David explained that "we didn't want to set up a dynamic in which the High Line was perceived as being in competition with these other good interests" (David and Hammond 2011: 65). It is not entirely clear, however, that the concessions associated with rezoning were purely about economic and legal feasibility.

In an interview in *The Edge Becomes the Center,* a city official who had served on the community board in Chelsea from 1996 to 2003 argues that a deliberate process of industrial and commercial displacement was under way: "There was an economic development analysis that determined you could invest in the High Line and make it a park without changing any land use along the corridor. The naturally occurring rate of return would be enough to justify the investment. But City Planning wanted to put that area on steroids and really capitalize on rapid large-scale development and that's what they've done. . . . When you go over there you see tourists from all over the world but you don't see local residents because it's not really a place for us" (Gibson 2015: loc 2197). As Darren Patrick points out in chapter 9, the High Line is estimated to have stimulated more than $2 billion in real estate development and to have increased property values within a five-minute walking radius by 103 percent. Michael Levere (2014) estimates that the opening of the High Line led directly to a 10 percent increase in home value within one-third of a mile of the park. At the same time, the green corridor takes up a disproportionate amount of the city's parks budget. It is, by far, the most expensive park per acre in the entirety of New York. Therefore, despite the fact that much of the High Line has been funded by philanthropic capital, the rezoning of West Chelsea and the significant public expenditure illustrate the ways in which the city has used the provision of urban green space to stimulate gentrification. Furthermore, the proportion of the High Line that was funded by multimillion-dollar donations and the disproportionate amount of public resources being poured into it raise some troubling questions about public space provision and its relation to real estate speculation (Millington 2015).

The real estate boom instigated by the High Line has raised concerns not only about the social and economic impacts of the new linear park, but also about the transformation of its surroundings. A widespread concern is that, aside from issues of crowding and domination by tourists, the experience of walking the High Line has been diminished by the proliferation of high-rise, luxury housing. David Halle and Elisabeth Tiso write this argument off, noting that, despite the fact that the 2005 West Chelsea rezoning allowed "developers to initiate a frenzy of high-priced new condominiums . . . giving [the area] a monied aura," ultimately it was worthwhile because the new, bold architecture "somewhat offset New York's reputation, earned over the previous three decades, for mediocre new architecture" (Halle and Tiso 2014: 154). Downplaying any displacement that may have occurred as outside the definitions of "traditional" gentrification, Halle and Tiso see the transformation as worthwhile in its monumentality and boldness of design. Still, with an aesthetic playing on the marginality, wildness, and industrial nature of its surroundings, the industrial landscape emphasized in the High Line's design is increasingly incongruous with its opulent surroundings. Though locations such as the Gansevoort Market Historic District retain much of their superficially industrial character, preexisting land uses are consistently displaced for high-end retail, dining, and other services targeting well-off residents and tourists. Furthermore, considering the number of luxury high-rises already built and reviewing visualizations of future development, the High Line's elevated status is becoming reversed: it increasingly becomes a canyon with a river of pedestrians flowing between towering edifices.

Herein lies an important consideration: whether or not the transformation and upscaling of an urban landscape was the intention of FHL, the park's creation cannot be understood without the rezoning that has ushered in these changes. As Alexandros Washburn, former chief urban designer for the New York City Department of City Planning, notes, "the High Line and its rezoning are one" (2014): the city had thought of the park and rezoning as a package deal to achieve its goal of boosting redevelopment on the West Side of Manhattan. Washburn celebrates the High Line as a "nested, iterative process of urban design where politics, finance, and design intersect," and where, "whether it is a rule . . . a plan . . . or a product . . . the process of urban design was used to make the transformation happen" (Washburn 2013: 137–138). In this conceptualization, the process of urban design is understood, almost primarily, as an adjunct to policy-led gentrification, all with an air of postpolitical consensus.

Regardless of the intentions of FHL, from the perspective of the city government and property interests along the corridor of the High Line, the rezoning and upscaling of the Meatpacking District and Chelsea was precisely the point. And, indeed, the increasing property values stimulated by the High Line have led not only to the displacement of residents and long-standing small industrial businesses and restaurants, but also to many of the art galleries that originally put Chelsea on the map (Bloomberg News 2015). It is against this backdrop of rapid urban change that the essays in this volume set out to critically analyze the High Line, paying close attention to the tensions, controversies, and contradictions involved not only in the park itself, but also in broader urban trends of postindustrial renewal within—and beyond—New York City.

FROM DESIGN TO EFFECT

This book is arranged in four closely related and interlocking thematic parts. Part 1, "Envisioning the High Line," focuses on the design of the park, including the vision and values informing its realization and operation. Emphasis is given to the High Line's significance to landscape architecture theory, the park's public programs, and the role of art and creative practice in popularizing the space. Part 2, "Gentrification and the Neoliberal City," examines the connections between the High Line, gentrification, and neoliberal urban redevelopment. In particular, the essays grouped here analyze the High Line's impact on the surrounding neighborhoods (real estate, business development, cultural life) and the ways in which the park has become enmeshed in broader processes and conditions of globalization. Part 3, "Urban Political Ecologies," explores the political-environmental aspects of the High Line's experiment in constructed urban nature. Essays in this section address issues such as private park conservancies, the incorporation of abandonment and ruin in the design and experience of the space, the use of nature as a tool for property revalorization, and the possibilities for alternative ecological politics. Part 4, "The High Line Effect," examines the influence of the High Line on other, similar elevated park projects in New York City (the QueensWay) and elsewhere (Rotterdam's Hofbogen and São Paolo's Minhocão). The emphasis in this section is on the circulation and

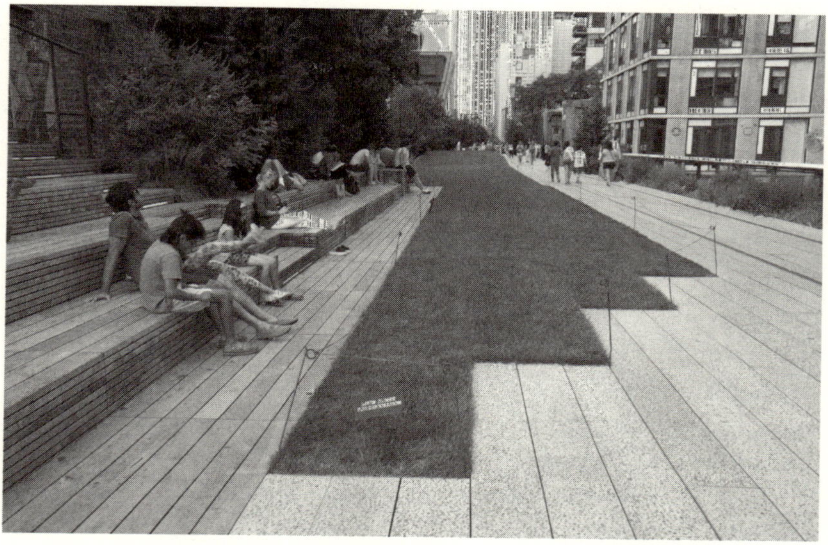

FIGURE I.3. Keep off the grass: "Lawn closed for restoration," 2015. Photograph by Brian Rosa.

exchange of landscape design and planning practice in the wake of the High Line. This section also questions the extent to which the High Line model of urban development is transportable to other locations in an era of global policy mobilities (Ward 2011).

Part 1 opens with a self-reflective essay on the vision and thinking behind the design of the park by James Corner, principal of Field Operations and lead designer of the High Line. In "Hunt's Haunts," Corner places his vision for the park in the broader context of the history and theory of landscape architecture—particularly the work of John Dixon Hunt—and reflects on how the High Line contributes to an extended genealogy of experimentation with constructed landscape. Corner's overall argument is that Hunt's notion of the "haunting excess" of good gardens—as both place and idea—is applicable to the High Line, but also complicated by the ways in which the park's design deliberately plays with memory, history, and imagination.

In "Community Engagement, Equity, and the High Line," Danya Sherman, urban planner and former director of Public Programs, Education and Community Engagement at Friends of the High Line, examines the High Line's changing visions of social inclusion, equity, and public participation in the creation and growth of a new public space. After outlining the various and evolving programs that FHL has created to encourage the participation of local residents, Sherman analyzes the uneven ways in which social equity has been addressed in the form and function of the High Line. Emphasizing the experimental and largely unprecedented nature of the project, Sherman considers how such projects can minimize the negative impacts on groups that have traditionally been marginalized in urban redevelopment, and how the political, aesthetic, and economic programs of such flagship projects may sometimes hinder democratic inclusion.

In "Loving the High Line: Infrastructure, Architecture, and the Politics of Space in the Mediated City," architect and designer Alan Smart reflects on the design sensibilities of Field Operations and Diller Scofidio + Renfro, seeking to contextualize their work in the political and aesthetic regimes that contemporary designers occupy, and to understand how designers situate themselves within ecological, symbolic, political, and economic processes. In exploring the symbolic monumentality of the High Line in relation to other signature cultural spaces in cities, such as Frank Gehry's Guggenheim building in Bilbao, Smart emphasizes the limits of the social agency of architects within contemporary processes of urban transformation and questions how design may articulate a more collective politics.

In Part 2, sociologist Kevin Loughran shifts the focus from questions of vision and design to issues of privilege and power. In particular, his chapter "Parks for Profit: Public Space and Inequality in New York City" explores the ways in which economic, political, and cultural elites use the creation of new urban parks like the High Line as tools to leverage profit and boost public revenue. Through an ethnographic sketch of the High Line, Loughran identifies how privilege becomes spatialized and how cultural capital allows for elite forms of consumption that are, by their very nature, exclusionary. He notes the overt and subtle ways that the High Line employs surveillance and design to regulate behavior and exclude members of the public deemed undesirable. He also demonstrates how contemporary growth coalitions support neoliberal redevelopment strategies by tapping into elite cultural networks, solidifying difference and distinction, and steering away from the pluralism that has often guided the ideals behind the development and maintenance of public space.

Anthropologist Julian Brash extends the critique of contemporary urban parks as spaces to observe and analyze social inequities in his chapter "Park (In)Equity." Responding to Loughran's work, but attempting to escape the binary between celebrating the High Line as a cherished new public space or castigating it as a symbol of socio-spatial inequity, Brash suggests that the High Line may have inadvertently supported the demand for parks equity in New York City. Focusing on emerging demands of community activists in underinvested districts of the city, Brash uses the High Line as a case study to explore the equitable distribution and quality of public park spaces, raising larger questions about the distribution of resources and services within the city as a whole.

Approaching the High Line from a more theoretical perspective, the final chapter in part 2 considers how the park's "slow landscape" simultaneously interrupts and accelerates urban flows and mobilities associated with neoliberal globalization. In "Retro-Walking New York," cultural theorist Christoph Lindner critically examines the history and design of the park, paying particular attention to the ways in which aesthetics and memory, as well as industrial heritage and transport infrastructure, are used in the High Line design and its various spin-off projects, such as the QueensWay and the Lowline, to refigure the decelerated, pedestrian conditions of the street. It is this refiguring of the street, he argues, that stimulates surrounding conditions of urban speed, supergentrification, and neoliberal renewal—conditions that the palliative urbanism of the High Line is paradoxically designed to alleviate.

In the first chapter of part 3, journalist Tom Baker focuses on how the High Line emblematizes contemporary aesthetics of the "neo-pastoral." Drawing on the work of art critic Julian Stallabrass, Baker argues in "The Garden on the Machine" that the High Line serves as a particular form of romanticized, ornamental "urban wilderness," an update on the traditional pastoral ideal of designed urban landscapes such as Central Park. Unpacking the ideology behind pastoralism, he reflects on the contrived nature of the park's design while emphasizing that the aestheticization of "wild" nature is a testament to how much the supposed newness of the High Line falls within the legacy of highly domesticated pleasure gardens of the leisure classes.

In "The Urban Sustainability Fix and the Rise of the Conservancy Park," urban-historical geographer Phil Birge-Liberman connects the political economy of park provision to contemporary discourses of sustainability, and contextualizes the High Line by placing it in the historical geography of urban parks in the United States. His discussion analyzes the ways in which urban power regimes deploy nature and exert social and economic influence to produce a new kind of park typology—the conservancy park—which reflects the entrepreneurial values of neoliberal urbanism. In the process, he argues that, from a political ecological perspective, the High Line can be understood as an urban sustainability "quick fix"—one that helps to improve the urban environment but that also creates the conditions under which an improved urban quality of life can be used to promote ecological gentrification and neoliberal renewal.

In "Of Success and Succession: A Queer Urban Ecology of the High Line," urban scholar and activist Darren Patrick views the park as a novel form of both gay and green gentrification, while arguing that the "success" of the project needs to be critiqued in light of both its queer and ecological history. Drawing on substantial primary fieldwork, Patrick provides an original account of the High Line's redevelopment in terms that trace the complex relations between queers and the urban political ecologies in which they are constitutively immersed. Patrick calls for an ethics and politics of responsibility *to* and *for* abandoned spaces, which pay consequential attention to the queer, the ecological, and to their ongoing entanglements.

Part 4 opens with a chapter analyzing a High Line spin-off project also located in New York City. In "A High Line for Queens: Celebrating Diversity or Displacing It?," urban geographer Scott Larson examines plans to transform a 3.5-mile section of the former Rockaway Beach Branch of the Long Island Railroad into an elevated, linear park. As Larson discusses, the QueensWay project seeks to replicate many aspects of the High Line, including its grassroots community organization and key elements of its design vision. Led by the Trust for Public Land in collaboration with a private group calling itself Friends of the QueensWay, the proposal envisions the new park attracting tourists, catalyzing redevelopment investment, and enhancing area property values, while also preserving existing local businesses and celebrating the ethnic diversity of Queens. Questioning the project's claims while tracing the influence of the High Line, Larson considers whether neighborhood revitalization and community preservation are compatible goals.

Shifting attention from New York City to the Netherlands, cultural studies scholar Daan Wesselman offers a detailed analysis of the stalled Hofbogen project, which has been attempting to build a pedestrian public space on top of a disused railway viaduct in Rotterdam. His chapter, "Programming Difference on Rotterdam's Hofbogen," focuses on how the Dutch proposal assimilates and reconfigures the High Line's approach to urban renewal, including the aim to create a heterotopian space—that is, a space of radical difference and otherness. Wesselman shows how, despite the similarities between the projects, each space displays its own strategy of postindustrial urban renewal, cultivating difference from the surrounding city according to local conditions and needs. For Wesselman, the Hofbogen is made different by being a *double* space: both a strange obstacle that cuts across the city and a lived space that represents everyday life in Rotterdam. Wesselman concludes that the Rotterdam viaduct is an illustrative case for projects aiming for the "High Line effect" because it shows how both the High Line and the Hofbogen call not for some general design formula, but instead require a focus on what makes each space specifically different in its own urban setting.

The book's final chapter, by geographer Nate Millington, examines a structure that oscillates between being a congested inner-city overpass and a recreational public space. In "Public Space and *Terrain Vague* on São Paulo's Minhocão: The High Line in Translation," Millington examines São Paulo's Minhocão, a two-mile stretch of elevated highway running through the city center, that closes to traffic in the evenings and on Sundays, and reopens for public leisure access, accommodating a variety of activities ranging from jogging and soccer to skateboarding and performance art. Although the Minhocão shares the same infrastructural typology as the High Line—an elevated viaduct built for mass transit—and also similarly repurposes the space for public use, it differs in several important ways. Most notably, the Minhocão remains a functioning highway and therefore lacks the landscaping and park design elements found at the High Line. Related to this, unlike the High Line, the Minhocão is not permanently repurposed, but transitions almost daily between two seemingly incompatible functions. As Millington explores, the resulting ambiguity surrounding the overpass's shifting identity mirrors the uncertainty of the site's future, as various competing urban forces seek to claim and develop the space.

HUDSON YARDS AND THE END OF THE HIGH LINE

One purpose of this volume has been to assemble a variety of critical, theoretical, and disciplinary approaches to explore the effects of the High Line on contemporary urbanism. As this book goes to press, we are still in the midst of the dramatic transformation of the West Side of Manhattan, complete with the extension of the 7 subway line and the massive Hudson

Yards mega-project, itself a bold reimagining of an urban space explicitly oriented around infrastructure. As a field-test for the emerging "smart city" urban ideal, in which nearly all elements of the built environment are technologically controllable and measureable, Hudson Yards is currently being constructed as the largest private redevelopment project in United States history and the largest redevelopment project in Manhattan since the 1930s. In this district of corporate high-rises and luxury living, "circuits are the new topology of this terrain, once dominated by tunnels and tracks" (Mattern 2016), a landscape seeking to perfect the marriage of urban built form and informatics. In May 2016, the first of the site's towers was completed, straddling the High Line.

This linear greenway has, and will continue to play, an instrumental role in the ongoing transformation of this former industrial and arts district. Though the conversion of the existing elevated railway is ostensibly "complete," the imagined expansions of the High Line seem almost limitless. While the viaduct has been bookended at its southern terminus by the new Whitney Museum of American Art, a new spur has been proposed at Hudson Yards, extending a platform from the northern tip of the High Line through the development, leading to a tower called "the Spiral." Proposed by developer Tishman Speyer, the office tower, designed by Bjarke Ingels Group, would feature a gardened terrace spiraling up the building, appearing to extend the High Line further into the sky, twirling to the top of the sixty-five-story skyscraper. As a blogger for *Gothamist* has wryly commented, perhaps "The High Line won't stop until all of Manhattan's West Side is one sleek, vegetated sun deck" (Heins 2016).

Furthermore, with the construction of the new Whitney Museum in 2015 came the first new architectural interventions beneath the High Line: part of Renzo Piano's museum building beneath the Gansevoort Street entrance of the park for the Italian restaurant Santina. In 2016, London-based Lisson Gallery opened its first New York space in a purpose-built building under the High Line, consciously playing on a postindustrial aesthetic. Beneath the Standard Hotel lies a new German-style Biergarten. The voids beneath the viaduct, once seen as nearly valueless and relegated to parking and storage, are now slowly being filled in—a fate hardly imaginable by the Chelsea Property Owners in the 1980s and 1990s.

Critically analyzing a project such as the High Line requires understanding and coming to terms with the relationships between the material and the symbolic, the local and the global, the public and the private. We

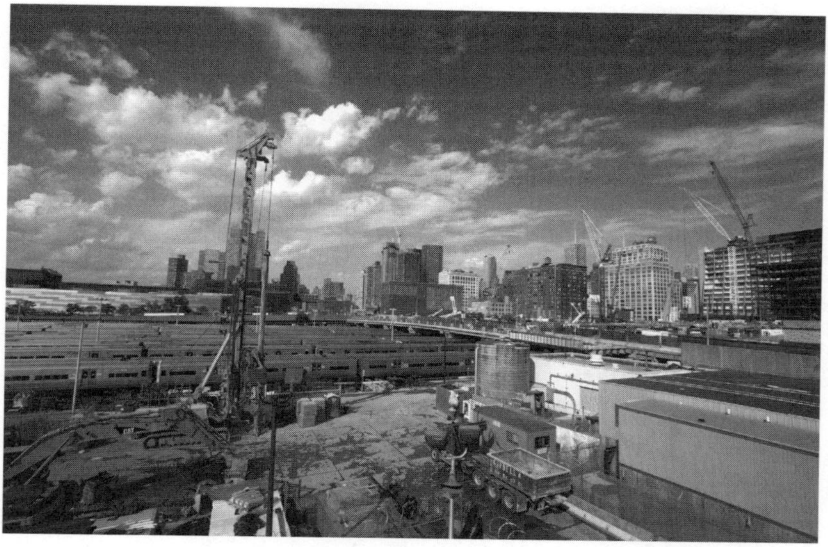

FIGURE I.4. Hudson Yards under construction, as seen from the High Line, 2015. Photograph by Brian Rosa.

consider this book a starting point in this endeavor. The volume provides a compendium of critical readings of the High Line, acknowledging that the linear park and its impact are still unfolding. While recognizing both the park's popularity and its provision of an innovative form of public space, the authors show that the High Line must also be understood as playing a key role in current urban transformations that are central to, but also transcend, the remaking of New York City. Accordingly, there are particular concerns to which the authors repeatedly return throughout the volume. These include the contested processes of gentrification, neoliberal urban redevelopment, the use of iconic design in urban restructuring, and entrepreneurial city branding. Each author addresses these concerns in a unique way and from different perspectives, and we see these thematic interrelations as a strength of the text, as they identify both dominant and emerging themes within contemporary urban theory.

Understanding the High Line as a result of political economic processes, while paying attention to the importance of culture, ecology, and aesthetics, demonstrates the extent to which the park is at once a highly local and a deeply global phenomenon. Issues raised by this volume's critiques of the High Line—as well as of other projects worldwide that have been inspired by the park—demonstrate the globalized (and frequently repackaged) nature of urban design, inextricably intertwined as it is with global finance capital and property speculation. The essays that follow explore the social, political, and cultural elements of policy-led gentrification and industrial displacement. They reveal the extent to which the aesthetics of the postindustrial built environment and the unruliness of urban nature have been mobilized as cultural drivers of urban redevelopment. And they provide a way into thinking about the condition and future of postindustrial cities, the role of urban green space in renewal strategies, and contemporary interest in redesigning landscapes rich in transport infrastructure.

PART I ENVISIONING THE HIGH LINE

1 ▪ HUNT'S HAUNTS

JAMES CORNER

By "HUNT'S HAUNTS," I am referring to the writings of John Dixon Hunt and the many discussions I have had with him over the years that have lingered with me in ways deeply enriching and, at the same time, oddly disquieting. After all, good criticism and difficult conceptual frameworks inevitably pose a challenge—one that can often agitate and haunt one's sense of direction if left unresolved. This same point regarding the *reception* of fecund and challenging ideas could also be said of some of Hunt's favorite physical haunts—some of the great gardens and places from which he has derived inspiration and about which his work is focused. Such places include Stowe, Stourhead, Bomarzo, the melancholic and hidden gardens of Venice, and the many others that have gifted him the feeling of a "greater perfection."[1] As he has written, such places are "haunted by undeniable spirits, [wherein] the environment can become landscape" (Hunt 2000: 223). By spirits, of course, he refers not to some mystical essence but rather to the human mind—to the imagination, to the fictions and designs that create a place of lasting presence, a presence that inevitably haunts precisely because of effects that tend to linger and escape any form of easy definition.

Good gardens haunt precisely because they inevitably exceed being thought. This phenomena of haunting excess—both as place and idea, and as developed through Hunt's writing on the subject—is both inspiring and elusive. It is a fascinating and fundamental topic of all art. Outlined here are three recurrent haunts in Hunt's work that I find particularly relevant for my own. In this context, I will use some images of the High Line project to suggest a certain striving in real-world practice to try to approximate certain ideas.

First is Hunt's work on site, the haunts themselves. Hunt has constructed an almost unassailable argument that the specificity of sites lies at the very core of any significant works of landscape architecture. In this vein, he has elaborated on key concepts such as the "genius of the place," "reading and writing the site," "place making as an art of milieu," "site mediation," and the nesting of "three natures" wherein the garden (third nature) is a focused concentration of its larger surroundings.[2] A close reading of a particular site's attributes—its history, its various representations, its context, and its potentials—conspires to inform a new project that is in some way an intensification and enrichment of place. Every site is an accumulation of local forces over time, and so, Hunt argues, any significant design response must in some way interpret, extend, and amplify this potential within its specific context. Averse to universal and stylistic approaches to design, Hunt demands inventive originality with regard to specific circumstance.

In the case of the High Line, a very close reading was made of the site's history and urban context. Two readings were particularly formative—one was the singular, autonomous quality of the transportation engineering infrastructure (its linearity and repetition, indifferent to surrounding context, and its brash steel and concrete palette), and the other was the surprising and charming effect of self-sown vegetation taking over the postindustrial structure once the trains had stopped running—a kind of melancholia captured beautifully in earlier photographs made by the artist Joel Sternfeld. These photographs were later used to great effect by those who sought the preservation of the structure in the face of impending demolition. The new design of the site, from its material systems (the lineal paving, the reinstallation of the rail tracks, the plantings, the lighting, the furnishing, the railings, etc.) to the choreography of movement (the meandering of paths, the siting of overlooks and vistas, and the coordination of seating and social spaces) is intended to reinterpret, amplify, dramatize, and concentrate these readings of the site.

The design is highly site-specific; it is irreproducible anywhere else without significant loss of origin and locality, partly owing to the history of the High Line itself and partly to the unique characteristics of its urban context and adjacencies. The design aims to concentrate these found conditions; to dramatize and reveal past, present, and future contexts; and to create a memorable place for all who visit. This brings me to a second theme of Hunt's haunts, the concern for reception. Over the past few years, Hunt has brought into sharper focus the importance for how visitors receive a given work—how they experience, understand, value, and extend various interpretations of the work. He says that "landscape comes into being as the creative coupling of perceiving subject and an object perceived" (Hunt 2000: 9).

As a landscape architect, I find it very difficult to believe that a designed work can determine a particular behavioral response; a good designer can at best influence, steer, or guide a particular set of responses, but can never overdetermine or script reception. Hunt recognizes such a distinction, explaining—in statements, such as, after W. H. Auden—that "a poet, especially a dead one, cannot control how we read and understand his poetry, but that—especially if it is good—we will constantly reread it in new ways; so even when later generations repeat the very same words that W. B. Yeats originally published, they will probably give them new meanings and new resonance." He continues the analogy: "When we are dealing with materials in a garden that have neither denotative basis (as words do in the first instance) nor precise declarations of idea or emotion, there is considerably more scope for reinvesting them with meanings, for seeing them in different ways than were originally intended or anticipated" (Hunt 2004: 12). Thus, he suggests that a good design must harbor sufficient room for a wide range of receptions and interpretations, if not actually instigate, prompt, and support open and indeterminate readings. As he quite rightly points out, "Here is the palpable, haptic place, smelling, sounding, catching the eye; then there is the sense of an invented or special place, this invention resulting from the creation of richer and fuller experiences than would be possible, at least in such completeness or intensity, if they were not designed. Like cyberspace, a designed landscape is always at bottom a fiction, a contrivance—yet its hold on our imagination will derive, paradoxically, from the actual materiality of its invented sceneries" (Hunt 2004: 37).

From such ideas, Hunt develops the concept of the *longue durée,* the long duration, the slow accrual of experience and meaning over time. Possibly one of the most fundamental, important, and difficult criteria for landscape architecture is the fact that the medium is bound into time. There can be no immediacy of appreciation, no fast way to consume landscape in any meaningful or lasting way. Landscapes can never be properly captured in a single moment; they are always in a process of becoming, as in a temporal quarry of accrual and memory—collecting experiences, representations, uses, the effects of weather, and changes in management, cultivation, and care, and other traces of layered presence.

In the case of the High Line, the experience of strolling is intentionally slowed down in the otherwise bustling context of Manhattan. Paths meandering in between tall perennial and grass plantings create an experience that cannot really be properly captured in a photograph, or even video. Like so many other gardens, the place must be walked, with scenes unfolding in sequence and in juxtaposition. The dynamic plantings are different from week to week, with varied blooms, colors, textures, effects, and moods, combined with the changing light at different times of day, varied weathers and seasons, and with the different microclimatic effects of the surrounding cityscape. The visitor is almost always experiencing the High Line in newly nuanced ways.

Importantly, the design does not employ signs or symbols of narrative intent; it does not try to tell a story or to embed meaning—rather, its very materiality, its detailing, its artifactuality elicits or prompts different associations and readings. Hunt has spoken in various essays of triggers and prompts in design, describing a number of theatrical devices such as entry thresholds and liminality, the passage from outside to inside, dramatic frames and scenes, displacement and collage, inscription and marking (Hunt 2004: 77–112). These precisely designed triggers and prompts are all concentrations of effect that draw the visitor into another world, heightening the allure and distinctiveness of a special place. The visitor becomes as much a performer as a viewer, more deeply engaged in participating in the theatricality of urban life—the promenade as elevated catwalk, urban stage, and social condenser.

And here words bring us to the third haunt of Hunt, the critical. When he declares that "to theorize about gardens is justifiable for its own sake; moreover it increases the pleasures of understanding," he is establishing the basis not simply for passive contemplation but for actively energizing fresh developments in the ideas and practices of landscape architecture (Hunt 2004: 107). His insistence on historical perspective is well taken, but his commitment to concepts, to critical discourse, to informed argumentation, and—most important—to cultural enrichment through imaginative and inventive place making continues to challenge us all. Hunt's haunts are quite simply those remarkable places and ideas where content concentrates, lingers, and accrues. The combination of physical, material places with cultural ideas points to the unity of theory with practice, of design with reception, and of experience with intellect, all dialogues that we strive for in the best of our work. That such experiences might also haunt our imaginations is perhaps the highest calling of art, and in gardens, as Hunt has so eloquently taught us, we might find the greatest perfections.

ACKNOWLEDGMENTS

Reproduced from "Hunt's Haunts." Paper presented at John Dixon Hunt—A Symposium, Philadelphia, Pennsylvania, October 2009. In J. Corner and A. Bick Hirsch (eds.) (2014) *The Landscape Imagination: Collected Essays of James Corner 1990–2010*. New York: Princeton Architectural Press, 340–349.

NOTES

1. See Hunt (2000) *Greater Perfections: The Practice of Garden Theory*. The title comes from Francis Bacon's "Of Gardens" (1625): "When Ages grow to Civility and Elegancie, Men come to *Build Stately*, sooner than to *Garden Finely*: As if *Gardening* were the Greater Perfection."
2. Most of these ideas come up in *Greater Perfections*, with a whole essay devoted to "The Idea of a Garden and the Three Natures" (32–75). See also Hunt's "Introduction: Reading and Writing the Site," in Hunt (1992: 3–16).

2 ▪ COMMUNITY ENGAGEMENT, EQUITY, AND THE HIGH LINE

DANYA SHERMAN

How can urban development projects build democratic capacity and address inequities? This was the key question I was engaged with during the seven years I spent working for Friends of the High Line (FHL), the nonprofit organization that saved and now runs the High Line on behalf of the City of New York. I was drawn to the organization in 2007 for two main reasons: because of its vision to create a high-quality public space on a forgotten industrial relic, but even more important, I was excited by the organization's focus on involving citizens in the politics and design of urban development. Aseem Inam (2014) calls this characteristic of the High Line's development "radical humanism"—"how human beings are capable of transforming cities through tremendous effort, creativity, and perseverance." While in hindsight it is easy to see the High Line's development as inevitable, as something that the city's power brokers were always going to support, I see an additional and equally important narrative: a group of urban residents, building on the long line of civic activists who have given time, sweat, and tears to organize and build political power in an effort to improve their neighborhoods.

Robert Hammond and Joshua David were so successful in doing this, whereas so many other similar civic organizing initiatives struggle, for several reasons. Hammond and David brought to the project skills as community organizers, strategists, and fund-raisers, and they were also able to leverage the significant privileges they had. Moreover, the High Line succeeded in large part thanks to timing: saving and designing the park in this specific way aligned with the political and economic agenda and conditions of New York City at that period.

As the founding director of Public Programs, Education, and Community Engagement for the organization from 2009 to 2013, I built on Robert and Josh's orientation toward civic organizing and their vision of the park as a piece of healthy social infrastructure. Simultaneously, I struggled with some of the decisions the organization had to make to get the High Line built, which I worried would unintentionally undermine the ability of the space to be accessible to, and a positive impact on, all citizens. In aligning with the Bloomberg administration's vision for the West Chelsea rezoning and adopting a pro-development stance, the High Line secured its success in creating a new public space (private development would have been the likely alternative). Yet in doing so, the High Line may also have undergirded the status quo of unequal power relations and impacts of urban development.

The park experienced a level of success that no one at FHL had anticipated when the organization began its initiative to develop a public space for the neighborhood. Recognizing that visitors to the High Line in the first few years did not reflect the diversity of the neighborhood, FHL began initiatives to better listen and partner with public housing residents in the neighborhood and other individuals and groups that are typically marginalized by urban development investments. It was through this discursive, relationship-building exercise that we began to consider what it might look like to intentionally develop equitable public spaces.

BUILDING A CULTURAL PLATFORM THROUGH PARTNERSHIP-BASED PROGRAMMING

While FHL had good intentions and public accessibility in mind while organizing to save, design, and manage the park, when the first section opened in 2009, visitorship immediately demonstrated that the park was not drawing all populations equally. Park visitors seemed to skew wealthier and whiter than the population of the surrounding neighborhoods and

New York City as a whole. I saw programming as a way to help fulfill the democratic ideal behind the park and, with consultant Abby Ehrlich, began to actualize this goal by building programs that directed resources where there was the greatest need and by encouraging social bridging across racial and class lines through carefully curated experiences.

Building on the deep relationships with community groups in the neighborhood that FHL had built in the previous ten years, we began to program the park with diversity, equity, and inclusion in mind. Emily Pinkowitz joined the small program staff soon after the park opened, bringing with her an intelligent and strategic theory about educational programming. We both came with community organizing experience and perspectives. We spent time meeting and brainstorming with many individuals in the neighborhood, including staff at Hudson Guild (a lauded community center in the neighborhood), tenant leaders at the Fulton and Elliott-Chelsea Houses (which together represented five thousand residents of public housing), the Meatpacking District Initiative, and many more organizations.

Through building trust and friendship in open conversations, we developed several new cultural programs in conjunction with the Hudson Guild in the years following the park's opening (Pinkowitz 2014). An innovative performing arts program called "Step to the High Line" (2011 and 2012) grew out of a conversation with Jim Furlong, director of the arts at Hudson Guild. The guild had released a report about the high number of what it termed "disconnected youth" living in Chelsea, which led me to wonder whether the park could become a better resource for teenagers, as few from the neighborhood were using it. Through a partnership with Youth Step USA's founder and executive director, Brock Harris, the three of us developed a unique series of performances and workshops that debuted with the opening of Section 2 of the park in June 2011. Five of the city's award-winning stepping teams came to the High Line and performed their routines. We repeated the program two years later and included a "Learn to Step" program. High school students from Brooklyn, Queens, and the Bronx—most of whom had never been to the High Line and the majority of whom were people of color—performed this African American cultural tradition before an international, intergenerational audience. After presenting their work at the park, the students noted that they saw it in a new way—as an art form—and perceived themselves as ambassadors of American culture.

Chelsea also has a large population that is advancing in age, or "aging in place." I observed and was told that they were not using the park much. Many of them (my own grandmother included) moved to the neighborhood long ago through developments in social housing, live in subsidized or rent-controlled units, and have limited incomes. Many residents utilize the services at the Hudson Guild Senior Center. Seeing an opportunity to address this discrepancy through the arts, we commissioned our first performing arts program specifically for the High Line with an organization called Dances for a Variable Population (DVP), led by the inventive and tireless Naomi Goldberg Haas. DVP's mission is to create performances that bring together people of body types and ages not typically thought of as ideal performers, and to do so through an inclusive, exuberant, and community-building rehearsal process. The unique performance, called "Autumn Crossing," was attended in 2011 by more than one thousand people and made an inclusive statement about whose faces should be seen as cultural creators in New York's new iconic space.

Early on, FHL also established teen employment programs to better utilize the park's resources to achieve diversity. A group of teens who graduated from the guild's youth job development program, with interests that overlapped with what we could offer, worked with FHL for three days a week in the summer as paid interns, beginning the first summer that the High Line was open. Youth who live in the neighborhood were especially encouraged to apply, and the program became an annual one.

While developing performing arts and teen programs, we also focused on expanding our opportunities for families and school-aged children. Emily Pinkowitz developed and managed inquiry-based educational programs that continue to utilize the High Line as a site for the exploration of New York City history, landscape design, and science education. She also initiated and grew, along with the help of programming consultant Abby Ehrlich, a series of thoughtful family programs focused on connecting thematically to the High Line. The understanding underlying these initiatives is that children's programs help to build ownership among entire families. Under Emily's guidance, we commissioned and built the High Line Children's Workyard Kit in 2011, a portable kit of parts designed by Abby and Cas Holman to allow children to build anything in their imagination, harking back to the High Line's industrial heritage.

These programs stake a claim for using a new space that goes beyond its initial blueprint: as a platform for creativity for artists, performers, and writers. They provide the opportunity for visitors to see not just the built environment, but also the sociocultural environment of New York, a diverse and vibrant place that is more complex than it might seem as one gazes down to the street. The intimate encounter that the High Line so beautifully enables creates a certain kind of openness in visitors, and doing cultural and educational programming in this environment is quite generative. As we had more and more success in our programs, we continued to expand our offerings. Consequently, more people found ways to help themselves grow as individuals as well as socially, and in the process developed stronger and deeper connections to the space. By the time I left in June 2013, the Public Programs, Education, and Community Engagement Department had grown from a staff of one (me) to comprise 5 full-time, 10 part-time, and 20 teen employees, as well as more than 125 active volunteers. Together we were producing more than 450 yearly programs and activities, serving tens of thousands of people annually (Pinkowitz 2014).

In many programs, staff may benefit more than participants. I observed that the volunteers, colleagues, teens, and others who were actively involved in shaping the program seemed to grow the most from the experience. This mirrors research on the beneficial aspects of active participation versus passive consumption of the arts (Brown et al. 2011). This is especially the case for teens, who are at such a crucial juncture in life, and for this reason we tried to create programs that were empowering and meaningful.

DEEPENING THE FOCUS ON EQUITY

By the summer of 2010, the programming department had begun to direct its activities toward better including those who had not been meaningfully involved in the community engagement process before the park opened. Our experience at the Hudson Guild's main headquarters on 26th Street in the summer of 2010 underscored the importance of this focus. Most of the people we spoke to that summer had not visited the High Line; many had not even heard of it. It did not make a negative impression on them; it was just seen as irrelevant. FHL, and in particular the programming department, began earnestly seeking to understand why these dynamics existed. Was it the design of the park, the fact that it was elevated? Would the reaction have been different if these communities had played a more active role in the design and development? These questions made larger issues—which had generally been underexplored and unarticulated throughout the past decade—impossible to ignore. Who was this park for? What were the consequences of building a new public amenity that prioritized design and material excellence? That summer was in many ways a turning point for the organization.

Concurrently, the Nathan Cummings Foundation (specifically Maurine Knighton and Peter Teague), an institution focused on social justice initiatives in the United States that had previously supported the High Line, approached us with an opportunity and a suggestion. This partnership launched what we called a community engagement initiative, or a "listening initiative" focused specifically on the five thousand residents living in public housing near the High Line. The word "community" in the external communications of the organization (and in my own title) was, in many ways, used as an unspoken metaphor for low-income communities, communities of color, and others who had perhaps not been considered central to the community of people who were the agents of the redesign and management of the High Line.

Over the course of 2011 and into 2012, we worked with a consultant, Lisa Yancey, who helped us focus the work on a more collaborative and less extractive model of community engagement. This project was not to be a population study. Rather, the idea was to try honestly and openly to forge individual and institutional relationships, in an effort to understand how the space of the park and the resources of FHL could be useful to those living at Fulton and Elliott-Chelsea Houses. In addition to speaking with more than forty members of our staff, board, and community leaders, Lisa led us through a unique survey process that modeled the kind of work we were seeking to do. We hired six teens who lived in the buildings, trained them in interviewing and public speaking, and worked with them to survey nearly every one of the more than one thousand households in the two complexes. Unlike the work that many more traditional firms do, this survey process allowed us to meet people face to face, introduce ourselves as people who run the park, and talk to them about what they are looking for. We also gave out High Line T-shirts to everyone who participated. Several years later, we still meet neighbors wearing the shirts who have good memories of the process. Most important, this process allowed us to develop responsive programming based on stated needs and interests. It also helped us understand the barriers that may exist through the more in-depth relationships we created with teens and others we met.

Many residents mentioned that their most pressing needs included teen and adult employment opportunities and teen recreational activities. Many residents saw the park as an exciting space for cultural activity or for enjoying gardening and other environmentally related activities. Needing employment and job training is quite different from wanting a place to go for a walk. In realizing this, FHL saw an opportunity to serve people more deeply than before. Moreover, the results from the yearlong initiative successfully made the case for hiring a full-time community engagement manager, Erycka Montoya Pérez, and creating two comprehensive six-month teen programs, the Green Corps and the Teen Arts Council. Because of this enhanced capacity, the organization was able to offer more opportunities that responded directly to needs articulated by the residents.

More than providing service opportunities, the organization began to realize that it was going to need to change from the inside out, if it was to try more fully to address the structural issues at play. Erycka and the rest of our staff, having learned so much through our listening initiative, began to develop programs that tried to dig deeper and address underlying inequities in the neighborhood. As much as possible, FHL tries to help teens who graduate from our programs get placed in other positions and jobs, and it also hires many teens back summer after summer in increasingly demanding roles. Neighborhood residents Hyisheem Calier, Kylah Bruno, Carla Hernandez, and others, now in their early twenties, began as Youth Corps members from the High Line's second summer. All graduated from the Hudson Guild's Power-UP workforce development program and have returned to the High Line as program managers, park rangers, and more, having leveraged their experience with FHL to gain jobs and opportunities of increasing responsibility. FHL also began offering career fairs for neighborhood residents in partnership with Hudson Guild and Workforce 1, the city's workforce development program, to try to recruit more underemployed residents for open jobs on the High Line.

After I left in June 2013 to pursue a master's degree in the Department of Urban Studies and Planning at the Massachusetts Institute of Technology, FHL hired Gonzalo Casals, now vice president for Public Programs, Education, and Community Engagement. Gonzalo came to the High Line from El Museo del Barrio in East Harlem and is building a new vision for the growing programming and engagement initiatives.

A CIVIC VISION

The efforts to deepen relationships with, and provide opportunities for, specific segments of High Line neighbors through engagement and programming were built on FHL's original democratic dream and early engagement work. But the initiatives during this time also critically engaged with the way this dream had been only partially realized in the design and development of the park in the ten years prior to opening. Here I will briefly outline the early engagement efforts that FHL pioneered.

The High Line always had, at its heart, a public mission: to remake a piece of urban infrastructure into a public amenity that all neighbors and city residents would use. The campaign to save the High Line generated many positive impacts in and of itself for those involved. Campaigns like these provide citizens the chance to learn about urban policy and decision making, to forge new relationships between individuals and with local leaders and politicians, and to create new communities around commonalities (Rubin 2008: 187; Wells 1975). In the case of the High Line, the campaign brought together unusual political alliances: young creative professionals (artists, designers), the professional art world, queer Chelsea, neighborhood property owners, developers, urbanists, environmentalists, and lovers of New York City history. The hundreds of volunteers and donors I worked with to attend city council hearings, write letters, make signs, and more enjoyed being a part of the process because they met others with whom they had something in common, and they felt good about their support for a new, unique civic amenity. They felt proud to be part of a creative contribution to society. Many individuals who are still volunteering in the park as docents, gardeners, or otherwise, still wear with pride their red "Save the High Line" T-shirts, created and handed out by FHL before the structure was fully preserved.

FHL also created unique ways to be involved in envisioning and eventually designing the High Line itself. In 2003, the organization launched an open ideas competition to generate a wide variety of creative visions for what the space could become. Entries ranged from the whimsical (a roller coaster, a mile-and-a-half-long swimming pool) to the pointed (a prison, as a way of making public our increasing numbers of incarcerated people in the United States). The competition received more than seven hundred entries from over thirty countries. The results were displayed at Grand Central Station, generating citywide buzz about the project. The organization also organized the High Line Portrait Project, Chalk Shoes, and other creative civic projects, many in partnership with local public schools, businesses, and community centers, all providing fun and interesting ways to engage with neighborhood history, politics, environmental concerns, and the growing civic movement to develop the park.

FHL heavily managed the design process alongside the city, which not only ensured more community input than normal, but also that the organizers' aesthetic visions were prioritized. When considered along a hierarchy where citizen power is better than tokenist and superficial forms of engagement (Arnstein 1969), the High Line's process was a significant improvement on most public engagement processes (PolicyLink 2012). The design team was required to present plans publicly on a regular basis to community groups in the neighborhood surrounding the High Line, and input sessions were held at public housing sites, with the community board, and at public schools. If neighbors had severe concerns, FHL was able to take the time to meet with them, hear their concerns, and in almost all cases, find a way to address them. FHL had good intentions when it came to gathering input from the wide diversity of neighbors surrounding the park. Citizens had much more information about the design of the park than normal and developed relationships with staff and even some design team members over time, with repeated exposure to the process through the sessions.

FHL made a concerted effort to publicize the events widely and to invite community leaders with whom it was working hard to develop individual relationships. In many cases, the organization left flyers at each home and building for many blocks around the High Line. Meetings were held for the most part in neutral and comfortable locations, like public schools and community centers, though it was noted when meetings were held at less neutral locations, like within the West Chelsea gallery district. However, child care was not provided, and meeting notices were in English only, without translators available, despite the presence of large Spanish- and Mandarin-speaking populations in the neighborhood and the city as a whole. In order to truly involve communities who have traditionally been marginalized, more than just an invitation to a meeting is required.

On the other hand, the community design sessions suffered from the same issues common to other such input processes, which are not typically considered fully democratic exercises (Fung and Olin Wright 2003). Sessions were for the most part classic podium-and-audience arrangements, with community decision making being secondary to the primary purpose of sharing information and updating people. This format allowed some members of the public to be partially educated about the process, but did not encourage or leave open the possibility for a more in-depth partnership or community control with regard to the design itself (Foundation Consortium n.d.). And, as Michael Rios writes of typical community engagement processes, "in addition to discouraging dialogue outside of narrowly defined problems, these processes fail to acknowledge that some of the people most negatively affected by planning decisions are the least visible" (Rios 2014: 187).

Additionally, the designers and ultimate decision makers were still (generally speaking) a group lacking racial, ethnic, national, socioeconomic class, and to some degree, gender diversity. This allowed underexplored assumptions about what "good design" meant to work their way into the design, development, and management of the space. Overall, the design process was much more concerned with conceptual and aesthetic consistency and form than it was on creating a space inclusive of a wide range of spatial practices.

Part of this focus was enabled through the ongoing support of the Bloomberg administration, which was immediately supportive of the project when the mayor took office in 2002. In an era of declining federal funding for municipalities and increasing competition among cities on a global scale, cities' fiscal tax bases are increasingly vulnerable (Donald et al. 2014). Ensuring stability and fiscal health through the property tax base and bolstering the tourist economy has become a common response of cities facing these budgetary dynamics (Pagano, Hoene, and McFarland 2012). Developing flagship public spaces, generally through public-private partnerships, are key elements of this trend. Chicago's Millennium Park and Seattle's Olympic Sculpture Park are two prominent examples. FHL was not antibusiness or antidevelopment, especially if it meant the High Line would move forward quickly with the support of the city (David and Hammond 2011). Given the high price of environmental remediation on the old structure, not to mention future design and operations of a narrow, elevated park, FHL quickly realized it had to make a proposition of value to the city in order to get the park built. The organization also realized that it would have to raise a significant amount of funds on its own. These factors played a huge role in the project's focus on "high design" and created pressure for the High Line to succeed as a return on investment for the city.

Although the campaign and design were wildly successful in many ways, they largely lacked ownership from, and representation of, many demographic groups in the neighborhood and city: namely, low-income individuals, communities of color, immigrants, and others—groups that have contended with compounded effects of exclusion and marginalization over decades. There were no specific measures to institutionalize inclusion, nor was there a commitment to ensure that positive economic impacts were widely shared or even focused on those who may need them most. These factors may have contributed to the demographic trends among High Line visitors, as well as to the lack of familiarity with the park among local public housing residents after it opened.

IMPLICATIONS AND PROMISING PRACTICES

In its civic orientation, intended public impact, and innovative programming, FHL provides important lessons for public urban space development. What the organization has learned through its listening initiative and responsive programming is that true relationship building, especially across race and class barriers, takes time, humility, empathy, and a great deal of intentionality and purpose. It also indicates that this effort bears fruit for all parties involved. This work strengthened the High Line's ability to deliver on its civic ideals and truly be a democratic space. It also begins to counteract (if only on a small scale) decades of unequal resource distribution and exclusion. It is vital to consider how the High Line might have looked and what impact it might have had if this process had occurred prior to the park's conception, design, and development.

Specifically, these lessons provide several key insights for urban development decision makers who seek to leverage new public investments to equitably maximize potential impact: (1) be clear and intentional about which communities a project seeks to impact and how; (2) actively share power and institutionalize partnerships with diverse communities (with a specific focus on low-income communities, communities of color, immigrants, and others typically marginalized by these processes); (3) devote resources and time to enacting policies and programs that may counteract any negative consequences that result from increased investment; and (4) be clear and honest about who the governing bodies are accountable to, and institutionalize accountability mechanisms.

If an urban development project hopes to create a publicly accessible amenity, it must acknowledge that even with the best of intentions, new public investments will not benefit everyone equally. To benefit groups that are positioned in marginalized ways with respect to power and resources, the process must begin with a humble interest in learning the history of other communities and sharing with them. As Roberto Bedoya writes, "how race, class, poverty, and discrimination shape place—through a politics of belonging or dis-belonging—needs to be reflected upon whether one is engaged with Creative Placemaking practices as an artist, funder, developer, NGO, or governmental agency" (Bedoya 2013). The same applies to park-making and other public realm infrastructure provision.

Specific policies and programs can be built that counteract past histories of marginalization, segregation, and disinvestment, in order to ensure that positive impacts of any new investment or development are widely shared. John Powell's *Racing to Justice* (2012) may be a helpful resource here in thinking about how targeted programs that seek to counteract past exclusion are actually a necessary part of the ideal of universal democratic impact.

Organizations that are committed to this kind of change often conduct regular anti-oppression trainings, self-educate, and institutionalize open and trusting relationships with individuals and community representatives from impacted communities. These relationships may be fraught and difficult at times, but they achieve a crucial alliance-building effort required to maximize positive impact. They also recognize that equity and democracy are never finished. This is a stance requiring ongoing deliberation, rather than framing as a task to complete/check off.

Designers and urban planners themselves can also incorporate a willingness to bear responsibility creatively in the planning and design of a space, as Barbara Brown Wilson and Liz Ogbu discuss in the recent article "When Good Intentions Aren't Enough: Linking Intent to Impact" (2015). Brown Wilson and Ogbu suggest that designers and developers can introduce frameworks and practices that increase the likelihood of equitable impact into the design and development process of a building, plan, or space.

Several similar projects that are currently in development at the time of writing include the Atlanta BeltLine, the 11th Street Bridge Project in Washington, DC, and Denver's Artway. They all show immense promise in their commitment to equitable process and impact. The Atlanta BeltLine created a tax district around the new green development, helping to fund the creation of below-market-rate units near the park. A 2014 study showed that

985 such units had been created (O'Connell 2016). The 11th Street Bridge Project was only approved after a series of two hundred community meetings indicated that neighborhood residents surrounding the new park actually wanted it. That project has since gone on to include residents in the design team selection jury and to convene an Equitable Development Task Force. That task force is currently exploring a community land trust and small business incubators for minority- and women-owned businesses (11th Street Bridge Park 2015). "If the people who helped to shape this can't afford to live there, then we will have failed," Scott Kratz, the project's director, has said (O'Connell 2016).

Of course, even if these projects have meaningful and equitable positive impacts on their surrounding communities, there is an inherent limit to what place-based investments can achieve. Truly addressing long-standing inequities in current metropolitan regions will require a sustained commitment on the part of policymakers, investors, developers, and others to counteracting the uneven playing field that can cause negative impacts as a result of new public investment. Single place-based developments cannot alone be expected to remedy inequality.

New public realm developments, and the processes by which they are designed, funded, built, and managed, are key sites for staking a claim to the kinds of places and cities we can create. A nuanced look at the High Line's development reveals a complex story, and specifically the difficulties of developing a public, democratic space given an existing landscape of extreme inequality. Building an intention around equity and institutionalizing accountability and action that focus on equitable process and impacts can help public spaces deliver on their civic promise.

3 · LOVING THE HIGH LINE

Infrastructure, Architecture, and the Politics of Space in the Mediated City

ALAN SMART

THE HIGH LINE has been completed. Rather, the work of reconstruction, performed by contract labor under the direction of designers, project managers, and a constellation of consultants, is finished. The architects and landscape architects who have worked for so many years designing the project and managing its construction have finalized their plans, marked off their punch lists, and sent out their final invoices. In a city that often marks its historical periods by mayoral administrations, Mayor Michael Bloomberg, whose administration has claimed the High Line as a crowning achievement in an array of ambitious building projects, has left office with his legacy cemented and the narrative of his administration wrapped up more neatly for having completed it. The construction of the High Line has, however, also been a long process during which much has happened, other processes and cycles of longer and shorter duration have "progressed" forward or spun in place, and the world has changed. As much as the opening of the High Line is a set of conclusions, it is also the commencement of the project's existence as an architectural object or strand woven into New York City's tissue of public space.

In a variety of accounts, the High Line project has been discussed as being either itself a process piece, as a part or symptom of other processes, or in other time-based terms. A "High Line effect" (McGinn 2014) has been described that attracts "visitors" and makes the city more "livable" by creating what is supposed to be a green space apart from the somehow "crowded" and difficult-to-live-in city. This has been differentiated from the "Bilbao effect" (Rybczynski 2002), produced by the sculptural, monumentally scaled museum that Frank Gehry designed for the Guggenheim Foundation, that is claimed to have contributed to "revitalizing" a depressed provincial capital in Spain by providing a symbolic, though mute, "icon" for the city. Less clear, and certainly less explicit in the popular press, is the distinction between the "High Line effect" and the original referent, the "Beaubourg effect" that Jean Baudrillard (1982) described in his critical essay on another seminal project of systems-oriented, urban culture-making: the Centre Georges Pompidou in Paris, designed by Renzo Piano and Richard Rogers. Also a *longue durée* project manifesting a transition between paradigms, the Pompidou shares the High Line's quality of mediating, uncomfortably, between the registers of material systems (both natural and infrastructural, systems of signs and information, and the production of images and environmental conditions). If the High Line is organized by design operations effected within and upon dynamic systems and conditions of flux, then—just as in Beaubourg—these are simultaneously ecological, semiotic, economic, and political processes.

The High Line is unavoidably cast as a monument to the civic building initiatives of the Bloomberg administration, appearing as evidence of the working of a neoliberal urban policy organized by public-private partnerships and committed to a vision of enlightened economic development working in the public's interest. This can be differentiated from the (neo) conservatism of the Giuliani years, in which a narrative was constructed of the crisis and chaos of the 1970s and 1980s being pushed back by fiscal discipline and aggressive policing focused on "quality of life" issues and embracing the "broken windows theory" (Wilson and Kelling 1982), which links the visual appearance of disorder and the tolerance of social deviancy and political dissent with uncontrolled violence and criminality. The Giuliani years would find—perhaps too late—their ideal urban architectural project in the reconstruction of lower Manhattan after the September 11, 2001, attacks on the World Trade Center. In this, issues of symbolic monumentality would be engaged politically in the refiguring of office towers and the public spaces of a financial district as monuments to dead heroes and defiant assertions of national unity and strength. In contrast, the Bloomberg administration would struggle to maintain a narrative of prosperity and progress in the face of crises that were more in the register of the mayor's history of synthesizing media and financial information systems. If, in this narration, a claim was laid to elements of the legacy of progressive politics and their complex relationship to architectural modernism in New York City, then projects relating to the World Trade Center had provided a venue for the resurgence and reappraisal of conservative postmodernist discourses from the 1970s.

PSYCHOLOGICAL OPERATIONS

The rhetorical schema in which the High Line "succeeds" by attracting visitors or "revitalizing" neighborhoods is, more than architecture, that of planning. In this the patron, if not author, of the High Line has been Amanda Burden, director of the New York City Department of City Planning during the Bloomberg administration. In 2014, shortly after the end of her term, Burden gave a retrospective account of her career as a planner and public servant in a speech at the annual meeting of Technology, Entertainment and Design (TED). TED serves as something of a vanguard for the liberal progressive tendency in the United States by positing a conception of "design" that is at once expressive, innovative, and entrepreneurial. Technology is then figured as an updated version of the old modernist hybrid of science and industry, and "entertainment" is approached as cultural production and ideological formation. Burden concluded her TED talk with a discussion of her role in the reconstruction of the High Line, noting, "When I was appointed, saving the first two sections of the High Line from demolition became my first priority and most important project" (Burden 2014). In framing the High Line reconstruction as a project of preservation or "saving," she complicated the figuration of design as a uniformly positive, additive process in which creative actors insert or "place" designed objects into empty spaces. She also complicated distinctions between subjects and objects: those who act and that which is acted upon. Burden used several terms to refer to subjectivity in her talk. She began with the assertion that "cities are fundamentally about people" and that therefore the public spaces between buildings are "more important" than the buildings themselves, because they make the city "come alive." People, when taken together, for Burden constitute the public, and she identified herself as an "animal behaviorist" who understands how people behave in, or "use," public space. There are, however, distinctions within Burden's category of the public. New Yorkers "crave comfort and greenery," yet both "architects" and "developers" favor "bleak plazas" because, for architects, they are "plinths for their creations" and for developers they offer minimal maintenance and security costs. When people are constituted into smaller groups with specific, local interests they become, in Burden's view, "communities" who must be listened to so that their opposition can be overcome and their support secured for projects benefiting the "common good." Burden also introduced another, more problematic, collective subjectivity in the form of "commercial interests," whose goals, in her account, often do not align with the "common good" and who "will always battle against public space."

In Burden's zoological account of urban planning, only three subjects are given individuality: herself, Bloomberg, and her stepfather. Burden opened the narrative of her career by introducing her stepfather as the creator of Paley Park, the "pocket park" on 53rd Street that, since its completion in 1967, has been celebrated as a model for privately owned public space. Design work on the project was done by the landscape architecture firm Zion and Breene, but, according to Burden, the "dedication and enormous attention to detail" that defined the project came from her stepfather, William Paley, the chief executive who built the Columbia Broadcasting System (CBS) into a major national media firm that shaped the development of popular radio culture in the United States. An exemplar of the political pragmatism characterizing an American progressive tendency that managed to be technocratic without being socialist, Paley was a moderate Republican who collaborated with the Rockefellers on cultural philanthropy projects, but he also maintained connections to the Roosevelt administration during the Second World War. He served in the war, with the rank of colonel, in the psychological warfare branch in the Office of War Information, demonstrating that media could not only be an industry, but even part of the war industry, along with its "heavy" industrial counterparts that produced steel, oil, and arms.

In discussing Paley Park and public space in general, Burden used the terms of both media and psychological operations. Without acknowledging her source, she referred to the film study *The Social Life of Small Urban Spaces* by William H. Whyte (1980), sponsored by the progressive, and still influential, Municipal Arts Society. Burden had worked on the documentary early in her career and rehearsed its narrative of people as charmingly eccentric social animals, who are naturally attracted to one another and move their chairs just to feel that they are in control of their environment. She did not discuss the "bleak plaza" in front of the Seagram Building, the other public space observed in Whyte's film, but it is clear that this would, for Burden, represent the work of plinth-making architects rather than progressive civic place making. What she did discuss are specifically human feelings of attraction, desire, and belonging. Public spaces should be "friendly" and make people—even those who don't use them—feel good about their city. Despite her professional credentials, Burden asserted that the way to "turn a park into a place that people want to be" is to work "not as a city planner but as a human being. . . . You don't tap into your design expertise. You tap into your humanity" (Burden 2014). If this humanity is assumed to be shared and universal, then the feelings it experiences are mediated by images perceived as immersive environments. In this humanist conception, leaders and designers are defined less by their superhuman genius or technical expertise as by the perfect commonality of their humanity or, as Paley was famous for, their astute comprehension of popular taste and desire.

In beginning her account of the High Line project, Burden, however, introduced a strange anecdote that complicated and exposed contradictions in her humanist perspective. She described being taken to see the High Line and becoming convinced of the importance of preserving the elevated deck and making it into a public space. Burden made no mention of the circumstances of these events, of who made her aware of the situation, brought her to the site, or framed, analyzed, and proposed the project. This all seems to have melted away in the intensity of the encounter. "When I went up on that old viaduct," Burden recounted, "I fell in love the way you fall in love with a person" (Burden 2014). She described nothing more of what she fell in love with, but there is, perhaps, nothing more to describe. Burden, as an exceptional human subject, was able to look at the High Line and the resurgence of nature that it represents and, as if making eye contact with a lover across a crowded room, see another subject gazing back at her. The account of the High Line's development that followed this Jane-meets-Tarzan moment was rendered in the terms of a love affair.

Burden thought constantly about "saving" the High Line. She defended it from unnamed "developers" who would turn it into a mall or demolish it for not fitting with "their image of a gleaming city of skyscrapers on a hill" and she invested it with agency and admiration. "Public spaces have power," she asserted. "It's not the number of people using them; it's the even greater number who feel better about their city just knowing that they are there" (Burden 2014).

Burden's ardor served both to solidify her as the persona of the entire city and blind her to her paramour's past, other commitments and entanglements, and possible faults. Not only did the Friends of the High Line, who proposed the project, and the architects and landscape architects, who worked on it, fall outside her frame and recede from view, but the current struggles over the gentrification and economic inequality, along with the law-and-order "cleaning up" of the city under the Giuliani administration that set the stage for them were also effaced. Rather than attempting to rationalize and systematize these processes—perhaps as her caricature of a city planner would—Burden's practice of "tapping into [her] humanity" instead focused on the production and transmission of images of the city and investing these with narrative meaning. Despite the upbeat affirmativeness of Burden's TED talk, this process was not as simple as the conversion of a piece of utilitarian, material infrastructure—the rail line—into a symbolic, culture-affirming, social space—a park. Just as the building of CBS and Bloomberg Media involved the synthesis of social relations, communications systems, and material infrastructure, Burden's city is an infrastructural machine, engineered to produce value. The primary value produced here is, however, symbolic and constitutive of subjectivities. In this, the progressive modernist project of using built forms to effect "social engineering" is shifted to one of more explicit political economy, in which relational structures are designed to transform conditions both cultural and material.

INFRASTRUCTURE AND ITS DOUBLE

The original construction of the High Line as an elevated railway was part of a rebuilding of the infrastructure along the Hudson River, which inaugurated a much larger project of remaking the city through these means. This process advanced under the direction of Robert Moses, who would come to stand as both an avatar of technocratic city planning and a leading translator of modernist urbanism into the terms of American culture and politics. Moses's later work, driven by postwar prosperity and responding to the social transformation it brought, would be more explicitly high modernist in character. The High Line and the West Side reconstruction, however, took place during the Great Depression and mobilized labor from the Works Progress Administration (WPA) and others of the subsidy and stimulus programs that made up Franklin D. Roosevelt's New Deal. In addition to increasing the efficient flow of materials into the meatpacking and industrial facilities of Chelsea, the High Line served as part of a larger project to organize the city and region as an integrated socio-technological machine. Constructed and managed by collaborations between state and industry actors, this apparatus was directed toward both the production of value and the reproduction of a stable, rational social order. Because the WPA was initiated to keep people working and to facilitate the continued circulation of capital, its projects had the double purpose of driving this circulation while at the same time teaching, choreographing, and arguing for modern forms of life that would constitute a social body. Questions of materiality, and of what this social body could be, how it could be constructed or constituted in conscious, controlled ways, and to what degree it was either an artificially engineered machine or a "natural" living system would, however, remain open both as theoretical issues and as flashpoints of political contestation.

In the postwar period, Moses would mirror his reconstruction of the infrastructure along the Hudson with a waterfront parkway, named for Roosevelt, along the East River. This arterial road extended ribbons of circulatory infrastructure, looping and slashing through Queens and the Bronx to growing suburbs on Long Island and north of the city. Enfolded in the interwoven traffic streams of FDR Drive is an enclosed bubble of real extraterritoriality in which the symbolic utopia of the United Nations (UN) Headquarters would come to stand, designed by a fractious collaboration of modernist architects, among whom Le Corbusier was the most prominent. The UN Headquarters stands as a perfect diagram of the modernist differentiation between infrastructure and that which it serves and facilitates. A rectangular office tower, like a huge bookshelf or file cabinet, housing the organizational bureaucracy, stands next to the round congress hall containing the symbolically constituted whole of a united world community. The true dichotomy, however, lies not within the architecture of the UN Headquarters but between the architecture as superstructural symbolic object and the infrastructural armature that situates and supports it.

Modernism's abstraction made it possible to imagine a separation between the engineering of material infrastructure and the design of symbolic form. In the American context, this split was invested with significance in ideological struggles between progressive tendencies and the populist and conservative forces that would oppose them. The "bleak" minimalism of modernist aesthetics may have been comfortably applied to "corporate" modernism and conventional domestic projects, but, when it came to housing, infrastructure, and public space projects organized by efforts to construct new social subjectivities, resistance was mounted to "utopianism" and "social engineering" that were seen to threaten the wholeness and naturalness of the human subject. The rhetoric and antinomies of these oppositions shaped the aesthetic and cultural politics of postwar modernism and the various strains of postmodernism that followed it. These symbolic politics are resurgent in discussions of the High Line, now that the possibility has been opened of its becoming "Architecture" in the more rarefied sense. What the High Line does, however, is to make uncomfortably clear the ways in which differentiations between the material and the symbolic, which underpin the opposition between the modernist social engineers and their postmodernist agonists, have not held up and perhaps never did.

Writing from the vantage point of the late 1970s, Rem Koolhaas (1978) described the condition of architectural islands within infrastructure as "delirious" in his "retroactive manifesto" of New York City. Koolhaas found a proto-postmodernism in "the city of the captive globe" in which separate, microcosmic worlds are created within a presumed-to-be-neutral grid of streets. In this, and his other early, polemical project *Exodus, or the Voluntary Prisoners of Architecture,* he asserted the possibilities of an architecture of icons—or rather iconic objects—and the enclaves of autonomy enclosed by them, which would grow like the fruiting bodies of a fungus from the invisible substratum of infrastructure below. The utopian enclaves that Koolhaas described, however, were not progressive modernist projects like the UN Headquarters (or, for that matter, the UN). Rather, he looked to commercial social spaces, created as entrepreneurial ventures that constitute identity through leisure consumption: downtown clubs and uptown hotels for the wealthy, amusement parks for the working class, and spectacular music halls for the middle class with some money to spend on entertainment. The delirium of Koolhaas's city comes from the dissolution, or liquidation, of subjectivity within the disjunction between symbolic and material orders effected by capitalism. The potential politics of the subjects reformed when this liquidity once more solidifies is, however, schizophrenic and alienated as much from the conditions of its reproduction as it is from the processes of production within which it is entangled. In writing a retroactive manifesto, Koolhaas was able to indulge in one of the principal conceits of neoliberalism by displacing the work of reproduction to some already-occurred time in the past or by pushing it into the dark jungle of a naturalized culture.

As postwar reconstruction processes developed and expanded into the creation of increasingly globalized, integrated systems of production and logistics, material and semiotic infrastructures would overlap, sometimes competing with one another for space and resources and bandwidth and, at other times, hybridizing and blurring one into another. A condition that was, on a global scale, hyperindustrial, and perhaps hypermodern, would be experienced in urban centers like New York City as postindustrial, as economic expansion and consolidation would increasingly push the processes of material production away from the city, first to the suburban periphery and then overseas. In architecture and urban planning this would exacerbate the difficulties of mediating between material and symbolic production.

The architectural process piece that would manifest these difficulties most starkly would take place not in New York but in Paris, in the Centre Pompidou. Rogers and Piano were awarded the commission in 1971 after winning a competition, initiated in 1969, for a new type of museum that would expand the exhibition of art into a wider range of cultural activities that engaged with a larger public audience. Their original proposal, rendered in cartoonlike collage images, promised to realize a project in which the architecture was reduced to a flexible scaffolding and infrastructure supporting dynamic systems for creating and conditioning environments. In addition to the playful dynamism of the Centre Pompidou's ducts and pipes making visible the mechanical workings of the building, they were also intended to demystify the flows of energy and material through the building and the mechanics of creating environmental conditions. Ironically, the project was planned to reinforce the "return to order" after the strikes and uprisings of 1968 and was situated on the site of the Les Halles market that Émile Zola called the "belly of Paris," both because it was where food came into the city from farms in the countryside and because of the seething foment of vice, criminality, filth, and radicalism that frothed up from the churning circulation of food and bodies and money and ideas. By relocating Les Halles to the suburbs and replacing it with the Centre Pompidou, an actual infrastructure of circulation was replaced by a symbolic representation of material circulation, whose primary function was to create a circulation of signs. The project went through a long and contentious public process before it was completed in 1977. During this process, openness and flexibility were largely designed out, and the circulation of the public through the building—like the symbols through the public consciousness—became more controlled and efficient. When the Centre Pompidou did finally open, it was against the background of the oil crisis—in which the flow and exchange of energy and capital was impeded by political forces—and the building's vectors of signification seemed to point more emphatically toward refineries and trans-shipment hubs than the construction scaffolding or stage sets that were the architects' intended citation.

In his sharp critique of the Centre Pompidou, media theorist Jean Baudrillard described the project as "a carcass of signs and flux, of networks and circuits . . . the ultimate gesture toward translation of an unnamable structure: that of social relations consigned to a system of surface ventilation (animation, self-regulation, information, media) and an in-depth, irreversible implosion" (Baudrillard 1982: 3). Baudrillard criticized the Centre Pompidou for sanitizing the city around it, but more important, he condemned the clarity and authoritarian coherence of the story it told about social construction and the creation of subjectivity. He referred to the Centre Pompidou as "Beaubourg" both in reference to the neighborhood in which it was built and so that the concept of the "beautiful city" could universalize his critique to include the postmodern city as a whole. In this utopian conception he sees an end, or collapse, of both politics and culture.

"This thing," Baudrillard asserts, "openly declares that our age will no longer be one of duration, that our only temporal mode is that of the accelerated cycle and of recycling: the time of transistors and fluid flow. . . . The very ideology of 'cultural production' is, in any case, antithetical to culture, just as visibility and multipurpose spaces are; for culture is a precinct of secrecy, seduction, initiation, and symbolic exchange, highly ritualized and restrained. It can't be helped. Too bad for populism. Tough on Beaubourg" (Baudrillard 1982: 5). Baudrillard writes that the architecture—and perhaps all architecture of this type—treats "the masses . . . like a converter, a black box, or in terms of input/output, just like a refinery handling petroleum products or a flow of raw material" (1982: 6). In this mixing of the metaphors of cybernetics and oil, a conflation is made between information, energy, and "raw material" that describes a too-bright interiority that condenses or constitutes wholes. To this Baudrillard opposes the dark space of another sort of infrastructure. "From today," he writes, "the only real cultural practice, that of the masses, ours (there is no longer a difference), is a manipulative, aleatory practice, a labyrinthine practice of signs, and one that no longer has any meaning" (1982: 6).

FRAME AND FRAMEWORK

In New York City, the practice that has been able to engage most successfully with this mode of anti-architectural architectural production is Diller + Scofidio (now Diller Scofidio + Renfro, or DS+R). Together with the redesign of Lincoln Center, the High Line project has been one of two long-duration projects that have defined DS+R's development from a specialized conceptual practice whose work was often dismissed as "not architecture" by conservative disciplinary border guards, into a major feature of whatever international avant-garde there can be said to be in architecture at this point. This transition has taken place even as New York City has itself moved from the authoritarian clamp-down of the Giuliani-era cleanup, to a new gilded age of spectacular prosperity, coinciding with the High Line's long redevelopment process, and now into the uncertain present, where the project has arrived, already an artifact from several different pasts.

The early work of DS+R includes buildings that can be described as "iconic" (if that was what a critic wanted to see), including the Institute of Contemporary Art in Boston and their proposal for a building for the Art + Technology Center that, had funding been secured, would have been built next to the High Line. Another sequence of projects, however, engages with the capacities of architecture as frame and mediator. The Brasserie restaurant in the Seagram Building, around the corner from Mies van der Rohe's "bleak plaza," uses surveillance camera technology to materialize the otherwise tacit voyeurism of the bar. A beach house for a couple of art dealers named the Slow House, which deployed a frustratingly curved axis of vision approaching the high-value ocean view, which was then framed, targeted by cross-hair window mullions and reproduced repetitively on video screens, most explicitly manifests linkages between the framing, objectification, and commodification that take place as architecture projects its field of effect into the surrounding context. Less literally a frame but equally a study in mediation is the Blur Building, which adapts technical elements from one of the most exemplary projects of socially affirmative, environment-conditioning media/systems architecture—the Pepsi Pavilion designed for the 1970 Osaka Expo by the design collective Experiments in Art and Technology (E.A.T.). Its tensegrity structure scaffolding creates not a spherical interior, but a reactive intervention in the open system of the climate: an artificial cloud of water vapor over a lake. This project was particularly transgressive of the compositional, object-making imperatives of architectural convention, less in being unformed and indeterminate in its objecthood, and more in being an intervention in the material dynamics of natural systems that was able to cut across the clean, safe separations between the real and the symbolic that these conventions were made to enforce.

In both the High Line and the redesign of Lincoln Center, these two modes of practice are combined. For all of its spectacular moments, Lincoln Center was a process piece, worked out through a laborious series of interventions into both material structures and infrastructures, and the social and political machinery of New York City. The diverse, but largely conservative, client group originally sought to hire a master object-maker to be the architect, someone whose humanist ideological orientation more closely matched theirs. They found this in Gehry, but it quickly became clear that the project would require the ability to design both globes and that which they are captured by. The project was shifted to DS+R in the hope that their critical approach to systems would allow the project to navigate the social ecology it grew from and was sustained by. In the High Line, this mode is even more radically operative.

In a blog post by Anna Winston in *Dezeen Magazine*, Ricardo Scofidio describes the project as a "pulling back from architecture" (2014). The political will and shared public narrative that drove the conversion of the High Line into a public space initially coalesced around a collection of images by photographer Joel Sternfeld, published in the book *Walking the High Line* (2001). Taken over a period of years, the photographs present the High Line as a "natural" space, recolonized by plant and animal life that had reestablished an advancing "soil cycle" and become a microcosmic ecosystem within the city. The images are mostly composed so as to contrast this lush, second landscape with the surrounding urban context. Rather than a simple opposition between the natural and built environment, however, Sternfeld's images suggest there are also ecologies at work within the changing city. As one of the founders of Friends of the High Line, Sternfeld has worked in more conventional ways to mobilize public support and organize capital for the project of preserving and converting the High Line into a public space. It was, however, his deployment of images that enabled the formation of a public capable of visualizing the conversion process and projecting a desired future condition for the High Line. Nevertheless, the qualities of the resulting condition remain heavily marked by the doubly visual character of a project founded on a process of making visible—and therefore accessible, and therefore public—and then creating a structure from which to look at the city differently and visualize alternative possible conditions.

As an urban architecture project, the design of the High Line is forced to negotiate between the imperative to create a space that is public, accessible, visible, and "safe" for its range of imagined user groups, and desires to retain the potentials of alteriority, disjunction, and difference that had defined the site. In *Dezeen Magazine*, Elizabeth Diller asserts that the High Line "became a ruin and it was self-seeded, all of that was what we built the thing out of, so our feeling was that our biggest work was not screwing it up—because it was already there" (2014). The thing that was "already there," however, was as much a precarious microclimate of social ecology or "political landscape" as it was a growth of literal vegetation. If the steel deck of the rail line was a "ruin," then so too were the remnants of industrial production that had organized modernism, upon which had "grown" the living systems of postmodern culture and postindustrial symbolic and image-producing economies. In light of this, the great, lost cause of "not screwing it up" is reduced to the preservation of at least a ghost of the relational structures—turned into the relations of production by the High Line's "friends" in the art world—that create autonomy in the unvalued, invisible, and alien. And all of this had to be achieved while providing for public safety, access for Americans (and foreign visitors) with disabilities, emergency egress and unimpeded access by the fire department, prevention of the breeding of rats and other vermin, mitigation of liability, and doubtlessly claiming to reduce the risk of terrorism, vandalism, and so forth.

A strange paradox of the High Line reconstruction—and one that seems to have in fact driven its success both in being realized and in being received as a model for urban development—is that the project's architects have attempted to turn away from architecture and operate more as gardeners in the urban jungle. Its landscape architect, James Corner, on the other hand, has striven to claim for his work some of the totalizing vision and authorial agency that has defined and often burdened architecture in its conventional figurations. In an essay titled "Terra Fluxus" (2006), written just as the reconstruction of the High Line was getting under way, he writes of a resurgence of interest in landscape, conceptualized as the plane of "complexity" where built infrastructure and ecological systems interface.

In "Terra Fluxus," Corner attempts to selectively draw elements from modernist systems thinking and use them—along with a large measure of optimistic affirmation—to mediate between the neoliberal ideologies of growth, development, and hyperconnectivity, and the mythic romanticism of a conservative postmodernism figured as the (eternal) return of neoclassicism. Corner begins by invoking the shift from the progressive loading of what he calls the "green complex" of functionalist urbanism to conceptions of systems ecology. "This 'green complex,'" he states, "comes in the form of parks and green open spaces, accompanied by the belief that such environments will bring civility, health, social equality, and economic development to the city. More than aesthetic and representational spaces, however, the more significant of these traditional urban landscapes possess the capacity to function as important ecological vessels and pathways" (Corner 2006). He, however, turns this analysis not toward utopian ecological management, but instead to the neoliberal hybrid of technocratic control of market forces imbued with an almost mystical vitalism and claimed as a "new nature," in which are synthesized biological systems, the plane of the circulation and accumulation of value, and the territorial domination of power. Corner writes that he would emphasize an

> understanding of surface . . . as urban infrastructure. This understanding of the urban surface is evident in Rem Koolhaas's notion that urbanism is strategic and directed towards the "irrigation of territories with potential." Unlike architecture, which sums the potential of a site in order to project, urban infrastructure sows the seeds of future possibility, staging the ground for both uncertainty and promise. . . . [I]t is much more strategic, emphasizing means over ends and operational logic over compositional design. For example the grid has historically proven to be a particularly effective field operation, extending a framework across a vast surface for flexible and changing development over time, such as the real estate and street grid of Manhattan. (Corner 2006)

Corner introduces a distinction between projecting and speculating on the future in both conceptual and financial terms and suggests, in his invocation of "operational logics," a potential politics.

When he arrives at the point of articulating the promise held out, however, he resorts to romantic conceptions of constituting community founded on a mythos of symbolic order. Corner claims that "public spaces are firstly the containers of collective memory and desire, and secondly they are places for geographic and social imagination to extend to new relationships and sets of possibility. Materiality, representation and imagination are not separate worlds; political change through practices of place and construction owes as much to the representational and symbolic realms as to material activities" (Corner 2006). In his more recent writings, Corner no longer refers, as he did in "Terra Fluxus," to the socially engaged naturalism of Frederick Law Olmsted, but rather to picturesque garden design and its tradition of composing pictures with the uncomposed realness of the material world and using these to construct or bolster the solidity of the viewed subject. In his 2014 essay "Hunt's Haunts," reprinted in this volume, the humanist world-picture-making is coupled with the romanticism of ruins and conceptions of the "spirit" or "genius of place." In the case of the High Line, this *genius loci* is construed as a kind of nature spirit that emerges from the history and culture of the city taken as a preexisting ground to be projected upon. This reservoir of contextual meaning is taken as a thing to be discovered, tapped, extracted, and speculated on—like oil or the remnants of antiquity redrawn by oblivious British neoclassicists on the grand tour.

In this sense the High Line is a border. It is a thick border with an interior that accommodates voluntary prisoners, as in Koolhaas's exodus project. Here Sternfeld's much-discussed images of the High Line as a "natural" space are restaged—now with benches and lighted footpaths—for a procession of tourists who have come to experience the space. The High Line is not, however, either Koolhaas's wall or a Beaubourg. As much as it is a cinematic procession of picturesque views or a closed system of social massification, it is also a viewing apparatus for looking at the city and objectifying its visible valence.

If the High Line steps away from architecture, then architecture has taken several steps toward it. The icon makers have contributed many more-or-less inspired confections to the Flemish still life of architectural opulence that Chelsea is developing into. Gehry's lustrous fruiting body springs from an invisible mycelium no less banal—though perfectly Koolhaasian—than the Shopping Network. Neil Denari's luxury condominiums appear in an elegantly engineered, diagonal frame that expresses, on an architectural scale, all the fluid plasticity of a beautiful piece of nonfunctional sports equipment designed for never-performed labors of self-improvement. Here the masses passing along the High Line can gawk at the carefully "staged" interiors, notionally inhabited by the global super rich, who for the most part fail to "appear" as political subjects or otherwise. For the less spectral rich there is a proliferation of more livable condos that, to greater or lesser degrees, choreograph luxurious forms of life while remaining inscribed with vestiges of nonalienated "loft living." At the southern end of the High Line, in the Meatpacking District, Renzo Piano has again designed a culture refinery for the Whitney Museum that will, this time, be itself more refined and—in an era when "data is the new oil"—more sophisticatedly integrated into the circulation of signs that is the city's metabolism.

STEPS TOWARD THE POSSIBILITY OF A "NEXT"

Through financial crisis and (possibly jobless) recovery, the force field emanating from the High Line (or whatever is behind or beneath it) will retain its charge and continue to generate its effect. This new infrastructure of symbolic immateriality will go on imbuing the objects accreting around it with value, and the machine that is the High Line will continue to make the "land"—both the literal earth and the cultural ground—pay. It will pay and keep paying even as a new municipal administration has arrived with a mayor who invokes a return to the projects of progressivism (and who was noticeably absent from the opening of the final stage of the High Line) but who has appointed a police commissioner who was the architect of the city's "broken windows" approach to law enforcement. What remains to be seen is whether and which subjectivities will be able to claim these channels of circulation and the infrastructures of the new logistics as spaces of appearance. If postmodernism effected a liquidation of politics and culture into fluid streams of signs, then we are now in the desperate era of hydrofracking where the last drops of value—that "untapped potential" so sought after by neoliberalism—are being wrung, in atomized droplets, from the city, its ecologies, and its people through pressure, along with the grinding, crushing rupture of production detached from reproduction and consumption split from signification.

Like the Centre Pompidou, the High Line has arrived late and will be judged—fairly or not—in a context different from what it was designed in response to: the discussions of gentrification and development that had been structured by issues of lack of affordable housing and loss of "neighborhood character" or "sense of place." A popular blog titled *Jeremiah's Vanishing New York* exemplifies a set of discourses in which the appearance of the High Line and its effect of making-through-making-visible is paradoxically framed as a disappearance of some older, more human city. What seems lost, however, is disappearance itself: a space that had been able to be inhuman and escape the front-of-house/back-of-house diagram of the stage-set city, in which increasingly the audience watches only itself. Character has been imparted and sense-of-place enhanced. If anything, the picture is too perfect and the space too precious. The construction of inhabitable world-pictures and microcosmic utopias, blind to their infrastructural support has, in many places, achieved a density that threatens to displace and suffocate all that is other to it: the city of the captive globe becomes a dense foam of spheres captured only by each other.

The next step—whether it is toward or away from architecture, forward or back, keeping up, moving on, or just keeping going—must be to find ways in which the liquefied and diffuse objects of both architectural and political practice can coalesce, not into symbolic orders and micro-spectacular phantasmagoria, but into real, material, alternative infrastructures that support life, whether "natural" or not. If rupture and ruin is to be the field condition established by the strategic operations of power and capital, the tactics of condensation, blockage, and functional realignment must be found. If a thing like the High Line is to be useful as a ruin, it will not be as a shrine to a cultural mythology that composes world-pictures while causing displacement, disruption, fracturing, and dissolution of reality outside its frame. Rather, it will be as a memento mori in the still life image of the banquet: a reminder that all infrastructures—whether material or social—are always also ruins or potential ruins, that the flows can coagulate, and that the subjugated barbarians can smash the empire's aqueducts and turn them into houses.

It is seductively simple to frame this next step as a call to refuse the reification and personification of dead things that Burden exhibits in professing her love for a derelict rail line, even as she abstracts living people into populations and "communities" and constituent components of the urban apparatus. This paraphilia can be seen as the spatial expression of a passion that animates social formations from the "black box" high-frequency trading algorithms of postmaterial finance, to the geekiness of "big data" cultural ideology, to the ecstatic techno-vitalism of "parametric" architecture.

It would be easy to be overcome by an ethical revulsion and demand the stamping out of this perversion and the creation of, or return to, a city where people address one another as subjects—whether to confront one another, struggle with each other, or fall in love. However this city of human relations, lucid communication, and gazes met and returned may relate to Baudrillard's conception of Paris, New York has always been an inhuman city, made more so by its humanist rulers. The potential architecture, and potential politics, that, despite the mystifications, is implied by the High Line is one that, rather than claiming humanity and making places, struggles to keep moving and keep working, namelessly and without hope of definitive success. The radical potential in this struggle will lie not in the creation of spaces that supply a "sense of place" and affirm feelings of humanity but rather in the setting up of conditions of possibility in which subjectivity can be broken and reformed and the city made and unmade responsibly, if often blindly, from within its dense meshwork of infrastructures, plans, and agencies. There is no need for another Beaubourg, as the "beautiful city" has already been built. From now on, the task of architects working in the abattoirs of the Meatpacking District and wherever the High Line effect is manifest will be to process and package the "carcass of signs and flux" and thereby feed the city.

PART II GENTRIFICATION AND THE NEOLIBERAL CITY

4 · PARKS FOR PROFIT

Public Space and Inequality in New York City

KEVIN LOUGHRAN

AT THE OPENING ceremony of New York's High Line in 2009, billionaire Mayor Michael Bloomberg declared that the new park was "an extraordinary gift to [the] city's future" (Pogrebin 2009a: C3). His statement placed him in a long tradition of politicians, city boosters, and urban planners who have collectively asserted that parks are built for the public good (Low et al. 2005). For centuries, parks have been closely related to ideas about democracy, public health, and civic virtue (Wolch et al. 2005). But park development in the contemporary city has taken on a different complexion. Rather than existing for the broad public, new spaces such as the High Line in New York and Millennium Park in Chicago represent an effort by city governments and elite private interests to leverage parks for profit.

The group of elite political, economic, and cultural actors that came together to redevelop the High Line represents what Harvey Molotch (1976) famously termed the "growth machine." Molotch argues that "growth" is the driving force of all cities, as the economic benefits that accumulate through urban growth provide incentive for elites to act collectively in ways that structure further growth. In New York under Bloomberg, neoliberal economic doctrine and an overarching "growth" ethos exacerbated social inequalities of all kinds (Brash 2011); these effects are particularly visible at the level of public space. City governments and developers build luxury public spaces to lure tourists and wealthy consumers for leisure and consumption—the High Line and the Brooklyn Waterfront Greenway are two prominent New York examples—while parks catering to poor communities and immigrants are underfunded and forgotten unless they can serve "growth" schemes—as seen, for example, in the case of Flushing Meadows–Corona Park in Queens, which in 2013 was leased to a billionaire to build a new sports stadium (Powell 2013a).

The High Line thus represents an archetypal urban park of the neoliberal era, where the rising inequality of economic and cultural resources produces a spectrum of unevenly developed public parks, ranging from elite, privatized spaces in wealthy districts to neglected parks in poor neighborhoods (Boone et al. 2009; Wolch et al. 2005). Developed for profit and spectacle by New York's contemporary growth coalition—the city government, real estate developers, and financial and cultural elites—the High Line has become one of the city's most popular tourist attractions and an anchor for the super-gentrification (Lees 2003) of western Chelsea. While Jane Jacobs's "urban village" offered a community-controlled model of urban space (Shepard and Smithsimon 2011: 38–44)—one that could be exclusive, elitist, and undemocratic—today's urban spaces are the province of global capital and culture, where the "community" is transnational and the "control" is elusive, privatized, and panoptic (Flusty 1994; Madden 2010; Mitchell 1995; Shepard and Smithsimon 2011).

NEOLIBERAL PUBLIC SPACE

Much scholarship has identified important changes in the form and function of parks and public spaces that parallel transformations in capitalism, urban politics, and culture. From the first planned parks of the modern city, parks have fostered social control and shaped the social construction of "the public" (Madden 2010; Taylor 1999). Like urban parks in previous eras, public spaces such as the High Line express the relationships among citizens, the state, and other institutions of power. These expressions take on many forms. The neoliberalization of public parks is far from complete, and an amalgam of city parks districts, private conservancies, and business improvement districts increasingly control public spaces (Shepard and Smithsimon 2011;

Zukin 2010). Overlapping administrative units and "revanchist" police tactics also blur the public/private distinction of spaces (Smith 1996; Vitale 2008). As Sharon Zukin argues, privately managed spaces like New York's Zuccotti Park can be the sites of populist expressions and political actions, while state-run public spaces can sometimes be "more repressive, more narrowly ideological, and not representative [of democratic principles]" (Zukin 2010: 158). The inequality of urban public spaces in contemporary cities—expressed by the contrast of luxury spaces such as Bryant Park (Madden 2010) and marginalized spaces of gun violence (Nickeas and Gorner 2013; Schweber 2012) or sidewalk "stop and frisk" policing (Beckett and Godoy 2010; Vitale 2008)—mirrors the "savage sorting of winners and losers" in the global economy (Sassen 2010). In the contemporary city, there is growing unevenness in the economic, political, and cultural resources that structure and sustain the spaces, squares, and parks that materialize the "public sphere" in physical space (Low and Smith 2006; Madden 2010).

We are also witnessing a parallel divergence of cultural practices in space and the ways in which public space is experienced. In wealthy, predominantly white sections of the contemporary city, "entrepreneurial" public parks (Hall and Hubbard 1996; Zukin 2010) create both the subject of the citizen-consumer (Scammell 2000) and a heavily (if discreetly) surveilled, depoliticized public realm. In gentrified neighborhoods like Manhattan's Lower East Side, community gardens that once served to "take land out of the market economy and 'decommodify' it" (Zukin 2010: 211) now function as symbols of "authentic" urban communities, more apt to structure the consumption habitus of the new urban middle class, such as preferences for "local, organic" foods, than to offer refuge for rural migrants and radical environmental activists (Eizenberg 2012; Martinez 2010). In less affluent areas like East New York, community gardens lie mostly outside of the purview of developers and gentrifiers (Zukin 2010). While some large parks, like New York's Central Park, host daily cultural events and are funded by wealthy conservancies, there are other large parks, like Chicago's Washington Park, that serve more as lines of race and class demarcation than spaces of consumption, and where the trend is not one of development, but disinvestment (Boone et al. 2009; Wolch et al. 2005).

Analysis of privileged public spaces such as the High Line requires consideration of history: stratified, nominally "public" spaces that reproduce existing power relations have always been a part of cities, dating to the agorae of Greek antiquity (Low and Smith 2006: 4). Likewise, cities have always contained spaces of violence and exclusion, and counterhegemonic spaces are often fleeting, at constant risk of co-optation or destruction (Eizenberg 2012; Shepard and Smithsimon 2011). Therefore, to examine changes in the social production of urban public spaces is not to glorify Frederick Law Olmsted, Jane Jacobs, or community gardens. If elite spaces like the High Line are not fundamentally "new," they are at least spatial representations of the ongoing redefinition of citizenship and the state under neoliberalism, as privatization and commerce structure the convergence of consumption and citizenship (Jubas 2007).

The High Line case reveals how this redefinition is occurring in a context of economic power and social privilege. In a super-gentrified section of one of the world's wealthiest cities, elite actors developed a public space to spur economic growth and structure the leisure and consumption patterns of the new urban middle class.

A WALK ON THE HIGH LINE

It is 3 P.M. on a cool Friday afternoon in September 2011, and the High Line is at its verdant, vibrant best.[1] As one walks from the east, the dingy streets of the West 30s give way to the elevated green space, brimming with people after the summer's final gasp of heat and humidity. From the sidewalk, the High Line's black undercarriage is striking, as are the tufts of tall grasses and people peeking over its edge. Below the viaduct is the Friends of the High Line's (FHL) seasonal complement to the new park, an entertainment complex on a soon-to-be-developed parking lot that abuts the High Line's northern terminus. A tall fence plastered in Uniqlo and High Line Rink logos faces the sidewalk along Tenth Avenue. Uniqlo, a Japanese fashion retailer, is expanding its New York presence and has partnered with FHL to bring an open-air roller skating rink to the park. At the entrance, a uniformed security guard stands watch over the sidewalk, defending the space like a bouncer. His shirt is emblazoned, fittingly, with "Citadel Security" (see Friedmann and Wolff's [1982] discussion of urban citadels). A handful of people—all white, in their twenties and thirties—casually skate. Beyond the rink stand a Uniqlo "pop-up" store and half a dozen food trucks offering some of New York's upscale "al fresco" options—including CoolHaus, selling "architecturally inspired gourmet desserts," and Taïm Mobile, offering "Tel Aviv street food with a gourmet twist." The trucks are complemented by an arrangement of picnic tables and a long wooden bar—"The Lot on Tap," a collaboration between FHL and celebrity chef Tom Colicchio. A few dozen people—here too, predominantly white young adults—snack on falafel, dumplings, and beer, while additional Citadel Security personnel stand watch.

A few flights up from the street, the High Line's northern terminus offers vistas of Midtown and the skating rink below. This second section—which stretched the nascent park from 20th to 30th Street—had just opened in June, and plans for the third section—which would bring the High Line to the rail yards at 34th Street—are progressing. A few men are already working beyond the chain-linked fence that halts the line of pedestrian traffic. Looking northward over the rail yards, it is easy to see what had attracted Bloomberg and the cadre of real estate developers to the High Line: twenty-six acres of effectively undeveloped space sitting right in Midtown Manhattan.

An outcropping of benches provides seating for the dozens of people gathered at the edge of the park. Others press against the fence, eagerly taking photos of the Hudson River and Midtown's skyscrapers. Like the crowd at The Lot, everyone is white; the park's Latino construction workers are the only people of color in view. As one walks south, the wide landing area gives way to the narrow pedestrian corridor that defines much of the High Line's one-mile linear space. A long line of benches hugs the western edge of the passageway; a few people read books, click on iPhones, and chat in pairs, but at this time of day, the benches are mostly unoccupied. Opposite the benches is a row of tall grass, protected by a rope that hangs twelve inches off the ground, keeping stray feet at bay. A hundred yards south, the High Line careens through old industrial buildings and brand-new "starchitect" condominiums. Here the viaduct slices the blocks between 10th and 11th Avenues; the feeling of connection with the city's street grid begins to dissipate as taller, lusher plants overtake the space. The darkness provided by the plants and buildings makes this section a moodier, more contemplative space, though there is little room for people to linger. Like a conveyer belt, the rhythm of foot traffic forces everyone to keep pace.

Around 23rd Street, the park opens up again. A small patch of grass offers the first place where visitors can get inside the ropes to touch and feel the flora, and today it is full with people lounging and napping. Just ahead, a uniformed High Line official stops to collect plastic bottles from a recycling bin. A few paces further, an ice cream sandwich vendor stands alone behind a pushcart while several people take advantage of the view to Midtown's skyscrapers, taking photographs of themselves on their phones with the Empire State Building in the background. Just to the south of the skyscrapers, the nearby public housing towers also come into view.

The employee collecting plastic bottles highlights how startlingly clean the park is. Megan, a white food vendor in her twenties, discusses how the FHL regulate her immediate space. "[The FHL] are OCD [obsessive-compulsive] about it being clean up here. We aren't allowed to have any trash bags. We can't even give napkins to people unless they ask for them." She points to where she deposits her cart's trash, a small black box hidden behind a plant at the High Line's edge. "It has to be hidden back there so that people can't see it. I have to empty it away from the park at the end of the night." Another food vendor, Ricky—a Latino in his forties selling Korean tacos—discusses the process of obtaining a vending license from the FHL, a process that had been criticized by some politicians for its lack of transparency (S. Chan 2009). "It took about two months. [FHL] wanted to meet all our employees and taste all our food. It cost a thousand bucks to apply, too—non-refundable."

South of the vendors, near 17th Street, is one of the High Line's more sociable places. At the "10th Avenue Square," also known as the "Sunken Overlook," a glass cut-out affords people a view of the automobile and pedestrian traffic on the street below (see figure 4.1); the wide seating

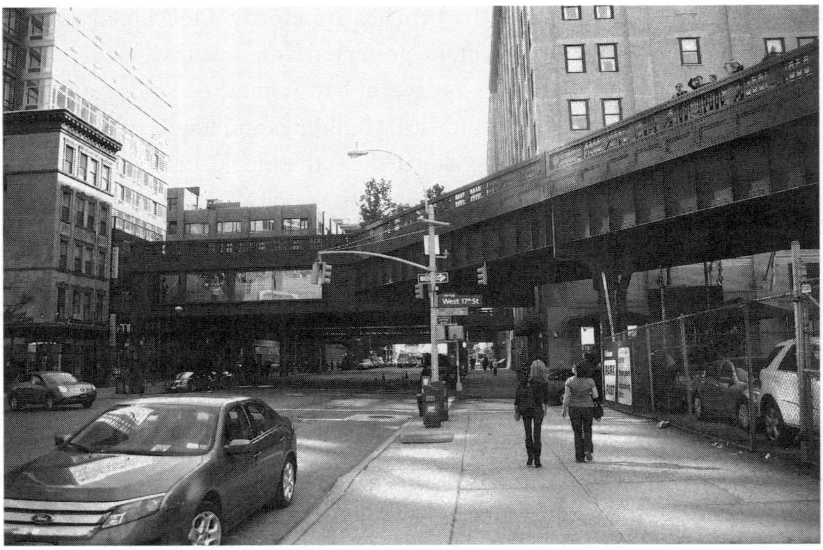

FIGURE 4.1. A view of the High Line from the sidewalk; the 10th Avenue Square is at the left. Photograph by the author, 2011.

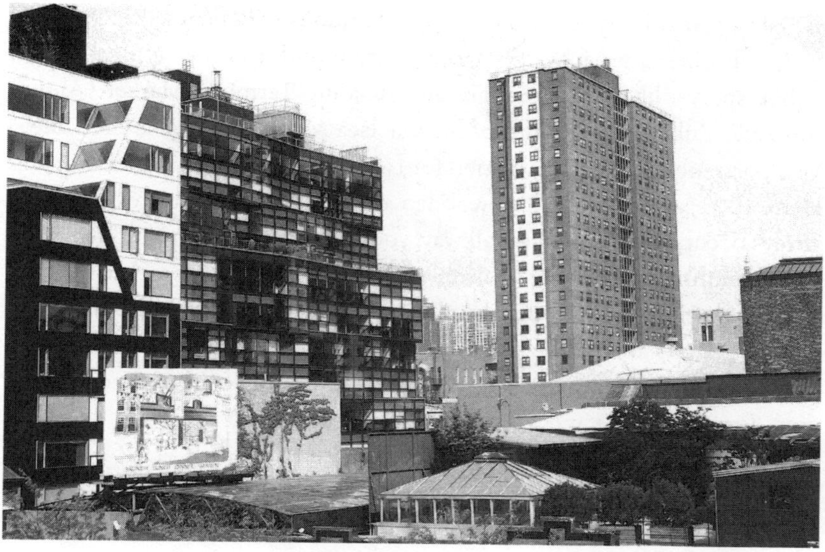

FIGURE 4.2. Public housing meets "starchitecture." Just to the east of the High Line stand (*left to right*) Della Valle Bernheimer's 459 West 18th Street (which *New York* magazine notes "suggest[s] an M. C. Escher print" [Davidson 2009]), Audrey Matlock's Chelsea Modern, and the Robert Fulton Houses. Photograph by the author, 2011.

banks provide room for groups of people to rest, and today many people are taking advantage. Overhead, billboards for luxury brands—Veuve Clicquot, Armani, and Hennessy—line the park. South of 16th Street is the Chelsea Market passage; here the High Line cuts through a section of a large industrial building that was originally a Nabisco factory. Inside, three art vendors sell their wares. One art vendor—James, a white man in his thirties—displays handmade mobiles with "inspirational" messages written on them. He sells them for $20 or $40 apiece, depending on the size, while he works on new pieces behind a large table. Nearby are competing gelato and artisanal popsicle carts and a full espresso bar. There's also an official High Line cart—selling books, apparel, and memberships—and a farm-to-table restaurant.

Scattered throughout the Chelsea Market passage are metal folding chairs and small tables, arranged haphazardly along the edges of the space. Many are occupied with readers, eaters, and people-watchers. A dozen people, mostly white young adults, are in line at the espresso bar; others wait for gelato and tamarind-flavored popsicles. With no plants, the High Line seems wider here, and the extra room, coupled with the bustle of the vendors, gives the space a feeling of continuous occupancy. It's here that the High Line approaches the conviviality found in more "typical" urban public spaces, like Union Square and Reading Terminal Market (Anderson 2012; Zukin 2010). South of the Chelsea Market passage is the Diller–Von Furstenberg Sundeck, named for two of the park's billionaire patrons. Here, there are a handful of wooden chaise longues that are seemingly always occupied. Across the walkway, young children splash barefoot in the small, centimeter-deep "water feature." Another High Line worker, this one walking north, stops to collect bottles and cans from a recycling bin.

The pedestrian traffic wends south through another "passage" at 14th Street. Today a predominantly white crowd of about a hundred is gathered, forcing north- and south-bound pedestrians to the park's edges. A sign announces an interpretive dance performance titled "Half-Mythical, Half-Legendary Americanism." The performance features a group of dancers clad in neon pink and white-and-black-striped spandex, parading in a style that supposedly mimics the nationalist sports demonstrations of the early Soviet Union. Blaring an off-key drone through a portable speaker, the group moves southward through the park, while onlookers stand on chairs to catch a glimpse over the crowd. The performance continues under the Standard Hotel—a luxury hotel literally built *over* the High Line in 2009—before ending a hundred yards from the park's southern terminus at Gansevoort Street. Immediately to the west is a newly minted construction site, where the Whitney Museum of American Art will be relocating from the Upper East Side in 2015.

Exiting the High Line via a long flight of steps, there's another Uniqlo "pop-up" store and more art and food vendors on the sidewalk below. These food vendors are quite different from those on the High Line, however. Operated by immigrants, instead of recent college graduates and middle-class entrepreneurs, these carts sell Manhattan's more commonly found "street food" items—hot dogs, soft pretzels, and the like—rather than hand-crafted popsicles and ice-cream sandwiches. One hot dog vendor, Abbas, says that he enjoys working in the High Line's shadow: "People go, they drink, they relax [in the park]" before purchasing his food. The art vendors are selling items similar to those found on the High Line; three display original artwork, and a fourth sells movie posters and prints of *New Yorker* covers.

One of the artists, Patrick, discusses his resentment toward the FHL. Under the current arrangement, only five art vendors are allowed to sell on

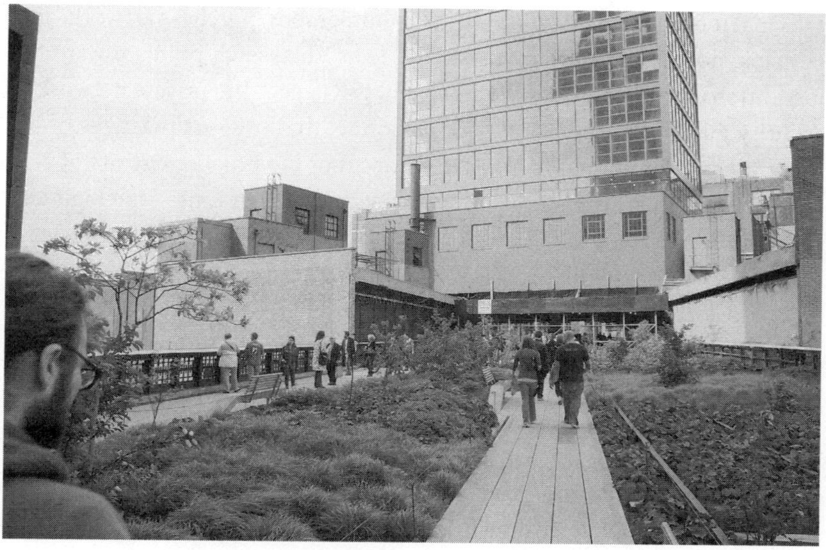

FIGURE 4.3. Much of the High Line's design channels pedestrians through narrow spaces. Photograph by the author, 2011.

the High Line each day, on a first-come basis. "I started selling up there right when it opened. Before [the FHL] cracked down on it, there were about twenty artists who sold up there. Business was great, really great. When you have a line of kick-ass artists, everyone does well." A few people poke around the art vendors' tables, but no one buys anything. Beyond the vendors, the sidewalk scene yields to the din of 14th Street and the Meatpacking District's luxury boutiques, restaurants, and cobblestone streets.

THE HIGH LINE AND THE UNEVEN DEVELOPMENT OF PUBLIC SPACES

The above ethnographic sketch of a typical sunny, summer day at the High Line illustrates how privilege is experienced in contemporary public space. Spatial "privilege"—the ability to make claims on public space, based on high standing within socially constructed and intersecting hierarchies of gender, race, class, sexuality, and national origin—reproduces social advantages in a process that both affirms individuals' existing cultural capital and enables "practices of consumption that open up multiple arenas for the expansion of other forms of capital" (Centner 2008: 195). Visitors to the High Line eat artisanal foods, drink microbrews, take photographs, purchase artwork, and, perhaps most remarkably, occasionally sleep. The sketch points toward the institutional underpinnings of this spatial privilege—the private network of security guards, vendors, and park personnel that support practices of leisure and consumption. We also see glimpses of the broader circuits of economic and cultural capital that intersect with the High Line—the high-end residential buildings, the redevelopment of Hudson Yards, and the relocation of the Whitney Museum, as well as the branding of the elite philanthropists and corporations that helped finance the High Line's redevelopment.

The ethnographic sketch further reveals how the design of the High Line puts constraints on individual spatial practices. While the intentions of architects (and the elites who ultimately direct the production of space [Smithsimon 2008]) do not wholly determine how people will use public space (de Certeau 2000; Lefebvre [1974] 1991), the High Line's narrow, linear space—coupled with relatively few places to play, sit, or linger, especially for larger groups of people—structures the most typical movement within the park: a bucolic walk from one end to the other.

The FHL's spatial strategy is partly a product of its position as a private conservancy. Though the park was built largely with public funds (Friends of the High Line 2008b), the city government has outsourced its ongoing management to the Friends of the High Line. Like other "entrepreneurial" public spaces (Hall and Hubbard 1996; Zukin 2010), the High Line is therefore immersed in commercial activity—a product of the neoliberal prescription that public parks must be financially self-sustaining. Food vendors cater to privileged tastes for artisanal and comfortably "exotic" foods, art vendors add to the privileged consumption aesthetic, and corporate partners—Uniqlo, AT&T, Calvin Klein, Millennium Partners, and many others—underwrite the FHL's operating budget. Through the park's commercial and surveillance mechanisms, the FHL encourages privileged consumption and passive forms of leisure—in line with the design team's motto of "keep it simple; keep it wild; keep it quiet; keep it slow" (field notes, 10/3/11).

Surveillance and exclusion are discreet on the High Line, as tends to be the rule for privileged public spaces (Madden 2010; Shepard and Smithsimon 2011). Only certain portions of the park are policed by methods of overt coercion. Beyond the High Line's design, the FHL uses institutionalized social control to regulate the socio-spatial practices of park users. Private security guards—like those overseeing "The Lot" in the above ethnographic sketch—are most visible at the park's special events: lectures, dance performances, and private gatherings, such as a reception I observed at the "14th Street Passage" for a corporate law firm (field notes, 10/3/11). The majority of the time, the FHL relies on relatively inconspicuous surveillance methods, such as the uniformed park employees who regularly empty the park's recycling bins. This tactic is possibly designed to prevent enterprising bottle collectors from scrounging through the bins for bottles and cans, which are worth five cents apiece at city recycling centers. Acts like bottle collection are widely seen as the sort of "quality of life violation" that the city's "revanchist" policies have sought to erase from public space (Smith 1996; Vitale 2008).

Along those lines, the spatial practices that are supported within the privileged domain of the High Line further reveal the differential policing of public space characteristic of the neoliberal era. As Alex Vitale notes, New York's retaliatory policing strategies have targeted "squeegee men, panhandlers, and *people sleeping in public spaces*," whom he argues "came to be the most visible symptoms of an urban environment that many people felt was out of control" (Vitale 2008: 70, emphasis added). While the New York Police Department's removal of homeless individuals from Manhattan's major public spaces is more or less complete (Duneier 1999; Vitale 2008) and sleeping in public has been effectively criminalized (Vitale 2008), at the High Line, it is routine in warmer months to find people sleeping on the chaise lounges at the "Diller–von Furstenberg Sundeck" or on the grass at "the Lawn." Sleeping in public space reveals either a profound trust in one's socio-spatial environment or a dire lack of other options. For privileged individuals visiting the High Line, sleeping in public space represents an enormous luxury. For less privileged individuals—such as homeless people, poor people, and people of color—sleeping in public space carries the stigma of poverty and potential danger. The sleeping practices of High Line visitors, therefore, illustrate the profound inequalities that exist among contemporary urban public spaces. In the divergent conditions of neoliberal public spaces, not only are parks in poor neighborhoods underfunded and unevenly developed (Boone et al. 2009; Wolch et al. 2005), but the spatial practices engendered by differential methods of social control are similarly segmented along intersecting lines of race, gender, class, sexuality, and national origin.

The High Line's redevelopment also informs understandings of contemporary growth coalitions and the new urban politics. The High Line's redevelopment underlines the centrality of cultural elites to the neoliberal growth machine (Whitt 1987). The success of the Friends of the High Line's cofounders in broaching New York's elite cultural networks—recruiting wealthy donors from the realms of fashion and art—played an important role in shifting developers' and politicians' attitudes toward the High Line in the first decade of the twenty-first century. Joshua David and Robert Hammond were able to draw a new mayoral administration and a network of real estate developers into what was originally a grassroots movement, in spite of the fact that members of the growth coalition had spent decades agitating to dismantle the High Line. This suggests that the social spaces that foster "growth" are inherently malleable constructions: what was once seen as a spatial symbol of blight—a space that was the antithesis of urban development—became reformulated as a spatial vehicle for gentrification and capital accumulation.

The High Line's redevelopment further emphasizes the dialectical quality of socio-spatial contests (Lefebvre [1974] 1991). Today's grassroots contestation of urban development is tomorrow's co-opted centerpiece of a growth scheme, which is then subject to new contestations, like those of artist-activist Robert Lederman, who fought the FHL's regulations on art vendors (Polsky 2009), and environmental groups that protested the use of rainforest wood in the High Line's construction (Parker 2009). While some of these contestations occurred in the High Line's public spaces, many of the political negotiations surrounding the High Line's redevelopment took place within the "post-democratic" (MacLeod 2011) realms of city planning commissions and public-private partnerships, thus raising questions about the ability of contemporary public space to sustain meaningful democratic interventions.

ACKNOWLEDGMENTS

This chapter is adapted from Loughran 2014.

NOTE

1. This data is presented as a composite sketch of a "typical" day on the High Line, generated from four months of fieldwork. Some identifying information has been changed.

5 · PARK (IN)EQUITY

JULIAN BRASH

APPRAISALS OF THE High Line come in two distinct flavors. On the one hand, there are celebrations of the park as a new and exciting kind of public space, artfully bringing together the reuse of postindustrial infrastructure, urban design, culture, grassroots initiative, and sustainability. In this view, the High Line is "an invaluable and transformative gift" (Ouroussoff 2009), "one of our most important new models of public space" (Goldberger 2014), "a communal enrichment" (Filler 2009). Then there are critical takes, which argue that the park's aesthetic appeal and popularity disguise a far more troubling picture of a space that represents a new high (or low) in the ongoing privatization, post-politicization, embourgeoisement, surveillance, exclusion of undesirables, and subtle control of ostensibly public spaces. Seen from this perspective, the High Line augurs "the continued neoliberalization of public space [that] will only exacerbate longstanding socio-spatial inequalities" (Loughran 2014: 53). So which is it? Is the High Line an exemplar of contemporary public space, or of contemporary "public" space? Should we take the park at face value or see it as a pretty veneer on a far nastier assemblage that has evacuated the notion of public space of its radically, or even conventionally, democratic promise?

Or, perhaps we need to take a third approach and focus on the "public" in public space: not just as a normative measure or as a regime of power/dominance, but also as a dynamic conception embedded in ongoing struggles and debates concerning the production of space in New York City (and elsewhere). Doing so illustrates how the claims to, and the critiques of, the

High Line's "publicness" have political force in these struggles and debates, force that might overflow the intentions and control of the elite supporters and developers of the park. In fact, this approach helps to explain the rapid rise in 2013–2014 of the issue that came to be called "park equity," which stemmed (if it did not halt) the neoliberal tide of privatization and luxurification of the city's public spaces. For if there is one thing that the two positions described have in common, it is that neither anticipated the emergence of this issue, which made the equitable distribution and maintenance of public park space a proxy for larger debates about inequality, the role of the state, privatization and the public sector, and notions of the common good. In what follows, I aim to show how the High Line helped create the conditions of possibility for the emergence of the park equity issue, and, in doing so, argue that we need to see the High Line not as representing a new paradigm of public space, or as its betrayal: instead, we need to see the publicness of the High Line as an unfulfilled promise, and to understand the political work the gap between this promise and the reality of public space in New York City was made to perform in the first decade and a half of the twenty-first century.

THE HIGH LINE'S PROMISE

Fifteen years later, it is easy to forget the political-economic context of Joshua David and Robert Hammond's initial advocacy for the preservation and reconstruction of the High Line. The mayoralties of Ed Koch, David Dinkins, and, most of all, Rudy Giuliani all saw drastic, if varied, movements toward the privatization of public space. The post–fiscal crisis decades of the late twentieth century saw a multipronged campaign to impose "order" on the cities' public spaces, usually by ridding them of the homeless, "squeegee men," protestors, and the sundry other urban undesirables who made life in the city unpleasant for the (white) middle and upper classes, the attraction of whom was increasingly seen as the key to urban economic revival (Smith 1996; Vitale 2008). In combination with post–fiscal crisis norms of selective austerity, which saw public support shift away from the broad-based public provision of goods and services toward those that served the imperative of postindustrial growth, this campaign affected the city's public parks in three distinct ways.

First, there was an overall disinvestment in the city's park system. In 1960, spending on public parks had made up about 1.4 percent of the city budget; in 1991, the number was 0.65 percent, and by 2014 it had fallen to 0.4 percent (Committee on Parks and Recreation 2014; Levine 2014). Unsurprisingly, this decline in funding was felt most acutely in the great majority of the city's roughly 1,900 parks located in the poorer and more far-flung areas of the city, where the benefits of the city's reemergence as an economic and cultural powerhouse in the 1990s were apparent only tenuously, if at all—as opposed to the burdens of austerity and aggressive policing, which were pervasive. However, even the city's most prominent parks—Central Park, Prospect Park, and so on—were affected by this decline in funding.

Second, a certain form of public-private partnership, the park conservancy, sprang up to fill the funding gap, at least for those few parks lucky enough to be favored with media attention, private generosity, and booming nearby real estate markets. Most were in the privileged districts of Manhattan below 96th Street and in gentrifying Brooklyn. Chief among them was the exceedingly well-capitalized Central Park Conservancy, which essentially took over responsibility for, and control of, the park's budget, staffing, and operations (see chapter 8, by Phil Birge-Liberman). The exact strategies conservancies used varied. They included philanthropy, the introduction of retail and commerce, increased policing and surveillance, and free and paid cultural events. But one constant was that the establishment of conservancies and the increased role of private money and control led to the formation of individuated "communities of self-interest" around parks (Perkins 2009a, 2009b, 2010, 2013). The relation of a citizen to parks was no longer defined by the use of and access to the park system as a whole, but rather by a willingness to assume responsibility for the particular park to which one's attachment—whether financial (via its impact on real estate values), recreational, or social—was strongest. Moreover, the increasing role of conservancies helped justify public disinvestment: why should the public at large invest in parks that were not able to demonstrate the support of their "local community"? This neoliberal logic also eroded the long-held conception (often honored in the breach) of the city's parks as a single system to which all New Yorkers had access, and for which all New Yorkers were responsible (Rosenzweig and Blackmar 1992: 524).

Finally, parks were a central focus of stringent new regimes of surveillance, policing, and social control implemented in the city's public spaces.

Particular parks, usually located in areas where gentrification or redevelopment was under way, such as Tompkins Square Park (Smith 1996), Central Park (Rosenzweig and Blackmar 1992: 514–520), and Bryant Park (Madden 2010: 195–196), were prime targets for heavy-handed interventions. These park "cleanups" removed "undesirables" from urban space and, in so doing, helped reclaim space for development. More subtly, the legitimated uses of parks were reconfigured in ways that favored elite sensibilities and lifestyles, via the foregrounding of commerce and certain sorts of cultural events, aesthetics, and programming (Low et al. 2005: 66; Madden 2010; Rosenzweig and Blackmar 1992: 518–520). City parks, and particularly large and well-used ones like Central and Prospect Parks, continued to be used by a broad range of New Yorkers. But the question of who parks were for was being answered in a new, and restricted, way.

All this was especially notable in a city that had long been celebrated for, and proud of, the quality and accessibility of its park system. On the one hand, the design and programming of urban parks have often served to pacify the "lower orders," defuse social conflict, "reform" public culture, produce docile and productive subjects, "cleanse" the city in both moral and physical terms, and bolster patterns of profound racial inequality (Azzarito et al. 2004; Caro 1975; Cranz 1989; Draper 1996; Gandy 2003; Low et al. 2005; Madden 2010; Rosenzweig and Blackmar 1992). Yet parks in New York City—whether Tompkins Square (Smith 1992) or Zuccotti (Shepard 2012)—were also sites of ideological contestation, political gathering, popular organization, spontaneity, and counterhegemonic cultural appropriation. The city's most famous and celebrated public parks, and the "imaginary of an urban whole" that they evoked, represented "urban democratic symbolism at its most powerful" (Bender 2002: 225). Even as the post–fiscal crisis era saw already existing parks become less "public" in their funding and programming, and the park system become, like the city itself, more unequal, the publicness—the accessibility and collective "ownership"—of the city's parks remained a powerful, if increasingly threatened, ideal.

It was into this context of overall long-term public disinvestment and uneven private reinvestment that Joshua David and Robert Hammond made the initial push to save and redevelop the High Line, founding the nonprofit group Friends of the High Line (FHL). These two may have been well-educated white-collar professionals conversant in the language and practice of technical expertise, public policy, and the political process, and well connected to the city's movers and shakers. But they were not real estate developers, corporate executives, or elite planners driven by the desire to transform the city in line with the requirements of capital. Nor were they the typical authority- and agency-hopping creatures of the city's murky development apparatus. They could, with some credibility, claim to represent the "community" or the "grass roots." Such claims were bolstered by the initial opposition of local property owners and a scornful Giuliani administration, which had so enthusiastically implemented policies of privatization and revanchism in the city's parks, and by 1999 had begun a precipitous slide in popularity only arrested in the aftermath of the terrorist attacks of 9/11.

Moreover, from the very beginning, the advocates of the High Line stressed the importance of a park that was open to everyone: the oft-stated goal, "to get people up there," while clearly naive and perhaps even disingenuous (Which people? Under what conditions?), nevertheless evoked ideals of openness and accessibility. And despite some initial intimations from Philip Aarons, the well-connected developer who was one of the park's earliest backers, that the High Line might be developed as a "privately-owned public space" through the use of the city's zoning code (David and Hammond 2011: 10; Miller 2007), there was never any real doubt that the park would in fact be "public," in the sense of being owned by the city government and funded, at least in part, by city money. This was made clear by 2003, as both the Bloomberg administration and the city council had committed to purchasing the High Line structure and devoting significant public resources to its redevelopment.

Other factors helped reinforce the High Line's bona fides as "public" in more symbolic ways. The pervasive role of design, art, and culture in the park's development process signaled that the park was not just about attracting investment or increasing real estate values. The park's supposed "sustainability" also represented a claim to broader import and a commitment to higher values. Likewise, the refusal of FHL to endorse the Bloomberg administration's plans for a West Side stadium at the northern terminus of the High Line and its repeated criticism of elements of the larger Hudson Yards plan that might threaten the integrity of the structure established the organization's independence and willingness to stand up for its vision of public space. The fact that both Hammond and David (like many of its prominent early supporters such as local restaurateur Florent Morellet and West Side City Councilwoman Christine Quinn) were gay, and the fact that the pre-reconstruction High Line itself, along with nearby areas like

Chelsea, the Meatpacking District, the West Village, and Hell's Kitchen, were well-established sites of LGBTQ socio-sexual practice, lent the project an air of inclusivity.

Finally, there was the repeated, consistent, and vocal claim on the part of FHL and other institutional actors, such as the Design Trust for Public Space, as well as supportive architects, designers, philanthropists, critics, and politicians, that the High Line represented an innovative *public* park. The centrality of the concept of "public" to the skillful and ubiquitous marketing of the park, regardless of the intent of its users, had real force, particularly coming after decades of ideological and material assaults on the city's public spaces, its parks in particular. Suddenly public space was hot—perhaps best (if superficially) embodied by a series of photographs, published in the society pages of the city's newspapers in 2009, of fashionable partygoers at an expensive High Line benefit holding "We ♥ Public Space" signs. All this was a real departure from the post–fiscal crisis norms, and particularly from "Giuliani Time," when public space, and parks in particular, if not ignored, were construed as problems to be solved—either through private sector benevolence, commercialization, or social cleansing.

It is entirely appropriate to subject the High Line's claim to "publicness," and the varied bases of this claim, to rigorous critique. And in fact, the critical case has been cogently and powerfully made. David Madden (2010), in a discussion of Bryant Park that is equally applicable to the High Line, argues convincingly that efforts to make urban parks more accessible and open—that is, more public—may in fact embody elite projects of neoliberal rule and result in what he calls "publicity without democracy." Kevin Loughran takes apart the High Line's origin myth, noting that "the folksy legend belies the duo's sophistication and deep ties to the city's elite" and "that as the Friends of the High Line continued to gain momentum and financial support, idealistic sentiments were cast aside for pragmatic realpolitik" (2014: 55). Indeed, it is clear that the Bloomberg administration's embrace of the project—without which the High Line could not have become a nominally public park—was driven by its broader development agenda (Brash 2011) rather than any commitment to urban democracy: the High Line would be a driver of tourism and local development, another "asset" in the city's luxury-city brand (Halle and Tiso 2014: 164–165). A number of scholars (Foster 2010; Gandy 2013; Patrick 2011, 2014) have taken on the park's depoliticizing ecological presuppositions, demonstrating their role in naturalizing the particular shape redevelopment took and obscuring the park's links to real estate development, gentrification, neoliberalization, and displacement (of humans and nonhumans alike). The "queering" of the High Line has been challenged, most notably by Patrick (2014: 930), as eliding internal class, race, and gender divisions within the city's LGBTQ population, as well as pulling resources and money away from more pressing issues facing this population and destroying the very environment of gay sociality and sexuality that it supposedly celebrated (see also Cataldi et al. 2011: 369–370). Finally, the role of design and aesthetics in establishing the park's publicness can be questioned. This emphasis clearly coincided with efforts on the part of the city to stimulate investment and development in neighboring areas via their rebranding as centers of the arts, global architecture, and the culture industries (Halle and Tiso 2014). Michael Cataldi and his coauthors argue that the park's approach to the arts reinforces the commercialization and exclusivity of artistic production and that the reifying deployment of aesthetics, images, and narration on and about the High Line evacuate this public park of its democratic potential, serving to "diminish public space even as they purport to represent it" (2011: 358). Taken together, these critiques represent a powerful indictment of the High Line as an ostensibly public space, and even more so as an authentically democratic space. Taken one by one, they counter each of the ways in which I have argued that the High Line represented a break with post–fiscal crisis norms regarding public parks, and in which the park might have bolstered, rather than enervated, the power of the concept of publicness in the context of the city's parks system.

However, I think that all these critiques share a common problem: they overstate the power of the elite cultural, economic, and political projects that came to center on the High Line to accomplish their goals and to structure political practice and discourse. John Clarke has noted the danger of conflating the desires and goals of neoliberal projects with their advocates' ability to achieve them, calling for attention to "the instability and incompleteness of neo-liberal attempts at hegemony" (2004a: 100) and cautioning against "reading outcomes from strategies" (2004b: 44). And in fact, it has become commonplace for urbanists to acknowledge the contingency and incompleteness of neoliberal projects, at least in the abstract (for a review, see Maskovsky and Brash 2014). However, the call to resist analytical closure seems to have gone unheeded in the case of the High Line. By 2013, critical analysts of the High Line seemed to have reached a consensus:

not only was the High Line itself thoroughly neoliberal and undemocratic, but it typified a broader evacuation of democracy from public space and augured the ongoing growth and normalization of profound inequalities in the provision of public parks. Yet at the very same moment the verdict was rendered, political developments in New York City suggested that the High Line's (unfulfilled) promise of a park, and by extension a park system, providing accessible, high-quality space to all had taken on a life of its own, one unexpected (and, one imagines, unwelcome) to the various elites who had seen in the park an opportunity to implement their vision of a luxurified, competitive, and profitable city. I am referring to the emergence of the movement for so-called park equity.

"A SINGLE, UNIFIED SYSTEM": THE RAPID RISE OF PARK EQUITY

On October 7, 2014, Mayor Bill de Blasio announced the launch of the Community Parks Initiative, which would channel $130 million of city capital funding to thirty-five parks throughout the city. The parks slated to receive money were for the most part unknown to New Yorkers not living or working in their immediate vicinity. Among them were the Bronx's Seabury Park, Brooklyn's Thomas Boyland Park, Staten Island's Grandview Playground, Queens's Van Alst Playground, and Manhattan's Sol Lain Playground: all a far cry from the parks that had received so much attention in the recent past. As de Blasio's Parks Commissioner Mitchell Silver acknowledged, this was but a "down payment" on the pursuit of a more equitable city park system: the 35 parks had been culled from a list of 215 parks that had received less than the pitifully small sum of $250,000 in capital improvements in the past twenty years (the High Line had received more than $100 million of city money in the decade prior).

De Blasio's announcement marked the culmination of the year-and-a-half-long rise of park equity as a salient political issue. The long-term decline of city funding for parks and the growing divides between parks dependent on city funding and those supported by private conservancies had not gone without its critics (Rosenzweig and Blackmar 1992: 527–529). Indeed, there had been earlier attempts to address the issue. Among these were the 1995 founding of the Partnership for Parks, a partnership between the nonprofit City Parks Foundation and the city's Department of Parks and Recreation that sought to aid parks without well-funded private conservancies, and the 2001 "One Percent for Parks" campaign calling for the city to dedicate 1 percent of its annual budget to its parks system, which was doomed by post-9/11 political developments. The administration of ex-CEO billionaire Michael Bloomberg—who entered City Hall shortly after 9/11—did devote resources to public parks, but in a way that supported its luxury city development strategy and exacerbated inequities with the park system (Brash 2011: 122).

In fact, it was only in May 2013 that these inequities emerged into mainstream political discourse. In terms of the public funding of parks, the recent past had been nothing special. The year 2012 saw the familiar two-step of Mayor Bloomberg proposing cuts to the parks department budget, only to have funding (mostly) restored by the city council. But the twelve-month period ending in October 2012 had been a banner year for the private funding of parks in New York City. It began with a record $20 million gift to the FHL from the Diller–von Furstenberg Family Foundation (this was the third donation of $15 million or more made by Barry Diller and Dianne von Furstenberg), continued with a $40 million pledge by philanthropist Joshua Rechnitz for an indoor bicycle racing track (a plan that was eventually dropped) in Brooklyn Bridge Park, and ended with a staggering $100 million donation to the Central Park Conservancy by financier John Paulson. While the increasingly stark contrast between public privation and private abundance in the city's parks did not pass unnoticed among advocates and activists, it was a May 2013 *New York Times* op-ed piece by State Senator Daniel Squadron that shoved what he called "open-space equity" onto the stage of public debate. Along with more city parks funding, Squadron, a Democratic political wunderkind who had served as a top aide to US Senator Charles Schumer before being elected at the age of twenty-eight in 2008 to represent lower Manhattan and parts of Brooklyn, proposed that wealthy conservancies associated with one of the "marquee jewels" of the parks system commit 20 percent of their annual budgets to other, needier parks. Soon afterward, Squadron proposed legislation making such redistribution mandatory, much to the chagrin of the conservancies and their elite benefactors.

Squadron's op-ed and proposal struck a chord. While Squadron linked park equity (to use the term that replaced "open space equity" in public discourse) to broader patterns of inequality in the city, a much-circulated opinion piece by *Times* metro reporter Michael Powell, published three days after Squadron's, went even further, decrying the "feudal landscape of the privileged and underprivileged" offered up by the city's parks, lamenting the "condescension pass[ing] as realism" represented by claims that private funding was the only way to fund parks in an ostensible age of austerity, condemning the timidity of those who "would not upset the conservancy lords," and questioning whether "privatized parks serve the broadest public good." Powell's was the most widely read of a number of pieces over the next few months (Powell 2013b; Salmon 2013; Soskis 2013; Ulam 2013) that placed the private funding of parks and the conservancies themselves under an intellectual and political microscope—and found both wanting in terms of economic efficiency, philanthropic value, racial and class makeup of conservancy staff and boards, and basic standards of fairness and justice. Indeed, even the FHL, the newest of the city's powerhouse conservancies, acknowledged the importance and legitimacy of the park equity issue, holding a July 2013 panel discussion titled "Building Equitable Cities and Public Spaces," which featured Majora Carter, prominent Bronx activist and forceful advocate of park equity. Then-mayoral candidate Bill de Blasio, whose populist "Two Cities" campaign focused squarely on issues of equity and inequality, soon got into the parks equity game, endorsing the Squadron bill and promising to commit city resources to the park system broadly, and particularly to the many parks that had not benefited from the favor of the Bloomberg administration or the "conservancy lords."

Unsurprisingly, those defending and dependent on the city's elite attacked Squadron's proposal. *Crain's New York Business* (2014) called it an "Orwellian" idea that would "cannibalize" the successful conservancies and discourage charity. The notoriously neoliberal Manhattan Institute's Howard Husock decried its "leveling impulse," "politics of envy," and embodiment of "mediocrity, shared equally" (Husock 2013, 2014). Less stridently, various nonprofit park advocates voiced fear that such a bill would undermine private support for parks. While differing in tone, these arguments shared the premise that an infusion of private money was required if the city was to be able to "afford" decent parks (if not a decent park system), and that the wishes of private donors to guide their philanthropy toward the park of their choice had to be respected—either out of principle or out of fear that their aid would otherwise be withheld (Saul and West 2013).

While defenders of private funding of public parks might have objected to Squadron's proposal to redistribute conservancy funds, for the most part they called for better maintenance and funding of city parks. This included not just mainstream advocates for parks like *Times* architecture critic Michael Kimmelman (2014), but also neoliberals like Husock (though he predictably claimed it was public employees' overly generous salaries and benefits that were sucking money away from parks). Even the Central Park Conservancy implicitly acknowledged the validity of Squadron's critique, beefing up an existing program that had provided several parks, mostly in Harlem, with technical assistance: in October 2013, it introduced a team of gardeners dubbed the "Five Borough Crew" that would share the conservancy's expertise with ten parks throughout the city (Foderaro 2014a).

After his election, de Blasio backed off the conservancy tax idea, and by March 2014 it was essentially a dead letter. But the notion that the current level and distribution of resources to city parks was unjust and unsustainable had taken hold. Parks Commissioner Mitchell Silver explicitly placed the idea of park equity at the top of his agenda, and Mark Levine, chair of the city council's Parks Committee, became a vocal advocate as well. Levine held a well-publicized April 2014 hearing, addressing what he called "New York City's two tiered park system," and though ultimately rejecting Squadron's proposal, called for more equitable and transparent public funding, as well as for more community influence in park design and programming. Moreover, in a March 2014 op-ed, Levine lamented the "insidious effect" of conservancies: "they dampen the political will of the city's most influential citizens for robust public funding of the Parks Department, mostly because such high-income individuals live adjacent to parks benefiting from private donations" (Levine 2014). Such arguments subjected neoliberal parks provision to direct and public critique. Not only was the level of post-fiscal-crisis park funding scandalously low, but the logic of private funding and the "communities of self-interest" that it produced actively undercut public provisioning. The solution was the reassertion of the notion that the city's parks system was, as Squadron (2014) put it when testifying before the city council, "a single unified network," rather than collection of individual, self-sufficient parks.

With the first budgeting season of de Blasio's mayoralty under way, the drive for park equity began to affect policy. His preliminary budget made some small increases in park funding but proposed no major new investments (the $80 million in capital funding for "neighborhood parks" it contained was actually a carryover from the Bloomberg administration). The city council requested an additional $27 million in parks operations and maintenance funding, mostly for additional maintenance and security staff. The final budget agreement, passed in June 2014, contained a $16 million funding increase. Four months later, the mayor announced the launch of his $130 million Community Parks Initiative. While not sufficient to undo the legacy of inequality produced by several decades of public disinvestment cum targeted private investment, it represented a clear victory for the park equity movement. The neoliberal logic that placed responsibility for the quality and upkeep of parks at the level of the individual park was being eroded in favor of an ethic stressing the collective provision of a high-quality citywide parks system for which all New Yorkers would be responsible, and to which all New Yorkers would have access.

THE HIGH LINE AND PARK EQUITY

The High Line played an important role in the rise of park equity as a salient issue in New York City. The effects of its publicness were felt in ways both arterial—in the outlets of mainstream public discourse—and capillary—in the context of local organizing around parks in neighborhoods socially and geographically distant from the hyper-gentrifying districts of Chelsea and the Meatpacking District. How the High Line's publicness was interpreted, and how its interpretation functioned politically, varied from case to case. The High Line could be an example to emulate, an emblem of everything wrong with the provision of park space in contemporary New York, or a complex blend of both. While this much more localized "High Line effect" worked in different ways in different contexts, it was the park's multifaceted and ambiguous publicness that constituted its discursive and ideological power.

The most obvious way in which the High Line sparked debate over the equitable distribution of resources among the city's parks was as a paradigm of privatization, exclusion, and elitism. In an August 2012 op-ed piece in the *New York Times* that represented the first prominent disruption of critics' and commentators' overwhelmingly positive response to the park, pseudonymous blogger Jeremiah Moss decried not only the park's gentrifying impact, but the park itself. Moss argued that, with its manicured and museumlike design, it was turning its back on "regular New Yorkers" in favor of tourists, elite newcomers, and global corporations. While only obliquely raising issues of the park's funding and expensive upkeep, Moss focused attention on what kind of environment a truly "public" park should be—and who city parks should be for. Responding to the piece, FHL heads David and Hammond glossed over the sorts of socioeconomic divisions that Moss addressed, defending the park as rooted in the neighboring "community" and touting its success at drawing in some two million (undifferentiated) New Yorkers annually (the number of annual visitors has since more than doubled).

While the debate over the High Line's impact on Manhattan's West Side followed familiar grooves, with critics condemning it as a "monument to gentrification" (Bourne 2012) and supporters touting the tourism, economic investment, and architecturally sophisticated real estate development it had unleashed (see, inter alia, Filler 2009), one point quickly became common wisdom: if the park's design and backstory were part of what made it unique, so were the massive private and public resources that had been poured into its construction and upkeep. And as the debate over the investment in the city's park system emerged in late 2012 and early 2013 and the notion of park equity began to coalesce, the High Line became, along with Central Park, exemplary of one pole of the city's divided park system. Every major article and op-ed addressing the issue used the High Line as an example of the kind of park that had benefited from both public and private investment in the recent past. Moreover, that level of investment increasingly became the standard, sometimes implicitly but often explicitly, against which the condition of parks across the city was compared. The novelty of the High Line was particularly important here. Given the key role that other marquee parks like Central Park and Prospect Park had long played in both the city's everyday life and its democratic aspirations, higher levels of investment were more easily justified and accepted for those locations. But the investment of more than $100 million of public money (to say nothing of the hundreds of millions of dollars of private donations) in an entirely new park at the same time that hundreds, if not thousands, of existing parks lacked even the most basic amenities and upkeep, was more difficult to square with even the most rudimentary notions of fairness and democracy implied in the notion of a "public" park system. So while it was obviously too late for the emerging park equity debate to center on considerations of the wisdom of constructing the High Line, or even the expensive maintenance of the park, it was not too late to pose this simple question: if this high level of maintenance was appropriate for the (public) High Line, why was it not appropriate for Flushing Meadows–Corona Park in Queens

(Foderaro 2013b), South Lyons Square Playground in the Bronx (Foderaro 2014c), or Shore Park–Verrazano Narrows (Powell 2013b)? And it was not too late for this question to become a proxy for larger questions concerning broader patterns of inequality, inequity, and class in New York.

Crucially, this new positioning of the High Line and its publicness in the broader contexts of both the city's park system as a whole and the city's profound inequalities allowed for advocates of park equity to shift the debate in advantageous ways. Defenders of the park and of neoliberal patterns of development could—and did—dismiss High Line critics using a familiar stock of epithets: Moss and his ilk were stuck in the past, reflexively antidevelopment naysayers unwilling to accept the inevitability of urban change (Brash 2011: 194; Lindquist 2012). But by placing the High Line into a comparative frame that included the entirety of the city's park system, park equity advocates could strategically side-step the High Line itself, and shift the focus to the new norm of well-endowed and high-quality public park space that it had established. This increasingly common rhetorical move was demonstrated by Bronx activist Majora Carter during the previously mentioned July 2013 FHL-sponsored panel discussion. When asked by the moderator what she would do differently if she were building the High Line, after a pause and bit of filibustering that seemed to acknowledge the danger of taking on the design of the park, she responded: "Considering the level of interest and support that this geographic location was going to get, and support from real estate . . . I would have pushed the city to use their influence to make sure that other places around the Bronx, that were trying to build parks . . . got the same kind of support" (Friends of the High Line 2013a).

Moreover, the "scale-jumping" (Smith 1992) move to a citywide perspective allowed park equity advocates to delink criticism of the High Line from criticism of broader inequalities in the city's parks provision. Considering the High Line not in isolation but as one element of a large and varied system that could encompass many different kinds of spaces, from hyperdesigned tourist attractions to run-of-the-mill playgrounds, allowed a commitment to park equity to be expressed in combination with a variety of attitudes toward the High Line. Advocates of park equity could celebrate the High Line as a unique and valuable public space, as Councilman Mark Levine did when he attended the October 2014 commemoration of the opening of the third section of the park. Or they could express relative indifference to the High Line in favor of a more typical New York City park experience, as Mayor de Blasio did when it came out in October 2014 that he, much to the shock of the city's chattering classes, had never visited the High Line and did not intend to do so anytime soon (Grynbaum 2014). Daniel Squadron (2014) did something similar by refusing to offer any appraisal of the High Line beyond an acknowledgment of the importance of the city's marquee parks. By the time park equity had emerged in early 2014, the once-sacrosanct High Line was no longer exempt from public critique. Nonetheless, de-linking advocacy for park equity and criticism of the High Line allowed for just the kind of rhetorically effective, if intellectually suspicious, "both/and" position that is the grist of skillful political discourse.

And it was not just in elite and political discourse that the High Line, and its publicness, impacted the drive for park equity. In neighborhoods throughout the city, activists and everyday residents turned the High Line to their own rhetorical and organizational advantage. The so-called High Line effect did not just inspire similar projects in other US cities and abroad, it also inspired and bolstered projects entailing the reuse or revival of neglected pieces of infrastructure closer to home. A number of these came to be justified in part through explicit appeals to park equity.

This worked in ways I have already considered, as supporters of these projects argued that if the High Line was worth millions in public investment, than so was the High Bridge, and the QueensWay, and the Harlem Promenade. Moreover, these parks often were directly justified by their provision of public benefits beyond creating park space in relatively underprivileged areas of the city (even if, as Scott Larson demonstrates in chapter 10, this justification might not square with the fact that park proposals, like that for the QueensWay, were shaped by elite agendas). The rehabilitation of the High Bridge, the city's oldest standing bridge and a piece of the historic Croton Aqueduct, as a pedestrian passage between the Bronx and Upper Manhattan, along with the refurbishment of Highbridge Park on the Manhattan end of the bridge, was touted as a contribution to improved public health in the predominantly low-income black and Latino communities it would connect. It would provide much-needed space for walking and other forms of exercise, including swimming: the single pool built by Robert Moses in Upper Manhattan had been cut off from Bronx residents since the High Bridge was shut to pedestrians in the 1970s (Fullilove 2013: 172–184; Garcia 2012). The Harlem Promenade, proposed by the Housing Partnership, a nonprofit affordable housing advocacy organization, would, like the High Line, use the sale of development rights above a railroad line (in this case active) to fund some two thousand units of affordable housing in West

Harlem, improvements to nearby Riverside Park, and a "promenade" connecting the neighborhood to the park (Rosenberg 2014).

These projects had varied origins and had reached varied stages of completion at the time of this writing. The High Bridge project was actually conceived of soon after the High Line, received support from the Bloomberg administration in 2006, and opened in June 2015. The QueensWay began to solidify in early 2013 and by 2014 had received some preliminary state funding. In contrast, the Harlem Promenade, as of early 2015, consisted of little more than a website and a rough zoning proposal, which was expected to enter the city's land-use review process in mid-2015. However, what they all had in common was a claim to public support that was bolstered by the public investment in the High Line.

Another aspect of the High Line's publicness contributed to the growing sentiment that these parks were worthy of public funding. This became apparent to me via interviews with former staff members of the Partnership for Parks, which for a brief period from 2005 to 2010 served as a kind of fifth column of social justice activism in the heart of the Bloomberg administration, attempting to advance progressive aims within the context of neoliberal projects. My interlocutors (who wished to remain anonymous) tended to view the High Line and the hoopla that surrounded it with some suspicion, as more of a stadiumlike development project than a public park. They privately snarked at the slavish efforts of city officials to get themselves included in High Line–related photo-ops. Nevertheless, they saw the park as providing grist for those organizing for better parks in communities throughout the city. The "narrativity" of the High Line—the way in which the story of its development was inextricably linked to the physical space itself—served as an important precedent. Through sustained advocacy paired with the articulation of a "compelling narrative," the park's champions had achieved support and eventual success. Given the relative dearth of resources available to groups organizing around parks in poorer and less powerful neighborhoods, one informant told me, a compelling narrative was even more important, as it helped sustain the efforts of often overburdened people and imbued their struggles for park equity with meaning and sense of purpose.

"EVEN IF PEOPLE DON'T LIKE IT, THEY STILL FEEL LIKE THEY OWN IT"

In all these ways, the High Line played a crucial role in the development and emergence of the park equity movement in 2013 and 2014. The size of the public investment in the park, its celebrated design, the quality of materials used, the expense of its maintenance, and its origin myth all helped to create a new benchmark for what public space in contemporary New York City could, and *should*, be. Central to this was a rescaling of parks discourse and practice. Whereas city officials and FHL officers might want to focus on the park and its immediate vicinity, or on the global circulation of the park as an exemplar of innovative public space, activists like Majora Carter and politicians like Mark Levine and Daniel Squadron pitched their arguments at a citywide scale. They insisted that the city's parks had to be conceived of as constituting a single (if internally varied) entity accessible to all New Yorkers. They rejected the notion of a two-tiered system consisting of a few privileged marquee parks and a great mass of everyday parks, as well as the idea of city parks as a collection of "free agents," with responsibility for the maintenance located at the level of the individual park and its "community of self-interest." This rejection of neoliberal logics of inequality and individual responsibility in favor of an ethic of collective responsibility was reflected in the proposal to redistribute private conservancy money away from well-endowed parks toward those with few resources, as well as the eventual policy of increasing the overall level of public parks spending and guiding more of it toward parks in need.

The citywide perspective endemic to the park equity movement also allowed for new and politically compelling linkages and points of comparison to emerge: whereas the High Line had typically been grouped with "elite parks" like Brooklyn Bridge Park, Bryant Park, Central Park, and so on, now the High Bridge or the Harlem Promenade could be brought into comparison with the High Line—the natural consequence being the question "if the High Line, why not the High Bridge?" The only answer was that the High Line could generate private support that the High Bridge could not. The High Line's claims to publicness, compromised though they might be, increasingly made this a politically untenable response.

Finally, the centrality of the citywide scale of the park equity movement allowed for the linkage of the "top down" projects of mainstream elected officials and the "bottom up" efforts of activists focused on particular parks.

The push for park equity succeeded where many other challenges to neoliberal policies in New York City had failed (Brash 2011: 36, 279): by articulating a new, progressive, and *citywide* alternative to the prevalent, and ostensibly inevitable, neoliberal approach.

Some important caveats must be added here. As successful as the park equity movement has been, and as clearly as it challenges broader patterns of injustice and inequality in New York City, it remains to be seen whether it augurs shifts away from neoliberal logics in other policy realms. On the one hand, Mayor de Blasio and his political allies have expressed a broad critique of the stark inequality that neoliberal policies have produced and have taken action in areas such as education, affordable housing, and minimum wage policy. On the other hand, broader movements away from neoliberal policy are hemmed in by the extralocal factors that are crucial to its continuing power (Peck 2013; Peck et al. 2009; Peck and Tickell 2002). Without changes at the national or global scale, cities like New York are limited in the actions they can take. Moreover, powerful actors closer at hand also present obstacles to the development and implementation of a broader package of more just policies. Private wealth continues to unduly influence the provision of parkland, as witnessed by Barry Diller's $170 million ($130 million of which he would provide) proposal for a futuristic park on a publicly owned West Side pier, a plan developed with no public input whatsoever (Bagli and Pogrebin 2014). Also, the real estate development industry remains a dominant power. Indeed, unlike Mayor Bloomberg (Brash 2012), de Blasio has so far been unwilling to challenge its priorities, a fact expressed nowhere more clearly than his selection of Carl Weisbrod, an established advocate for the interests of real estate, as chair of the City Planning Commission. It is worth nothing that one explanation for the park equity movement's success is that it did not represent a profound threat to the interests of real estate. Moreover, the one policy proposal that might have impinged on its prerogatives—Squadron's proposal to tax private conservancies—was quickly dispensed with.

Despite all this, the rapid rise and relative policy success of the park equity movement, and the role that the High Line played in this, is cause for some optimism. What I hope this chapter has demonstrated is the continued democratic potential of the "public" in public parks. While critical urbanists have subjected the various ways in which neoliberal projects have sought to discredit, evacuate, transform, and reorient the notion of the "public" in keeping with their economic interests and visions, it is important to note that these projects have been, at best, only partly successful (Clarke 2004b). Cataldi and his coauthors quote Rosalyn Deutsche, who writes, "democracy is 'the legitimacy of debate about what is legitimate and what is illegitimate,' crucially sustained by the antagonism at the heart of the social that opens onto public space" (Cataldi et al. 2011: 382). The emergence of the park equity movement—and its implicit and explicit acknowledgment of the social and geographical antagonisms that structure the city's park system—was enabled in crucial ways by the publicness of the High Line. If the gap between the promises made by the park's claim to publicness and the reality of the city's "two-tiered" park system was a betrayal of the democratic potential of public space, it was a productive one—one that park equity advocates seized on to make their claims for a more democratic and equitable park system. As one of my park activist informants put it: "It's the debate [the park has inspired] that makes it public . . . even if people don't like it, they still feel like they own it. It feeds dialogue. . . . What is fair? What should a park be?"

6 ▪ RETRO-WALKING NEW YORK

CHRISTOPH LINDNER

IN THE SPRING of 2013, I visited the High Line as part of a research project on global cities and interruption (Jordan and Lindner 2016). Walking along the elevated walkway while reflecting on interruption, I was struck by how the site brought together various strands of thinking that I had been developing in relation to visual culture and urban space. The High Line is a site that I had been visiting for many years and that I had been writing about since before it opened (Lindner 2008). But this was the first time that my experience of the park had led me to see it as a site where the urban, the global, the aesthetic, and the creative mix together in a particular way that we might call interruptive, in the sense of an intervention in urban space designed to produce an intensification or defamiliarization of experience.

Far from being spontaneous, this interruptive experience is highly scripted and occurs in the context of a tightly controlled and planned environment. Just as important, the High Line is a space designed around—even designed *as*—an aesthetic, durational encounter. At one level, then, the High Line enables new forms of spatial and visual incursion into the globalized cityscape that deliberately disrupt familiar, everyday urban experiences. At another level, the High Line marks the reintroduction of mobility into a space of interrupted transit in the form of a defunct elevated railway system. It is, however, a mobility designed around detour and delay, rather than speed and destination, and in this respect the park comprises an experiment in slow urbanism aimed at countering, while simultaneously contributing to, the accelerated urbanism of globalization.

In the following discussion, I return to the space of the High Line to think through its interruptive potential, and do so in relation to what I see as the key factor behind its success as an engine of urban renewal: its refiguring of the street. One of the reasons why this refiguring of the street is significant is because, through various effects of deceleration, it enables a set of three interrelating practices I call "retro-walking": first, retro-walking as a nostalgic return and a conscious retracing of steps; second, retro-walking as a form of reflexive critical-spatial analysis; and third, retro-walking as a stylistic, performative practice connected to the generic urbanism of globalization and inherited from the leisure strolling traditions of the *grands boulevards* of urban modernity (Frisby 2001; Scobey 1992). Retro-walking is an integral part of the aesthetic and spatial experience of the High Line and the broader global phenomenon of the postindustrial elevated park.

SLOW NEW YORK

Writing in 2013 about plans to develop the defunct Bloomingdale rail line in Chicago into an elevated linear park, Amita Sinha notes the proliferation of such projects in the wake of the High Line's success. Echoing most commentators, she understands the growing phenomenon of the elevated linear park as reflecting the desire to "reclaim marginal sites with derelict infrastructure in post-industrial cities whose manufacturing base has shifted elsewhere" (113). What is somewhat different about Sinha's reading, however, is that she goes on from this general remark to make an explicit link between the trend of the elevated linear park and the rise of slow living movements:

> Slow food and slow city are recent reactionary trends to fast food and fast-paced urban life with a bearing on design of contemporary public parks. The slow food movement advocates . . . sociable eating at a calm, unhurried pace. Its influence on the urban landscape is seen in the popularity of community gardens, nowhere more so than in Detroit where their growth into urban farms in vacant lots has created the productive public park, in the process transforming industrial urbanism into agricultural urbanism. The slow city movement

> promotes leisurely rhythm of public life marked by conviviality. The anomie and standardization of globalization and corporate culture are countered by cultivating a sense of place and place making through local cuisines and arts and crafts. (Sinha 2013: 117)

Because they are designed around core values shared by the slow food and slow city movements—namely, decelerated practices aimed at improving quality of life and promoting urban sustainability and community—elevated linear parks like the High Line and the Bloomingdale Trail can be understood as "slow landscapes" in Sinha's thinking. These sites "where nature is calming and attunes the body's rhythms to its own, creating a sense of quiet, offer respite from the hurried pace of the city." The aim, she argues, is to create "sensuous and pleasurable experiences" that redefine "the idea of beauty in terms of the strangely familiar" (Sinha 2013: 117), effectively evoking the realm of what Anthony Vidler (1994) terms the "architectural uncanny."

Like Sinha, I understand the High Line as an iteration of slow urbanism designed around an aesthetics and spatiality of defamiliarization. Although I would hesitate to trace such a direct line of influence from slow-living movements to the rise of the elevated park, I do agree with the broader idea that both constitute deliberate counter-responses to the ever-accelerating pace of life in the era of globalization. What I seek to add to this line of thinking is the idea that, as illustrated by the High Line, the creative production of slowness in global cities is predicated on—and ultimately helps to sustain—the culture of speed it resists or, at the very least, modulates.

There are certain tensions, then, to be found in the history of the High Line's reclaimed infrastructure, given that the building of the elevated railway in New York City in the early twentieth century was designed in accordance with the modernist vision of urban planning to unclutter the streets for pedestrians, while unlocking new forms of rapid transit and separating traffic functions into different levels (Lindner 2015: 165–167). The High Line is therefore situated in a space that helped to produce urban modernity's early articulation of today's multileveled, multirhythmic city, as well as that city's initial culture of speed. By conspicuously preserving the form of the elevated railway while rededicating its use to slow human traffic, the High Line simultaneously activates yet distances itself from the site's history of acceleration and dislocation. It both extends and restricts the elevated railway's function as a conduit of urban flows.

The implication of the High Line's complicity in New York's culture of speed is that, like the slow-living movements (which now stretch to include slow money, slow fashion, slow media, slow design, slow science, slow parenting, and more), slow urbanism does not escape the time-space compressions of globalization (Harvey 1990) but instead remains deeply if ambivalently implicated in that condition, even as it interrupts it. In the case of the High Line, the experiment in slow urbanism is one that consciously draws on the perambulatory practices of the sidewalk, including its spatiality and aesthetics, to engineer an otherworldly encounter with the frenetic built environment of the global city. This encounter, in turn, is framed by the revivification of industrial ruins and the remobilizing of urban memory. One of the results is the nostalgic, reflective, and stylistic practice of retro-walking. Another, related, result is an urban pastoral walkway that removes pedestrians from the everyday city while still maintaining a visual connection to the street below. In such a reading, the High Line becomes a site of slowness from which to observe the city of speed.

In terms of design antecedents, the park is indebted to the Promenade Plantée in Paris, where a disused rail viaduct in the city center was transformed in the 1990s into an extensive green walkway, which urban historian Joseph Heathcott describes as a "classic Parisian bourgeois park, with its carefully crafted landscape and firmly controlled optics—a linear pathway for seeing and being seen" in the classic mode of the Benjaminian *flâneur* (Heathcott 2013: 289). The High Line shares the Promenade Plantée's concern with bringing nature back into the city, giving new life to a dormant space while blending traditional park elements—such as formal plantings, manicured lawns, and delineated paths—into the surviving transport infrastructure. It also shares the Promenade Plantée's emphasis on visibility, not only of the structure itself but also of its users and their practices.

In these respects, the High Line belongs to a broader, global trend in landscape urbanism, in which abandoned, postindustrial sites are creatively remade into eco-friendly, pedestrian spaces designed for conspicuous public leisure. In the New York context, I would cite the example of the Fresh Kills landfill on Staten Island being transformed into a wildlife preserve and recreation zone (Lindner 2008), which is also a project by Field Operations, the landscape architecture firm behind the design of the High Line. Other examples include the civic reoccupation of Governors Island and its abandoned military base in the form of a giant public park, the transformation of Brooklyn's Navy Yard into a green-tech hipster playground, and Brooklyn

Bridge Park's repurposing of defunct cargo-ship piers into playgrounds and sport fields jutting out into the East River.

What makes the High Line remarkable is its staggering popularity. From its initial opening in 2009 onward, the park has exceeded all expectations in terms of the volume of visitors (attracting upward of 4.5 million visitors a year) and has quickly established itself as one of New York's must-see destinations and an alternative green space to the more traditional, nineteenth-century landscape design experience of Central Park. This popularity has helped to regenerate and, in some cases gentrify, the surrounding neighborhoods (Halle and Tiso 2014), attracting property developers, businesses, and even major cultural institutions like the Whitney Museum of American Art, which strategically placed its new building at the southern entrance to the High Line.

The story of the High Line's success is much more complex, of course, and connects not only to the design of the park, but also to the high level of support and involvement it has received from the local community. In particular, the nonprofit organization Friends of the High Line (FHL), which led the campaign to build the park, has now assumed both operational responsibility and cultural stewardship over the space, as the organization's website explains: "We seek to preserve the entire historic structure, transforming an essential piece of New York's industrial past. We provide over 90 percent of the High Line's annual operating budget and are responsible for maintenance of the park, pursuant to a license agreement with the New York City Department of Parks and Recreation. Through stewardship, innovative design and programming, and excellence in operations, we cultivate a vibrant community around the High Line" (Friends of the High Line n.d.). As this mission statement articulates, the park consciously seeks to activate cultural memory and draw on the city's industrial heritage, but in doing so recasts that memory and heritage into an elaborate, forward-looking experiment with community activism, public art, urban design, and cultural programming. All of this, I would argue, hinges on the High Line's former identity as a disused elevated railroad and, in particular, on the way in which that identity shapes the perambulatory experience of the park's linear pathway.

This idea was made visible by FHL in an outdoor exhibition of a large-scale photograph displayed on a billboard adjacent to the park in 2011 (figure 6.1). The work, titled *Landscape with Path: A Railroad Artifact,* comes from a series of photographs by Joel Sternfeld, which was commissioned

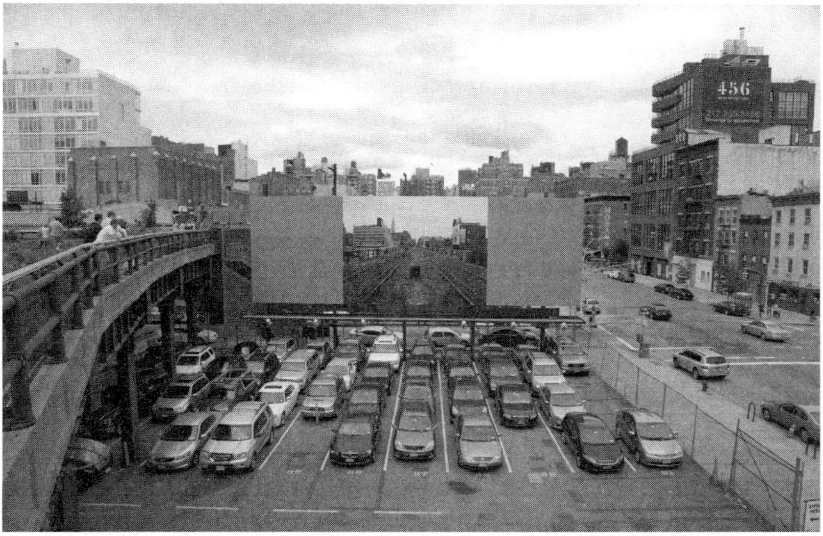

FIGURE 6.1. Billboard next to the High Line: Joel Sternfeld, *Landscape with Path: A Railroad Artifact*. Commissioned by High Line Art, presented by Friends of the High Line and the New York City Department of Parks and Recreation. On view June 2–30, 2011. Photograph by Brian Rosa.

by FHL. Taken in 2000, long before the park construction began, the image shows the tracks of the abandoned elevated railroad. The placement of the photograph on a billboard next to the High Line and directly above a parking lot is significant. The relationship between the photograph's image of emptiness and stillness resonates strangely with the congested stasis of the unoccupied vehicles in the parking lot. The more powerful resonance, however, occurs between the billboard and the park located beside it. This juxtaposition of the site's postindustrial history of abandonment next to its present day condition of revival and reoccupation delivers a poignant, visual reminder of the park's status as a transformed urban ruin.

In this respect, the High Line speaks to a wider cultural fascination with ruins. It is a fascination inherited from European romanticism (Hell and Schönle 2010) and the Renaissance turn to classical antiquity (DeSilvey and Edensor 2012), one that has been renewed and intensified in recent decades by the growing spectacularization of postindustrial abandonment, as in the case of ruined cities like Detroit, ghost towns like Japan's Hashima Island (which shot to fame after featuring in the 007 film *Skyfall*), and toxic disaster sites like Chernobyl. The result is what Tim Edensor (2005) describes in *Industrial*

Ruins as an aesthetics of disorder, sensuality, and enchantment. Through urban photography projects like Camilo José Vergara's *American Ruins* (1999) and Yves Marchand and Romain Meffre's *The Ruins of Detroit* (2010), as well as museum exhibitions like Tate Britain's *Ruin Lust* (2014), these ruin aesthetics have captured the visual imagination in much the same way as the global slum, which has also been experiencing a new wave of artistic and popular interest for much the same reasons and in much the same way (Jones 2011). What the global slum and the industrial ruin both evoke in their urban aesthetics is a condition that Sudeep Dasgupta (2013), writing about urban poverty in Mumbai, has called "permanent transiency" (148).

Crucially, the High Line's status as an industrial ruin (albeit a ruin whose qualities of decay and disorder have been carefully sanitized and contained) allows the park to reference the mobility and visuality contained in the structure's original function as an elevated railway. As Michael Cataldi and his coauthors argue in their analysis of the High Line's use of public art, Sternfeld's photographs thus "form a supplement to the High Line's development, evoking its precarious past to regulate its future" (Cataldi et al. 2011: 362). In other words, the positioning of Sternfeld's photograph in the direct view of the park's visitors helps to reinforce the desired public image of the High Line as a defamiliarizing space of memory and mobility, which James Corner, the park's lead designer, once described as "a postindustrial artifact maintaining a sense of melancholy and other-worldliness in a city context that, by contrast, [is] ever-evolving and modernizing" (in Fehrenbacher 2013).

The sense of melancholy and otherworldliness to which Corner refers is integral to the popularity of the park, which partly functions as a nostalgic memory walk for a bygone era of industrial urbanism and faded promenade culture. The elevated walkway lifts visitors up from the level of the street just enough to provide a different perspective on the city. Yet, unlike the original railroad that moved rapidly across the city, the park offers a decelerated encounter with the surrounding urban landscape. That landscape, in turn, is the product of the accelerated urbanism of globalization and, in the immediate vicinity of the High Line, the result of neoliberal gentrification gone wild—a phenomenon that Loretta Lees, writing about the proliferation of exclusive and expensive enclaves in Brooklyn, calls "super-gentrification" (Lees 2003: 2487). In the case of the High Line, this process of rapid and chaotic urban renewal is fueled by the popularity of the site to the extent that the view *from* the park is partly being shaped by both the presence *of* the park and the view *onto* the park.

This is evident, for instance, in the surge of signature architecture projects that have sprung up around the High Line, seeking to boost visibility through proximity to the park and, in the process, aiming to become new visual anchors in the cityscape views afforded by the High Line. Key examples include the new Whitney Museum building by Renzo Piano (figure 6.2); the Polshek Partnership's Standard Hotel, which straddles the High Line and has become something of a magnet for both performing and watching exhibitionist sex through hotel windows; and the Barry Diller corporate vanity project of the Frank Gehry–designed IAC Building. This dynamic of the High Line producing its own view also registers in the explosion of new luxury condo developments adjacent to the park, which frequently incorporate the High Line into their names and trade on their proximity. These include the much-hyped Soori High Line Condos, which come with private indoor swimming pools; the Zaha Hadid–designed starchitect condos at 520 West 28th Street (figure 6.3), which boast prices up to $35 million; and Neil Denari's HL23, the first luxury residential complex to be named after the park.

All of these factors give the High Line a strange doubleness. It is both an aging ruin and an object of newness. It is simultaneously abandoned

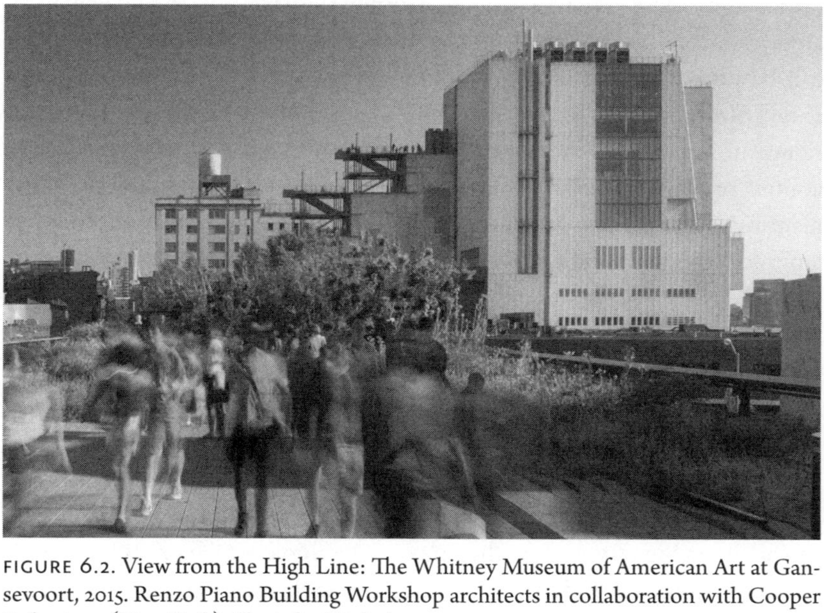

FIGURE 6.2. View from the High Line: The Whitney Museum of American Art at Gansevoort, 2015. Renzo Piano Building Workshop architects in collaboration with Cooper Robertson (New York). Photo by Nic Lehoux.

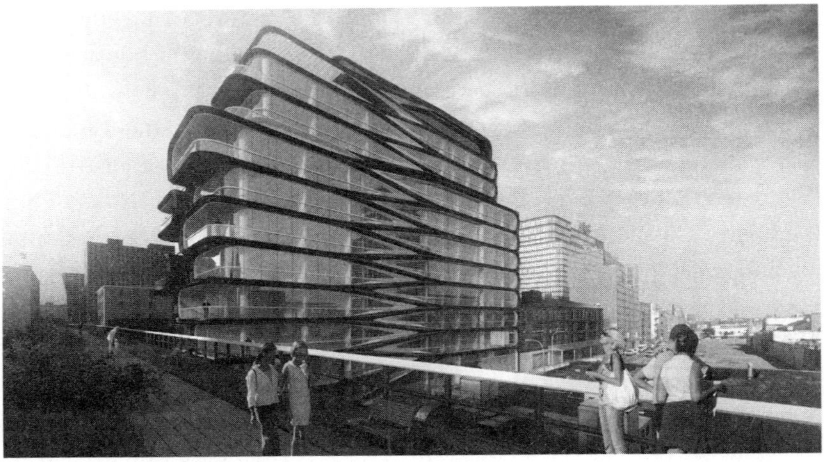

FIGURE 6.3. Luxury living at the High Line: Rendering of 520 West 28th Street. Courtesy of Zaha Hadid Architects.

and occupied. It is populist and accessible, but also exclusive and elite. The park is designed to generate precisely these kinds of tensions and, just as important, to provide opportunities to reflect on them under conditions of slowness. In an essay about the influence of landscape historian John Dixon Hunt on his design practice, James Corner is explicit on the deceleratory aims of the park and, in particular, on its insistence on slow walking: "There can be no immediacy of appreciation, no fast way to consume landscape in any meaningful or lasting way. . . . In the case of the High Line, the experience of strolling is intentionally slowed down in the otherwise bustling context of Manhattan. Paths meandering in between tall perennial and grass plantings create an experience that can not really be properly captured in a photograph, or even video. Like so many other gardens, the place must be walked, with scenes unfolding in sequence and in juxtaposition" (Corner 2014: 345). Despite overstating the uniqueness of the High Line experience (after all, no space or landscape can be fully grasped through mediated representation), Corner's comments are revealing for the emphasis they place on the design's resistance to speed. Pause, delay, and detour are all possible on the High Line and are encouraged by the meandering design of the central walkway and the various stopping places and viewing points spread along the way, such as the Sunken Overlook, which provides amphitheater seating suspended above 10th Avenue, facing a glass window that cinematically frames the street below. In these sorts of ways, the High Line keeps visitors close to the street, immersed in the city, yet released from the everyday.

THE HIGH LINE EFFECT

As a reinvention of the urban promenade, the High Line speaks to the depth of our cultural investment in streetwalking as an urban practice tied to leisure and embodied pleasure. It is therefore somewhat ironic that Paris's Promenade Plantée, although popular, has not attracted anything like the public attention of the High Line, since this earlier experiment with repurposing an elevated railroad cuts across the very city where the modern boulevard and its attendant promenade practices were invented. My view is that the High Line's greater public visibility as a landscape architecture project is connected to the cityscape it inhabits as much as to the park's design itself, in the sense that the extreme iconicity of the New York skyline and the opportunity provided by the park to encounter that skyline—even inhabit it—in a defamiliarized, intimate, and decelerated way is at the core of the High Line experience.

It is therefore worth noting that, as both an urban park and an engine of urban renewal, the High Line has directly inspired similar projects to repurpose abandoned railroads in cities as diverse as Bangkok, Sydney, Rotterdam, Chicago, and Philadelphia, to name just a few. Many of these projects have stalled or collapsed, but the trend of seeking to build elevated green walkways has been gathering momentum since the construction of the High Line. In New York, for example, a campaign was launched in Queens in 2011, led by the community coalition Friends of the QueensWay, to "transform the blighted structure that housed the Long Island Railroad and was abandoned over 50 years ago into a public greenway" (Friends of the QueensWay n.d.). Both the QueensWay proposal and its grass-roots community approach consciously seek to replicate the High Line model while connecting to both the geographic and cultural specificities of Queens.

Back in Manhattan, another High Line–inspired project was also announced in 2011. Called the Lowline, it takes the design concept behind the elevated railroad park in a new direction: underground. Still in progress at the time of this book's publication, the Lowline is a proposal by designers James Ramsey and Dan Barasch to build an underground park at the site of the abandoned Williamsburg trolley terminal, located under Delancey Street on Manhattan's Lower East Side (figure 6.4). The project is explicitly

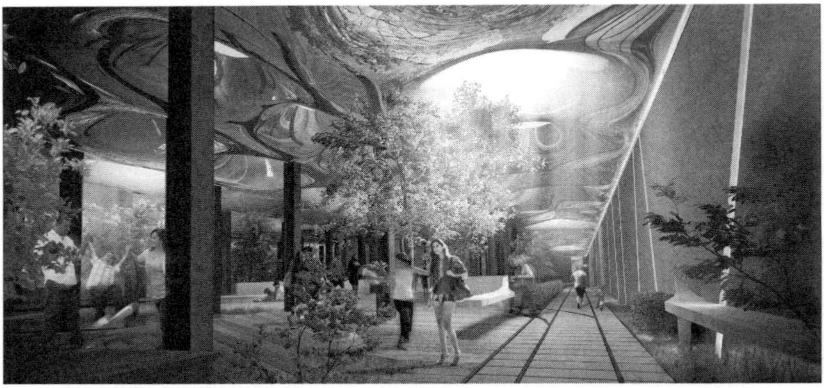

FIGURE 6.4. Rendering of the Lowline at Delancey Street, 2012. Courtesy of Raad Studio.

conceived as a spatial inversion of the elevated linear walkway comprised by the High Line and envisages a subterranean space with walkways, trees, plants, and abundant natural light, made possible by remote skylights using fiber optics. Unlike the High Line, the Lowline specifically places technology at the center of the park's design and experiments with how that technology can help to solve urban design problems, such as the lack of available space for public parks in dense urban environments. So although it shares the High Line's concern with repurposing abandoned railroad tracks for eco-friendly public use, the Lowline goes one step further by seeking to conjoin smart city and sustainable city design.

As an inversion of the High Line's spatiality, the Lowline differs in a few significant ways. First, its underground location means that it offers no city views. The project's flipped urbanism thus promises a kind of extreme visual self-reflexivity in which the only view available from the Lowline is the Lowline. Gone are the High Line's sweeping panoramas and any associated experience of inhabiting the New York skyline from a floating walkway. Second, the Lowline is not visible from the street and consequently lacks the conspicuousness and public presence that helps the High Line draw visitors and attract surrounding development. For instance, there is no possibility of building luxury Lowline condos overlooking the park, unless the buildings were similarly subterranean. Although entirely unlikely, such a project is technically feasible and, if realized, would represent another form of inversion: the upside-down penthouse, where the lowest floors of the building offer the best park views and become the most expensive and coveted levels. My point is that, because of its inversion, the Lowline is unlikely to have the same gentrifying effects on its surrounding neighborhood as the High Line, and it would most probably struggle to achieve a similarly iconic status in the urban imaginary.

Even so, public interest in the concept of an underground linear park has been strong enough for the Lowline to gather substantial community support and financial backing, and even to generate spin-off proposals of its own. In 2012, for example, Fletcher Priest Architects won a green infrastructure design competition in London with a proposal for an underground urban mushroom garden in a disused Mail Rail tunnel running beneath the congested shopping artery of Oxford Street (Bathurst 2012; figure 6.5). As illustrated by the transnational migration of the concept of the underground railway park, we can now also speak of a Lowline effect—a subterranean variation on the High Line effect—in which ruin lust meets green-tech fetishism.

Yet if we strip away all the high-tech solar technologies of the Lowline and set aside the absence of visibility, what remains is remarkably similar to the High Line: a green walkway shaped by the linear spatiality of a

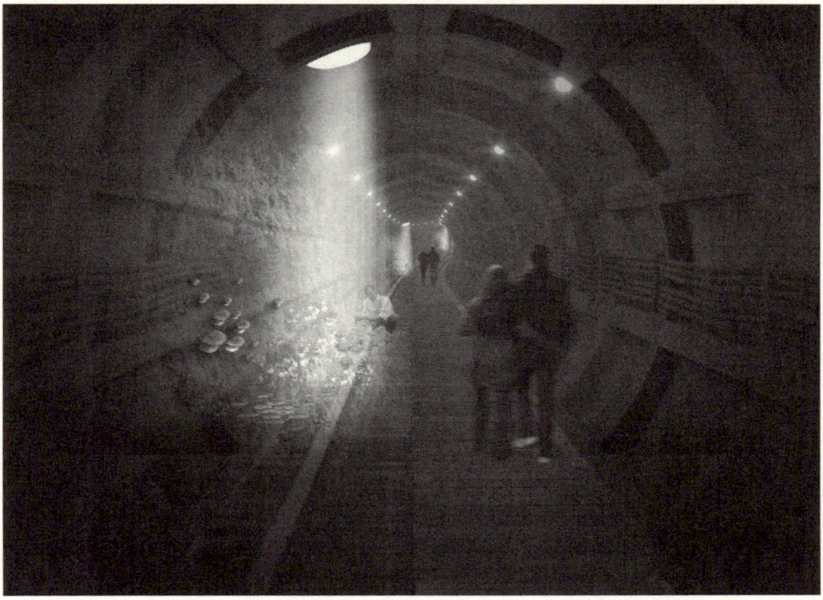

FIGURE 6.5. "Pop Down": Proposal for a Mail Rail urban mushroom garden in central London, 2012. © Fletcher Priest Architects.

railroad and made possible by the abandonment of that infrastructure in a time of postindustrial urban decay. More than that, all of these park projects hinge on producing what Sunny Stalter, writing about 1950s artists concerned with the obsolescence of the "el," has called a "nostalgic urban visuality" (Stalter 2006: 871) rooted in the transport history of the space. What makes the Lowline different is that it seeks to achieve its nostalgia and otherworldly transformation by submerging visitors beneath the street, whereas the High Line and the Promenade Plantée achieve these effects by elevating visitors above it. Yet, in both the elevated and underground versions of the railroad park, the aim remains the same: to refigure the street by relocating its sidewalk practices to a decelerated space of reanimated urban mobility—a space where those sidewalk practices do not conventionally belong but where they can be newly enacted through interruptive, otherworldly transformations of the space.

SLOW SPOTS

The important connection between the High Line and its spin-off projects is that they all seek to produce what I have called "slow spots" (Lindner 2013: 16)—creative spaces of decelerated practice and experience developed in response to what Paul Virilio, commenting on the architecture of velocity, describes as the amnesiac "speed-space" of the contemporary city (Virilio 2001: 69). These linear park projects may promote retro-walking within slow spots as an interruption of the accelerated city, but those interruptions are only temporary and superficial, ultimately reinforcing urban velocity. The reason is that their slow urbanism is also a palliative urbanism. It is designed to alleviate symptoms associated with life in the accelerated city, while simultaneously stimulating surrounding conditions of speed, anonymity, spectacle, and amnesia.

In an article on the poetics and politics of walking, David Pinder (2011) has argued that we need more nuanced, differentiated models for understanding pedestrian practices as resistance, nomadism, and subversion. I agree. One tendency in critical responses to the High Line's perambulatory conditions has been to label the space a heterotopia—a space of radical otherness that disturbs and transforms. For example, Daan Wesselman (2013) works through Michel Foucault's various writings on heterotopia and maps the concept onto the High Line, arguing that the elevated park perfectly fits the label, but he concludes that "the alternative offered by the park remains tied to the dominant surroundings, showing the limits to the suspension of the everyday that heterotopia can achieve" (Wesselman 2013: 25). While I think the label of heterotopia can work for the High Line, it is also far too generalizing to reveal much beyond the park's surface experiment with the idea of spatial otherness.

To contribute to a more nuanced, differentiated reading of the High Line—one that is more attuned to what Pinder describes as the potentialities of urban walking "for experiencing, researching, weaving, re-enchanting, or subverting spaces" (Pinder 2011: 676–677), I have proposed the concept of retro-walking. This concept does not disregard the heterotopic potential of slow practice and the spaces in which that practice occurs. Instead, the concept of retro-walking connects those qualities to the broader trend of slow urbanism. It is a trend that extends from architecture, landscape design, and urban planning, to art, urban heritage, and everyday life, and that is paradoxically being absorbed into the very conditions of neoliberal globalization and accelerated living that it seeks to interrupt.

ACKNOWLEDGMENTS

This chapter is adapted from an earlier version published as "Interrupting New York," in *Cities Interrupted: Visual Culture and Urban Space*, ed. Shirley Jordan and Christoph Lindner (London: Bloomsbury, 2016).

PART III URBAN POLITICAL ECOLOGIES

7 ▪ THE GARDEN ON THE MACHINE

TOM BAKER

THE HIGH LINE "is something of a New York fairy tale," according to Robin Pogrebin (2009a). In some ways, too, it is revealing of a city hell-bent on reinventing itself. Intriguingly, this "park in the sky" channels the aesthetics of two distinct eras in its own history. Of course, New York City is no stranger to nostalgia and timeless icons—the yellow taxi, the steaming manhole cover—but the socio-spatial configuration of the High Line brings together the themes of both the historical fabric of the urban industrial age and the strikingly verdant vegetation that grew while the railway line lay disused.

Two overarching concepts are useful when considering these strands that are so central to the High Line's visual discourse. First, the park can be read as a contemporary example of pastoral landscaping, an idealized construction of a particular vision of nature, that of the "urban wilderness," which is ornamental in essence. There is much in common here with understandings of the "traditional" pastoral landscape (Bachin 2003; Cranz 1978, 1989; Gandy 2003), though the term "urban pastoral" reflects the way in which the contemporary landscape of the High Line deploys a "traditional" pastoral impulse (associated with the great American urban parks of the nineteenth and early twentieth centuries) in the creation of a novel landscape. Considering the role of the industrial era in the contemporary landscape, Julian Stallabrass's 1999 work, *High Art Lite,* on the urban pastoral in art history is relevant. He argues that some of the subjects of pastoral art and literature are shifted from the rural to the urban in the work of the Young British Artists, saying they were more concerned with the aesthetics and materiality of the city, rather than with offering much in the way of substantive social commentary. The urban pastoral offers the language to describe and understand the cultural repurposing of industrial space and the domestication of a previously "illegible" landscape (Lynch 1960). Both nature and culture at the High Line are marked by a series of similarities with previous schemes of spatial production.

Thinking through the High Line as a landscape of the pastoral, one finds continuities and discontinuities between the broader historical usage of the pastoral as both an ideology and a vocabulary of landscape architecture, and its contemporary application. In American park design, the pastoral is most closely associated with the great urban parks of the nineteenth century, like New York City's own Central Park—both the continent's preeminent pastoral park, and what Matthew Gandy (2003) suggests was the most important public space created in nineteenth-century America—but there are also distinct connections to be made with the High Line. The similarity is not lost on critics either. A brief review by the *Telegraph*'s Melissa Whitworth (2009) is tellingly titled "The New Central Park."

Given the widespread application of the term "pastoral" to park design (and its mainstream cultural understanding), it is useful to think of it in terms of what might be considered pastoral ideology—the locus of several key ideas in literature and broader culture (Alpers 1996; Empson 1974), as well as in landscape architecture. These include artificial yet naturalistic design, the notion of nature as refuge, and the elevation of what might be considered "fundamental" values to a higher status. Urban pastoral, then, refers to the application of these broad themes to a new aesthetic production, in this case the landscape of the High Line. Simply put, urban pastoral reflects the way in which the High Line embodies the ideas of the pastoral, as produced through a similar cultural impulse, but appears beguilingly different from the traditional pastoral landscapes of the pleasure garden.

THE PASTORAL

Commenting on the place of the pastoral in literature, William Empson suggests that "the wider sense of the term includes such folk-literature as is by the people, for the people, and about the people. But most fairy stories and ballads, though 'by' and 'for,' are not about; whereas pastoral though 'about' is not 'by' or 'for'" (Empson 1974: 6). He argues that key to the pastoral is a sociocultural divergence between subject and object. The simple, wholesome, "fundamental" lives and emotions of the (rural) poor are offered up to a more elite audience—an audience that, in pastoral orthodoxy, accesses a more authentic experience through cultural consumption than is available through a life removed from the firsthand production of landscape. It is the elite with whom the message chimes most strongly, because the elite has left behind the simplicity of rural production. Naturally, the view of picturesque rurality is totally romanticized. This is the central conceit of the pastoral in literature. It relates to the *idea* of benign rural society more than the reality, and as such is a totally bourgeois vision, hence Empson's contrast to folk literature. The pastoral, as an idealized conception of a seeming reality, also flattens the messiness and antagonism of social relations. Pastoral literature does not reflect on the power structures in society that themselves produce the sociocultural divergence—land ownership, market economies, and so on. James Machor suggests that "our culture, as well as our literature, has tended continually to perceive environment through a pastoral filter" (Machor 1987: 4). The pastoralism of nineteenth-century park creation is the occasion for dialectically produced space, as rural landscape ideals—nature and culture in harmony—are embedded in processes of urbanization. These urban parks tended to be islands of "nature" in urban space, though admittedly often at the margins of cities as they were then (Cranz 1989). Nonetheless, the nostalgic and protectionist vision of rural life, and its embedded qualities, served as the inspiration for Central Park and the other reform parks.

The creation of pleasure gardens also saw the "Yankee predilection for the English picturesque landscape transposed to an urban industrial setting" (Gandy 2003: 86–87). Gandy usefully highlights the strange confluence between a developing American nature aesthetic and the preeminence of capitalist urbanization, the outcome of which saw an urban ideology of nature that embraced the commodification of nature for repackaging as an object of consumption. He notes the Sheep Meadow in Central Park, as well as the more picturesque Ramble. Besides the material features of the pastoral landscape, central to our understanding must be the conditions of its production. As Rebecca Krinke explains, "when Olmsted began work on Central Park, the site was virtually devoid of any vegetation and strewn with rubbish. . . . The park was a human-made construction, not a remnant of untouched nature as many people still believe. It is a powerful work of art and, as [Robert] Smithson underscored, it is a work of art that is ongoing" (Krinke 2001: 128). A landscape of artifice made "natural," the pastoral is a complex play on organicism and the human control of nature.

THE POWER OF CULTURAL PRODUCTS

Though it may seem to be stating the obvious to note that the inspiration for landscape production must come from somewhere, the extreme linearity between the High Line's influences and its finished form is striking. The nascent Friends of the High Line (FHL) and the Design Trust for Public Space commissioned Joel Sternfeld to photograph the extant landscape. His resulting photographic essay, *Walking the High Line*, published in 2001, was very influential in publicizing the site both as an object of interest and as a campaign for urban change. It is correct to make the distinction between the images in and of themselves—as cultural works of general interest—and their use for advocacy purposes, though their dual articulation is what makes them of most interest here. The perspective of the Sternfeld photos is particularly noteworthy. In every one, the orientation is as if one were traveling along the rails with the railway stretching toward the horizon, central in an urban vista. In this arrangement, one appreciates the High Line itself—its mixture of industrial and urban wilderness—as well as its place in the broader urban landscape. Adam Gopnik relates Sternfeld's fervor for the space: "These little shoots . . . see this! This is the *real* look of spring. Central Park is a construct in so many ways. A beautiful construct, but made for an effect" Gopnik (2001: 49). It is both the impressiveness of the scene, as well as the novelty of the naturally seeded growth, that captures Sternfeld's imagination. It is wonderfully ironic that his photographs were a major contributing factor to the development, and its own transition to a beautiful construct—but one made for an effect.

Robert Hammond, cofounder and executive director of FHL, said that "what happened is that's what people got attached to, that natural wildscape, and that heavily influenced what's up there now" (Hammond 2011). Leaving aside the conceptual tensions of whether plants growing on an elevated railway can be construed as "natural," the links between the popularized vision of the abandoned space and its eventual development are key.

As Gillian Rose argues, representations are "important to understand . . . because they are intimately bound into social power relations" (Rose 2007: 9).

CONTINUITIES AND DISCONTINUITIES

"This was completely new, a new beast for us. It was something that hasn't ever been done in this city for sure," Karen Tamir, project manager for James Corner Field Operations, told me in 2011, in an interview about the landscape architects' work on the High Line project. Although this claim may be true for the kind of industrial reuse to which she was specifically referring, it is in fact an uncritical statement. While the production of the High Line may seem like something out of the blue, there are significant pastoral continuities. For the pleasure gardens of the nineteenth century, landscape transformation drove the wish to fix a pastoral landscape for posterity in the form of the urban park. At the turn of the twenty-first century, it was the will to fix the "urban wilderness" that provoked so much interest in the High Line, as evident in many press reports. For Albert Amateau "the challenge was to keep the viaduct's wild look—which evolved as weeds and grasses covered it" (Amateau 2007). Taking influence from what might be thought of as the "wilderness era," the designers produced a landscape that evokes natural seeding, environmental dynamism, and a real sense of wilderness.

The design of the High Line is highly naturalistic, with the interplay between path and planting being one of the essential features. The concrete planks taper into the vegetation, allowing the greenery to push up and through the gaps. This vegetation and the hard engineering hold each other in tension. The species were chosen to be very resistant, a hint to the inhospitable conditions thirty feet in the air and with only seventeen inches of soil in most places. There are more than one hundred thousand plants, arranged in what is made to seem an arbitrary fashion. In fact, the approach of Piet Oudolf (the lead planting designer) to specifically reference the predevelopment "urban wilderness" is both thoughtful and playful. The plants are perennial, four-seasonal species that were chosen to be appreciated all year round. Melissa Fisher, the High Line's director of Horticulture and Park Operations, reported that seed heads are not removed, in the hope that they are appreciated as much in the autumn as the blooms were in the summer. The apparent arbitrariness is also clear in the way that the path meanders back and forth across the structure, with the planting emphasis first on one side and then the other.

As Charles McKinney, principal urban designer for the New York City Department of Parks and Recreation, says, "the idea was that by having those planks that dissolve into fingers, by having it move in kind of a serpentine fashion, that sometimes when you look at the end of a view the path will appear to dissolve into the weeds" (McKinney 2011). The "dissolving" landscape makes claims on the traditions established in the nineteenth-century pleasure garden. As Cranz argues, in Olmsted and Vaux's Central Park and elsewhere, there were arranged "masses of trees to formulate long vistas leading into imaginary distances to create the kinesthetic experience of moving through spatial sequences" (Cranz 1989: 37). Likewise at the High Line: Tamir (2011) explained the attempt to create a series of episodal sequences, orchestrated moments of landscape experience.

What we have, then, is a designed approximation of an urban wilderness. As Central Park is to an idealized rural idyll, so the High Line is to an idealized urban wasteland. During a tour of the park's art installations, the High Line's curator Lauren Ross described the park as "an elevated meadow . . . organic in many senses of the word" (Ross 2011). As I have shown, the "many senses" to which Ross referred is really only one sense—the biotic reality of the plants and animals. She makes claims on the myth of the pastoral by implying that the planting arose from the structure without intervention, whereas the truth is that in creating the park, all of the wildflowers were removed in order that the structure could be renovated and cleaned.

Charles McKinney told me "there's a desire not to have a vocabulary of 'stuff' that makes it look like a park. Like a normal park . . . there should be nothing that makes you think 'New York City park'" (McKinney 2011). As a result of this structuring approach to the design vocabulary, facilities that offer something akin to a "traditional" park experience are conceived to work with the urban pastoral landscape. For example, instead of a paddling pool or fountain, the High Line hosts a linear water feature consisting of a long strip of concrete over which a shallow stream of water flows into a drain. In the summer months there are usually people to be found paddling, splashing, and even lying in the water. Such a design approach actually marks a reversion to the pastoralism of the pleasure garden: "According to picturesque theory the designer avoided calling attention to the individual tree, its bark, leaves and other details" (Cranz 1989: 37). The point to make here is that individual elements are less important than the whole. The details are subordinated to the landscape.

ORNAMENTAL WILDERNESS

McKinney says, "[It's] fun to explore; you don't outgrow that desire, curiosity. It's different from a formal landscape where it's all laid out for you and it's all controlled" (McKinney 2011). In fact, the High Line is both tightly controlled and highly managed, particularly the relationship between people and nature. The High Line is, first and foremost, a *landscape* park, with the overall design details subordinated to the landscape vision. More than this, however, the whole experience is one that privileges the visual consumption of the landscape over other kinds of interactions. Contrary to FHL's rhetoric, there is evidence to suggest that this is a place of limited environmental dynamism. For example, some of the small trees planted on the structure at 14th Street are held up by cords, in order that they can withstand the strong winds that blow in from the Hudson River. The maintenance of the plants is very demanding, too. The watering system is more akin to a botanical garden than a public park, with Section 1 watered extensively by hand and with drip irrigation throughout the whole of Section 2. The financial and ecological costs of maintaining the landscape as envisioned by the designers are high.

As in pastoral orthodoxy, the landscape is designed with vistas and view corridors intended to draw visitors through the park, guiding their movement. But whereas in other parks one may be drawn away from the path, through the trees and perhaps even the undergrowth, the High Line leaves no room for such exploration. During one lunchtime visit I saw two children playing on the "wrong" side of the green cordon that serves to dissuade people from interfering with the planting. The High Line's naturalistic planting is inviting, with the concrete planks tapering into the vegetation, but sadly for those children, the landscape is delicate and ornamental, a combination of the ideology of nature that prioritizes noninterventionist human consumption (what Paul Gobster [2007] calls the "museumification" of nature) and the reality of having constructed such a dense and diverse planting regime in such an objectively unsuitable site (that is, one with little soil and water). Having noticed a "stay on the path" sign, an accompanying adult called the children away.

There is further evidence of the High Line's generally deterministic ornamentality at the 23rd Street Lawn, an expanse of mown grass on which people can walk, sit, and play. Since its opening, it has become one of the High Line's most popular features, which is telling of the tensions inherent in the model of the landscape park. It contrasts starkly with the pastoral aesthetic of the rest of the park and is more reminiscent of the "meadow" spaces of the pleasure gardens and manicured grass used for recreation elsewhere. However, the lawn is so popular that at times during the summer it has to be closed in order to protect it from overuse and to allow it to regrow. The incongruous lawn is justified by the designers with reference to "community wishes" (Hammond 2011), but this claim raises questions about the feelings of the community with respect to the rest of the design. If there is such a public appreciation for sitting on the grass (and so little issue with the lack of aesthetic coherence), why is there a lack of provision for this kind of use throughout the park? The lawn seems like merely one concession to the community, rather than a sincere reflection of a broader need and desire for public space. If so, then it is a concession in both design terms (given its aesthetic dissonance) and institutional terms (in respect to the lack of community oversight of the decision-making processes of FHL). Clearly anguished by the lack of play equipment, a young girl I met during my ethnographic research was overheard complaining, "Mom, this is not a park!"

The aesthetics of the High Line make it seem to be a more nuanced proposition than the kind of blunt encirclement of nature by global capital described by Cindi Katz (1998), yet in my view its status as ornament suggests otherwise. As Tamir says, "Trying to keep it wild in its own right, but . . . to the degree that it's a heavily populated park—it's hard" (2011). Such difficulty is perhaps the inevitable consequence of a park in which the urban pastoral landscape and its visual consumption are prioritized above other uses. Indeed, Hammond describes nature at the High Line as "*amped up*" (2011, emphasis in original). The abstracted state of decay (the allusions to urban entropy) at the High Line is the logical—and expensive—conclusion to this process of design intensification.

According to McKinney, "Central Park, you know they turned the swamps and they made them lakes, and they took the soil and they made the mountains taller, so they amplified it. That landscape design technique is applied on the High Line" (McKinney 2011). Richard Lacayo (2007) argues that we live in a time where the most intrepid designers create parks that are plainly human-made endeavors. Of course this is true of the High

Line in one sense—it exists atop a human-made structure—yet at the same time, the park's deployment of a pastoral aesthetic fixes the landscape in a way that is reminiscent of the pleasure garden. It is odd that in New York, a perennially unfinished city, the urban wasteland has been fixed as a natural/cultural phenomenon. Many of the press reports from the time of FHL's advocacy—by Julie Iovine (2004) and Meera Subramanian (2006) for example—employ a trope that might be understood as "nature reclaims the city." I would argue that the High Line landscape park is marked instead by the city reclaiming nature.

REFINING THE URBAN PASTORAL

If, according to James Machor, the pastoral ideal "constitutes a vision of environment in which city and country are equally valuable components in an evolving landscape best served when those components operate in harmony" (Machor 1987: 14), how is it that we can come to develop a pastoral critique of the landscape through a concept that moves away from the primary consideration of "nature"? As before, we may begin with a key theme of the pastoral. "The essential trick of the old pastoral, which was felt to imply a beautiful relation between rich and poor, was to make simple people express strong feelings (felt as the most universal subject, something fundamentally true about everybody) in learned and fashionable language (so that you wrote about the best subject the best way)" (Empson 1974: 11). Essentially, this strand of the pastoral rests on exhibiting something "fundamental" in a sophisticated way. Leo Marx (1964) provides a link between the "natural" and the human-made in consideration of the pastoral, as he examines how room was made for industry in the American myth of the pastoral—what he describes as "the machine in the garden."

Stallabrass (1999) works with the term "urban pastoral" without reference to Machor's earlier considerations. He teases out pastoral tendencies from the work of the Young British Artists of the 1990s, suggesting that the general theme of drawing on icons of "Britishness" produces a unitary and nostalgic image of the nation as a whole. As for Empson, "the work is about seeing something valuable in something trivial and associated with the less advantaged sections of society, and bringing that to the attention of art-lovers" (Stallabrass 1999: 237). He continues, "My argument will be that the outlook embodied in the pastoral has been turned from the rural to the urban, particularly to the landscape of the inner city" (1999: 238). Detailing the reasons why the city has become a site about which a pastoral narrative can be constructed, Stallabrass cites the industrialization of agriculture, the reduced number of people with a personal connection to the land, the ongoing transformation of the rural landscape, and the repackaging of much of the countryside into fenced nostalgic experiences. With this in mind, we can say that the High Line is a site of the urban pastoral.

Regarding the application of the concept to New York City, the urban pastoral, with some exceptions, has "more to do with the artefacts and appearance of the urban environment than with its inhabitants" (Stallabrass 1999: 247). The urban rejuvenation of the High Line very much rests on the materiality of the industrial West Side—the meat lockers of the Meatpacking District, the warehouse space of Chelsea, and the elevated railway. When memories of people are gone, it is the built fabric about which the nostalgic landscape is articulated. This is precisely Stallabrass's point. By highlighting a lack of social critique, he draws out the divergence between subject and object central to the urban pastoral. One effect is that the industrial landscape is then expressed in the terms of a cultural elite, as an aesthetic construct.

The production of the material landscape may be subject to a structural critique too. The neoliberalized funding strategies of public space in the city reproduce class-based inequalities between those who can mobilize to create a new multimillion-dollar park and those who cannot. As so often happens, it is those who lack the means to procure private access to leisure and recreational facilities who would have benefited from a less structured, landscaped park in the first place. The deployment of capital at the High Line was patently not for utilitarian social purposes. The micropolitics of the provision of park spaces under the status quo is such that new parks will only be built in the areas where private funds can be raised. Critics such as William Menking, the architectural writer, cite the unlikelihood of ever having acquired the levels of funding that were bestowed on the High Line, had the structure been located in the southern Bronx or eastern Brooklyn (Menking 2011). Though Stallabrass's neo-Marxian critique of the new appropriation of urban space is somewhat blunt, with its emphasis on class differentials between producer and consumer, it nonetheless provides a useful concept for thinking through the cultural significance of the industrial landscape.

GRIT WILDERNESS

It is commonly accepted that what might be considered "incidental landscapes" are increasingly being protected. That is to say that buildings constructed without particular reference to norms of beauty or the picturesque are being thought of as worthy of preservation. The fabric of the industrial city is one such incidental landscape. I do not suggest that there has been no appreciation of the kind of structures seen in urban industrial city centers across much of the world, but rather that such appreciation has moved right into the mainstream, to the extent that, for example, the High Line now attracts many millions of visitors a year. While seemingly removed from the city, the "grit wilderness" produced through historical contingency and deliberative landscape construction offers up a previously working landscape for the edification of visitors. This is a new kind of experience among the factories of the West Side. Where once production was central, a landscape of heritage and leisure now prevails. As Tamir puts it, "It wasn't looked at as creating a glamorous . . . glitzy place, it was 'hey, this is an abandoned rail, it's part of New York history' and how do we keep it in a way that . . . respects that?" (Tamir 2011).

Sharon Zukin, reflecting on the sociological production of postindustrial urban space and its increasing hold on consumption, refers to "the beauty in the tumble down and excitement in the rough" (Zukin 2008: 726). In the post–Jane Jacobs era of the appreciation of urban cultural diversity, interest in the industrial fabric has continued to grow. This is of course the classic argument developed by Zukin in *Loft Living* (1989) in relation to the occupation of loft spaces by yuppies. In her later work, Zukin (2008) relates this tendency to the structuring framework of authenticity, noting that, in reaction to the increased artifice and false morality of society, people began to think about the authentic self as honest and true. This specific point of analysis cannot be extended directly to the landscape of the High Line, but the broader cultural impulse that drives the "rediscovery" of the industrial city is similar.

So while Zukin and Stallabrass refer explicitly to cultural capital and population displacement, the High Line is a different case, given that the working-class population never occupied the structure itself and that the disinvestment in urban industry occurred long before the reinvestment associated with the project. Nonetheless, it represents a cultural expression of the kind of land use change that has occurred in the Meatpacking District and Chelsea. The elevated railway is reproduced as a pedestrian space a stone's throw from the lofts and renovated tenements and row houses. The value of Stallabrass's (1999) work is that it encourages us to discern the opening up of a previously culturally and pragmatically "forbidden" space into one that is both accessible to cultural elites and brought back into the market. The development of the High Line is marked not so much by the discovery of working-class space by elite groups, but more by the ongoing securing of the city by capital and the middle classes—what Neil Smith (1996) calls the "revanchist city."

INDUSTRIAL STRUCTURE

Niall Kirkwood is right to remind us of the value of industrial reuse: "Unlike past innovations in landscape design and city planning, which responded to economic changes, or growing alterations to population or technological innovation, this type of design work is a return to the productive use of exhausted and currently undervalued plots of ground—a tidying up of the past industrial environment" (Kirkwood 2001: 9). The redevelopment of the High Line was conducted specifically in order to preserve some of the key features of the railway, always with an eye to "authenticity." For example, the rail tracks that still remained on the structure (the majority, except for a few that had been dislodged and looted) were mapped, removed, cleaned, and stored, ready to be returned to the exact same place on the structure. A set of rails now runs the entire length of the landscape park, an immutable icon of its former life. On the Diller–von Furstenburg Sundeck, some of the wooden lounge seats even have wheels, allowing them to be moved a short distance along the rails. Memories of the working landscape are manufactured in conjunction with the rusted rails and factory buildings. Though cleaned, the rails were left with a patina of age—to do otherwise would be to interrupt the nostalgia for the industrial city that pervades the site. Elsewhere, some original signal lights are still attached to the wall by the Chelsea Market Passage of the park, as pointed out to visitors during regular guided tours. The objects of industrial New York are museumified in a landscape of nostalgia. Hammond explains, "What the design team did was expose the structure and add very subtle changes, but that really refocus you on the structure itself rather than become a means of their own" (Hammond 2011).

The approach to which Hammond refers is particularly striking in the design of the stairs that lead from ground level up to the High Line.

The stairways up from the street feature long landings below the level of the park, designed so that a cross-section of the structure, several meters in length, is directly at head height. The so-called slow stairs invite visitors to engage with the structure even before they step foot in the park itself. As with the episodal planting design, the orchestration of the visitor experience again exposes the High Line as a landscape first and foremost. Its use-value as a park is devalued in comparison with other spaces of recreation. The parts of the structure visible as one moves up and through the space of the stairs are not all original. The riveted surfaces were cleaned and painted, but the cladding is additional. Unlike the rails, however, this surface is pre-rusted—the aesthetics even of nonoriginal features tie them into the visual discourse established throughout the park.

RUST TO RUIN

The appeal of the urban pastoral park lies partly in the attraction of the High Line as a found space, an industrial ruin—the follies and artificial ruins of the English pastoral landscaped garden find their contemporary equivalent in Manhattan. For Peter Mullan, vice president for planning and design at Friends of the High Line, "this is a piece of lost New York that still exists" (quoted in Kilgannon 2010). The nods to urban exploration, and indeed to the predevelopment, unmanaged space, reflect the particular inflection of the pastoral: the landscape draws together the urban pastoral and industrial elements. On the part of FHL, cofounder Joshua David notes that the park's genesis was of the modern era, at the apotheosis of land use separation. The technological modernist legacy of the High Line is irreplaceable, and for David "new development should expand upon this historic and architectural identity, which is still a defining characteristic of the neighborhood" (David 2002: 20). The attitude toward the structure as a ruin, a vestige of another time, is highlighted by Glenn Collins (2008), who reports that the configurations of bolted steel plates were thought of as "industrial folk art" by those whose job it was to survey and clean them, again reflecting the tendency toward romanticism. As McKinney puts it, "Thank goodness the public has a taste for this postindustrial picturesque, that we can see past that it's a factory and we can see it in a romantic way, and so this piece of defunct industrial fabric has an appeal to our cultural, you know, enjoyment of ruins" (McKinney 2011).

As if the design team needed any encouragement, Tamir says, "A lot of this was required by what was . . . there, by the railroad, by the trains sometimes surrounded by buildings, so things sort of evolved within those kind of cues . . . certain views" (Tamir 2011). It is in the context of the High Line, of the West Side, and of industrial New York City, that these monuments work through their collective appeals to nostalgia. They are features of the landscape of the urban pastoral. As a cultural movement, the will to preserve and elevate industrial landscapes—to repackage them as sites of leisure—requires a certain sensitivity. The attention to detail marks it out as far more sophisticated than another example of the kind of "Disneyfication" bemoaned by Paul Gobster (2007) and Alexander Wilson (1991), but, as Tamir continues, "Places are just starting to turn into, they're so much more authentic, you know, if you work with them" (Tamir 2011). The kind of authenticity to which she refers is material. Put simply, developments must complement what is to be found at the site. The bridge to the Stallabrass critique of the urban pastoral here is obvious. Christine Boyer cites Magali Sarfatti (1993) thus: "Commodities (among them buildings), valued more for what they mean in terms of status than for their actual use, are the lifeblood of late capitalist commerce" (Boyer 1996: 165). The High Line is a good example of this privileging of status over use, as earlier argued in reference to the lack of provision for "normal" park uses.

DOMESTICATION

As Tamir (2011) states, building regulations and health and safety codes in New York City meant that the structure had to be totally cleaned and decontaminated if people were to be allowed to use it, but it is the aspiration to grand public enjoyment that compromised the magic of the High Line as it stood in its abandoned state. Domestication is a useful heuristic for comprehending this process. Annuli Ayer (2009) refers to the "humanization" of the landscape, but domestication speaks better to the need to make it "safe," both in terms of physical safety and in terms of legibility. The landscape can be experienced by the general public without needing to climb up onto an abandoned railway line for a genuinely "edgy" experience, as some did before the redevelopment. Zukin (2010) presents consumptive domestication as a means to secure the landscape. Instead of "domestication by cappuccino"—a process cited by Zukin in her work on gentrification—the

High Line features gourmet gelato. Of course, not all have been as receptive to the domestication project as the legions of visitors. "It was very pleasant, but I felt as though something had been lost," says Ashley Gilbertson (2009). Karrie Jacobs (2009) complains, "I thought—and still think—it was sad that Manhattan had been developed to the point where there was no room or tolerance for decay." Decay is now fixed into the landscape as a monument rather than a process.

It is worth noting that in the first two years of the High Line's opening not a single major crime (assault, larceny, robbery, or worse) was reported there, according to *New York Times* reporter Michael Wilson (2011), leading some to call it the safest place in New York. The securitization of the public realm in New York City over the past fifteen years has been well documented, marked by the convergence of the privatization of public space (Sorkin 1992), the proliferation of Business Improvement Districts and their private security guards (Boyer 2001), and the oft-noted—though contested—zero-tolerance crime agenda of former mayor Rudy Giuliani, and the associated "broken windows" approach of Police Commissioner Bill Bratton. For the landscape of the High Line, "It's important that it not be cleaned up too much; it still has to look . . . rough-*er*" (McKinney 2011, original emphasis). The aesthetic is slightly "edgy," but this can only be the case as long as visitors are allowed to feel totally safe. Poignantly, this is the same along the cobbled streets of "dark and melancholy" Gansevoort Street (Cunningham 2001) and the rest of the Meatpacking District, remembered by some as "an outlaw neighborhood, a working neighborhood on the edge" (Gay 2004). Drawing the discussion back to the urban pastoral, Stallabrass remarks that "a little edge, just the right amount, is energizing, and is necessary to spark off pastoral fantasy" (Stallabrass 1999: 246). Just the right amount relates to the materiality of urban industry, without the threat associated with public space.

AMPING UP: A CONCLUSION

Considering the High Line as an urban pastoral space, there are historical legacies of two crucial phases: the industrial era and the High Line's wilderness years. The resultant landscape is one that draws its power from the combination of the biological and industrial elements—truly, the garden on the machine. Although the continuity between the aesthetic of the High

Line before and after its redevelopment has been noted, so has the "amping up" of the landscape as it is today. One may consider the park to be a site of urban palimpsest, since there is no denying the layers of history on display. At the same time, the architectural deliberation is such that what is evident is largely contrived.

The continuities from the period of the great pastoral landscaped parks of the nineteenth century are evident. The High Line exhibits an aestheticized vision of one formulation of nature, that of the urban wilderness. The space of the naturally seeded era was reworked, made more lush and bombastic. Whereas before, none of the wild flowers grew above waist height, the High Line now features trees of nine feet and more. With aspirations to timelessness typical of the pastoral trope, future dynamism is limited. What's more, the designed wilderness is intended not to look like a park. This spatial-temporal fixing, combined with the fragility of the planting scheme and the high level of use, have resulted in the creation of an ornamental wilderness. As befits a landscape masquerading as a park, visual consumption is prioritized above all else.

Following Stallabrass (1999) on the urban pastoral, we can say that the landscape of the garden on the machine is marked by the opening up of a previously working landscape for the edification of the urban leisure classes. The "grit wilderness" highlighted by Tamir depends on the kind of place making that is familiar from other forms of industrial preservation and the projection of "authentic" urban experiences, with value imbued in the landscape through the evocation of memory. The postindustrial picturesque flows from design details like the emphasis on the structure on the "slow stairs," the subtle placement of the rails, and the assorted monuments to past times, like the faded advertisement. The process through which the landscape is domesticated not only makes it feel safe—a fundamental character of a space that must look but not feel too wild—but also legible. It has come to seem entirely natural to be strolling along a promenade in the sky among the factory buildings of the West Side. The true (social) "grit" is drained from the landscape, and, "partly (and ironically) out of designers' efforts to make them more legible, even the most complex industrial ruin parks tend to operate as themed follies" (E. Chan 2009: 27). The overall effect of the High Line's design—produced by simultaneously reinterpreting both the industrial and postindustrial eras of the site's history—is one of the pastoral.

8 ▪ THE URBAN SUSTAINABILITY FIX AND THE RISE OF THE CONSERVANCY PARK

PHIL BIRGE-LIBERMAN

> To the extent that cities are produced through socio-ecological processes, attention has to be paid to the political processes through which particular socio-environmental urban conditions are made and remade. . . . [T]he material conditions that comprise the urban environment are controlled, manipulated, and serve the interests of the elite at the expense of marginalized populations. (Heynen et al. 2006: 2, 6)

THE REDEVELOPMENT OF postindustrial American cities is closely linked to the economic and cultural processes of gentrification. In an economic sense, the gentrification of postindustrial American cities represents a strategy through which homebuyers and real estate developers reinvest capital in areas hurt by disinvestment and neglect. Culturally, this back-to-the-city movement results in the displacement of working-class residents by a new, upwardly mobile professional class seeking a hip, urban lifestyle (Florida 2002; Lees et al. 2008; Ley 1996; Zukin 1989, 1991, 1995). In terms of urban redevelopment, gentrification "is a consummate expression of neoliberal urbanism" (Smith 2002: 446).

Since the 1970s, American cities have experienced a neoliberal turn whereby they engage in economic strategies that, geographer David Harvey argues, helped them "re-establish the conditions for capital accumulation and to restore the power of economic elites" (Harvey 2005: 19). To many, the processes of gentrification converge in the housing market, but in recent years these processes have become more insidious, as they have increasingly been used to target a wholesale "class remake of the central urban landscape" (Smith 1996: 39). Through the use of public-private partnerships, the redevelopment of attractive, affluent neighborhoods with environmental amenities suitable for a hip leisure class has become the cornerstone of urban growth strategies (Bryson 2013; Checker 2011: 216; Veblen [1899] 2007). These eco-entrepreneurial strategies represent an urban sustainability fix (While et al. 2004). Employing environmental discourses and policies, such as urban sustainability and park restoration, these powerful partnerships produce a form of eco-gentrification where "the environmental improvements result in the displacement of working-class residents as cleanup and reuse of undesirable land uses make a neighborhood more attractive and drive up real estate prices" (Curran and Hamilton 2012: 1027; see also Bryson 2013; Checker 2011; Dooling 2009; Pearsall 2010; Quastel 2009).

Urban regime analysis helps situate these discourses and redevelopment strategies within broader political-economic-ecological contexts by taking into account the management of stakeholder interests necessary to achieve consensus strategies for urban growth (Gibbs and Jonas 2000; Mossberger and Stoker 2001; Ward 1996). In his seminal work on urban politics, political scientist Clarence Stone defines an urban regime as "an informal, yet relatively stable group, with *access to institutional resources* that enable it to have a sustained role in making governing decisions" (1989: 4, emphasis in original). He further explains the power held by the regime as the "power to," or the ability to act, instead of a form of "power over" others, even though the power to act can ultimately end up being construed as power over others (Stone 1989: 229). Urban regimes (e.g., politicians, business owners, institutions, real estate developers, nonprofit groups) act to influence cooperation and consensus from government and nongovernment actors.

The focus on urban sustainability means that urban regimes incorporate environmental goals into broader redevelopment strategies. Projects such as brownfield remediation and redevelopment, urban stream restoration, and park restoration may be considered forms of eco-gentrification, since they act as spatial fixes and have been "important in opening up actual urban spaces for new waves of investment and bringing back the middle classes in the city" (While et al. 2004: 550). By investing in urban infrastructure, urban regimes invest in "the whole suite of physical installations that sustain and enhance the system's ability to create wealth" (Schoenberger 2004: 429). In this way, nature becomes more than just a set of resources. Urban regimes deploy nature as a "key component of the total package required to . . . generate economic growth" (Florida 2002: 50). They invest in parks and green spaces as forms of "green infrastructure" to produce aesthetically pleasing environments to attract mobile capital, global tourists, and middle- and upper-middle-class professionals (Sandström 2002; Tarr 1984; Tzoulas et al. 2007; While et al. 2004). Urban parks, therefore, are one dimension in the increasing use of environmentally friendly urban design and have become necessary amenities for urban redevelopment.

The redevelopment of the city, specifically the manipulation of the built environment, is the result of, and results in, inequality. By examining these processes we can see that "environmental transformations are not independent of class, gender, ethnicity, or other power struggles," but instead these transformations "produce socio-environmental conditions that are both enabling, for powerful individuals and groups, and disabling, for marginalized individuals and groups" (Heynen et al. 2006: 10). In controlling the transformations of the urban landscape, urban regimes possess the ability to determine which environmental imaginaries get constructed, which in turn informs the material appearance of the landscape. In his environmental history of Seattle, Matthew Klingle argues that the history of urban space "emerges from how humans wield power over one another with nature as their instrument" (Klingle 2007: 198). The production of urban public parks, like the High Line, therefore, reflects a symbolic economy associated with cultural production and consumption, redevelopment, and gentrification in postindustrial neoliberal cities (Zukin 1995).

By looking closely at the "greening" of the High Line it is possible to see the ways in which powerful urban regimes deploy nature, wield power in the city, and produce particular urban landscapes. I frame the greening of the High Line in two related ways. First, by considering the park's *political* ecology to examine how efforts of the Friends of the High Line (FHL) represent a new park typology—the conservancy park—and reflect the entrepreneurial dimensions of neoliberal urbanism. Second, by considering the political *ecology* of the park to explore the ways in which this park acts as an urban sustainability fix, whereby the design relies on specific environmental imaginaries to produce aesthetically pleasing and "sustainable" landscapes. The critical perspectives offered by urban regime analysis and urban political ecology help to clarify who produces what kinds of socio-ecological configurations. The High Line is an important site for this examination, since it is a postindustrial urban site that has undergone cultural and ecological succession and is now the model for the adaptive reuse of urban infrastructure (Foster 2010; Patrick 2014).

THE HIGH LINE AS CONSERVANCY PARK

Since the 1970s, New York City, like other deindustrializing American cities, sought to replace its former manufacturing base and adopted an urban growth strategy that focused on service industries (Hackworth 2007; Logan and Molotch 1998; Smith 1996; Zukin 1995). Recently, this shift has included the commodification of urban spaces through the replacement of older industrial spaces with trendy restaurants, hip boutiques and shops, high-end lofts in converted mills and warehouses, museums, historic districts, parks, and other urban spectacles that incorporate historical or cultural themes (Boyer 1992; Harvey 1989a; Zukin 1995). With the emergence of present-day neoliberal governance within American cities, the burden to restore and preserve these urban landscapes has shifted away from municipal government to the private sector.

As cities faced shrinking budgets and imposed austerity measures in the 1970s and 1980s, public parks became low budgetary priorities. After decades of deferred maintenance and neglect, urban parks had become derelict spaces, havens of crime, and degraded ecosystems in need of restoration (Caro 1975: 331–34; Rosenzweig and Blackmar 1992: 469–504). Frustrated with the state of their parks, local citizens in cities like New York, Boston, and Buffalo began forming private park friends groups and conservancies in the 1980s to act as stewards and take control of their local parks, improve the landscape, and make them more ecologically, economically, and socially sustainable (McPeck et al. 1983; Rogers 1987; Rosenzweig and Blackmar 1992: 505–30; Taylor 2010). To fulfill their missions, these conservancies rely on public involvement and stewardship, where volunteering and fund-raising are just as, if not more, important than hiking, nature appreciation, bird watching, and environmental education.

The era of the conservancy park reflects the strategies of neoliberal urbanism, and a fine line exists between what might be perceived as the top-down role of urban leaders, the bottom-up efforts of grass-roots groups, and the privatization of public spaces associated with late-twentieth-century entrepreneurial forms of urban governance. As cities set about creating and restoring their urban parks, urban regimes rely heavily on private park conservancies to engage in the re-imaging of the city according to their environmental discourses and imaginaries. The increased reliance on private park conservancies helps create "markets for park stewardship by the local state as municipal parks are spun off to corporate and/or citizen regimes who act as their stewards with, or in place of, their former caretakers" (Perkins 2009b: 2616; see also Pincetl 2003). Perhaps the best example of a park being controlled by a private park conservancy is New York's Central Park. While the city's Department of Parks and Recreation still maintains nominal responsibility for the park, the Central Park Conservancy (CPC), a private nonprofit organization, has been the "official manager" of the park since 1998, when the city and the conservancy entered into its management contract (Central Park Conservancy 2014; Gandy 2003; Katz 1998). Since it began managing the park, the CPC has invested nearly $700 million and helped make it a model for park restoration (Central Park Conservancy 2014). Providing 90 percent of the park's $58 million annual operating budget, and employing 80 percent of the park's maintenance staff, the CPC is responsible for all essential park operations, as specified in its contract with the city (Central Park Conservancy 2014). The FHL drew heavily on the CPC's model of park production in order to improve both the physical landscape and social attributes of the High Line.

In 1999, Joshua David and Robert Hammond founded the FHL, eventually evolving into the private partner to the New York City Department of Parks and Recreation. The FHL funds virtually all of the park's operations (the group provides more than 90 percent of the park's annual operating budget) by soliciting donations. Its mission is "to engage the vibrant and diverse community on and around the High Line, and to raise the essential private funding to help complete the High Line's construction and create an endowment for its future operations" (Friends of the High Line 2014). The kind of public-private partnership exemplified by the FHL and the City of New York represents the shift from a managerial to an entrepreneurial form of urban governance (Harvey 1989b). In this way, the efforts of the FHL to produce an elevated green space symbolize the rise of the conservancy park. In creating the FHL, David and Hammond worked to preserve a piece of the city's history and tried to make the city more sustainable. To justify the public expenditure necessary to preserve the High Line, the FHL emphasized the ways in which the new park would improve the land values in the neighborhood.

Reflecting the entrepreneurial strategies of the conservancy park, the FHL immediately began to solicit private donations to help preserve the High Line and create the new park. The first FHL fund-raiser was held in December 2000, with several celebrities in attendance. A photo of Hollywood VIPs Kevin Bacon and Kyra Sedgwick appeared in the *New York Post* the next day, helping to brand the High Line as a "celebrity project," which would be useful for future fund-raising (David and Hammond 2011: 27). The event raised $60,000, but according to David, the connections and commitment to the fledgling organization were more important than the money: "In the early stages of fund-raising, the money is almost a secondary benefit. What you are getting is a group of people who have literally bought into your mission. That bonding—especially to a young, new organization—is a statement of partnership, or commitment, or belonging, or family, that is irreplaceable in any other way" (David and Hammond 2011: 27). The never-ending process of fund-raising continued as the organization began a $50 million capital campaign. The High Line continued to be a celebrity project, and in 2002, Martha Stewart agreed to host a summer benefit event at her home, with actor Edward Norton as event chair (David and Hammond 2011: 51). Calvin Klein Collection celebrated its fortieth anniversary by hosting a party on the High Line during Fashion Week in 2008 and "each time someone stepped onto the red carpet—Halle Berry, Brooke Shields, Naomi Watts, Anna Wintour—hundreds of flashes fired off. The High Line was packed with magazine editors, designers, stylists, models and actors. . . . The party had the kind of exuberance that makes you feel that New York City is the only place in the world" (David and Hammond 2011: 113; Trebay 2008).

By 2009, the FHL were raising extremely large sums of money for their celebrity project. In June, they held a fund-raising gala dinner with numerous "luminaries of the New York social circuit" in attendance, including Jerry Seinfeld, Harvey Weinstein, and Martha Stewart (Pogrebin 2009b). At this dinner, the FHL announced a $10 million challenge grant by media mogul Barry Diller and his wife, fashion designer Diane von Furstenberg. Billionaire hedge fund manager Philip Falcone and his wife, Lisa Maria Falcone, met the challenge that evening, donating another $10 million (David and Hammond 2011: 115; Pogrebin 2009b).

At a public event announcing the opening of the High Line shortly after the gala, Mayor Michael Bloomberg acknowledged these private gifts:

"Rather than destroying this valuable piece of our history, we have recycled it into an innovative and exciting park that will provide more outdoor space for our citizens and create jobs and economic benefits for our City. Ten years ago, detractors thought the High Line was an eyesore. Thankfully, there were a handful of people who looked at the High Line and saw also an extraordinary gift to our city's future. Today, we will unwrap that gift" (City of New York 2009). Hammond was clear about what such a donation meant to the FHL: "Ten years in the making, the High Line is a testament to what New Yorkers can accomplish if they dream big and work together. In these challenging times, gifts like those from the Diller–von Furstenberg Family Foundation and Philip and Lisa Maria Falcone will allow us to finish construction on Section 2 and help build an endowment for the future maintenance of the High Line" (City of New York 2009).

In 2011, the Diller–von Furstenberg Family Foundation followed up its $10 million challenge grant with a $20 million donation to help complete the third section of the High Line. In announcing the donation, Barry Diller noted, "In a hundred years, people will be amazed that this park was ever built, and during all that time it will have given pleasure to such great numbers of people. I'm glad that our family is able to play a small role in making the High Line a reality" (Foderaro 2011). Since 2009, the FHL have raised more than $90 million in private funds to maintain and operate this public park (Friends of the High Line 2010–2012). Though it provides 90 percent of the operating budget for the park, the FHL relied on funding by city, state, and federal governments to convert the derelict space into a new urban green space. The cost to construct Sections 1 and 2 amounted to $152.3 million, less than $10 million of which came from the FHL (table 8.1).

In addition to private donations, the effort to create the High Line also benefited from zoning changes made by the city. In 2005, the city rezoned the area and created the Special West Chelsea District to encourage the creation of the park and to facilitate real estate development. From the city's perspective, this rezoning was the main reason to support the reuse of the High Line. Along with the creation of the park, rezoning would provide opportunities for new residential and commercial development. But perhaps most important, new zoning regulations would ensure that the form and design of new buildings would enhance the character of both the High Line and the neighborhood, helping to strengthen the area as a "destination" (New York City Department of City Planning 2013b: 3).

TABLE 8.1 Funding the High Line Construction

Park section	Cost	Funding sources	Contribution
Sections 1 and 2	$152.3 million	City of New York	$123.2 million
Section 3 (expected)	$86.2 million	Federal government	$20.3 million
Total cost	$238.5 million	State of New York	$400,000
		FHL and other sources	$44 million

SOURCE: New York City Economic Development Corporation (2014).

The city also helped to establish the area adjacent to the High Line as a Business Improvement District (BID) to help fund the maintenance and operation of the park. Similar to traditional BIDs, businesses, property owners, and residents within the High Line Improvement District pay a supplemental assessment that goes directly to the FHL to pay for park maintenance (Friends of the High Line 2009). In terms of operating costs per acre, the High Line is the most expensive park in the city (table 8.2). The FHL estimated operating costs at between $3.5 million and $4.5 million, of which the city will contribute less than $1 million. The new district will generate approximately $1 million, and the FHL will raise the remaining $1.5 million to $2.5 million dollars through private donations. According to the FHL, the district is essential for the development of the neighborhood because "having an exceptionally well-maintained, world-class open space and truly unique amenity will benefit you in many ways, from increased business revenue, the ability to attract high-quality employees and tenants, and increased property values, to a generally improved quality of life for all of us every day" (Friends of the High Line 2009).

The notion of urban parks enhancing real estate prices is not new or unique to the High Line: less than twenty years after beginning the construction of Central Park, Frederick Law Olmsted reported that the value of properties within three blocks of the park increased by nearly $210 million (City of New York 1873; Fox 1990). Like Central Park, the creation of the park on the High Line represents the cleanup and reuse of undesirable land to help make the neighborhood more attractive and drive up real estate prices (Curran and Hamilton 2012). In this way, the High Line epitomizes the class remake of the urban landscape associated with the gentrification of postindustrial American cities. The rise of the conservancy park, represented by the semi-privatization of urban parks, highlights the ways in which powerful groups and regimes manipulate nature and use it as a tool

TABLE 8.2 Comparison of NYC Park Operating Costs

Park	Annual operating costs per acre
High Line	$672,000
Bryant Park	$480,000
Central Park	$32,000
Average NYC park	$9,555

SOURCE: New York City Economic Development Corporation (2014).

for urban redevelopment. The success of this redevelopment depends on the environmental imaginaries used to create or restore urban parks.

ENVIRONMENTAL IMAGINARIES ON THE HIGH LINE

Urban parks have historically operated as part of a specific spatial fix to a variety of economic, social, and environmental problems associated with major crises of production within American capitalism (Birge-Liberman 2010; Harvey 1981, 1999, 2001). Within capitalist development, the processes of recovery and creative destruction entail economic decision making, the reworking of social relations, and the transformations of the socionatural environment (Page 1999; Schumpeter [1942] 1994). As part of an urban sustainability fix, the production of park landscapes has been based less on scientific or technical criteria than on aesthetics and economic interests. By fetishizing the aesthetics of particular urban natures, the production of the High Line reflects the symbolic economy associated with redevelopment and gentrification of postindustrial cities (Harvey 1981, 1999, 2001; Smith 1996, 2000, 2002; Zukin 1995, 2008). A critical urban political ecology focused on the production of urban parks allows us to "disentangle the interwoven knots of *social process, material metabolism*, and *spatial form* that go into the formation of contemporary urban socionatural landscapes" (Heynen et al. 2006: 8, emphasis in original). Disentangling these socionatural relations allows us to explore the particular sustainability discourses and environmental imaginaries used by the FHL to produce a "native" landscape atop the elevated railway to improve the look of, and quality of life in, the neighborhood. Together, urban sustainability (as an environmental discourse and policy) and landscape urbanism (as a design approach) play important roles in contemporary urban redevelopment strategies.

Landscape urbanism, as a theoretical and design approach to the city, proposes to address the interconnected ways in which infrastructure, natural systems, and human activity operate in the city (Waldheim 2006). In general terms, practitioners of landscape urbanism seek to use nature and landscape to replace architecture as the basic building block of the city. One basic tenet of the field is to make the invisible visible, by reversing the historic trend of hiding urban infrastructure (for example, sending streams underground in culverts) and emphasizing the role of infrastructure in shaping the landscape. Landscape urbanism emphasizes "the use of infrastructural systems and public landscapes they engender as the very ordering mechanisms of the urban field itself, shaping and shifting the organization of urban settlement and its indeterminate economic, political and social functions" (Waldheim 2006: 39). In this way, the field's most pervasive design idea is "to emphasize the natural systems that already exist in the metropolis, recovering them and foregrounding them as shapers of metropolitan image" (Scheer 2011: 614). James Corner, one of landscape urbanism's most influential practitioners, whose firm Field Operations was one of the primary designers of the High Line, echoed this sentiment by declaring that urban parks now had "new roles as essential infrastructure renewal, colonizing no-man's land, healing abused sites, and overcoming barriers connecting communities" (in Tate 2015: x; also see chapter 1 in this volume, by Corner).

The design approach of landscape urbanism is based on the notion of "terra fluxus," which represents "the fluid, process-driven characteristics of the city" (Corner 2006: 30). In focusing on process over time, Corner claims that his design strategy is derived from ecology, and he addresses how the city operates in space and time to create a "more organic, fluid urbanism" (29). Similar to Jane Jacobs's ballet of the sidewalk, Corner stages the horizontal surfaces of the landscape as the "field" of action, where he views the park landscape as a choreography of visitors using the space in different ways over time, to create "an ecology of various systems and elements that set in motion a diverse network of interaction" (30). Finally, he argues that park designs must be creative to invoke the imaginary, whereby their designs help users achieve a sense of place attachment, since urban spaces act as "containers of collective memory and desire" as well as "places for geographical and social imagination to extend new relationships and sets of possibilities" (32). All of these elements of landscape urbanism can be found in both the designs and the material landscape of the High Line.

To make the case for this park's role in making the city more green and sustainable, the FHL hired Field Operations, along with Diller Scofidio + Renfro (DS+R) and Piet Oudolf, to collaborate on the design for the new park. This multidisciplinary team of designers emphasized the park's ability to help "re-wild" the industrial city. This theme of re-wilding came directly from the derelict landscape that first drew David and Hammond to form the FHL and preserve the High Line. As a neglected space, the tracks on the railway became a self-seeded landscape that had some aesthetic appeal owing to nature's ability to re-wild this former industrial space. Corner's Field Operations based the design on the principles of landscape urbanism: process over time, staging the horizontal surface, and the imaginary.

From the beginning, Field Operations / DS+R approached the High Line as "a ruin, a found object," and the goal of the design was to show the evolution of this once industrial landscape. Corner acknowledged, "The High Line had its own mythology long before we came along. In particular, the 'Friends of the High Line' were instrumental in creating this distinct image around the High Line—they established an aura that projected an idea that this was in fact a postindustrial artifact maintaining a sense of melancholy and other-worldliness," with a major goal of the design being to "give people the feeling that they've come across a secret, magic garden in the sky" (in Fehrenbacher 2014).

In keeping with the tenets of landscape urbanism, the designers focused the core of the park's design on a new walkway system—the horizontal stage upon which to set the scene for the re-wilding of this former industrial space (figure 8.1). Corner used tapered concrete planks that would "comb into the landscaping" to blur the boundaries between the hard spaces of the walkway and soft spaces of the plantings (David and Hammond 2011: 77). With these boundaries blurred, it would appear that the plants were growing up out of the concrete walkway "like nature trying to claw back the man-made structure and reclaim it" (David and Hammond 2011: 77).

One of the critiques of landscape urbanism is that this design approach is really not new, that it is merely a different representation of landscape architecture and urban planning, but with a new ecological aesthetic. Landscape urbanism, as practiced by Corner, focuses more on the environmental discourse and imaginaries than on the actual material ecology inherent in park designs. Therefore the most appropriate theoretical approach to examine the manner in which Field Operations / DS+R designed the High Line is to utilize the perspective of urban political ecology, requiring

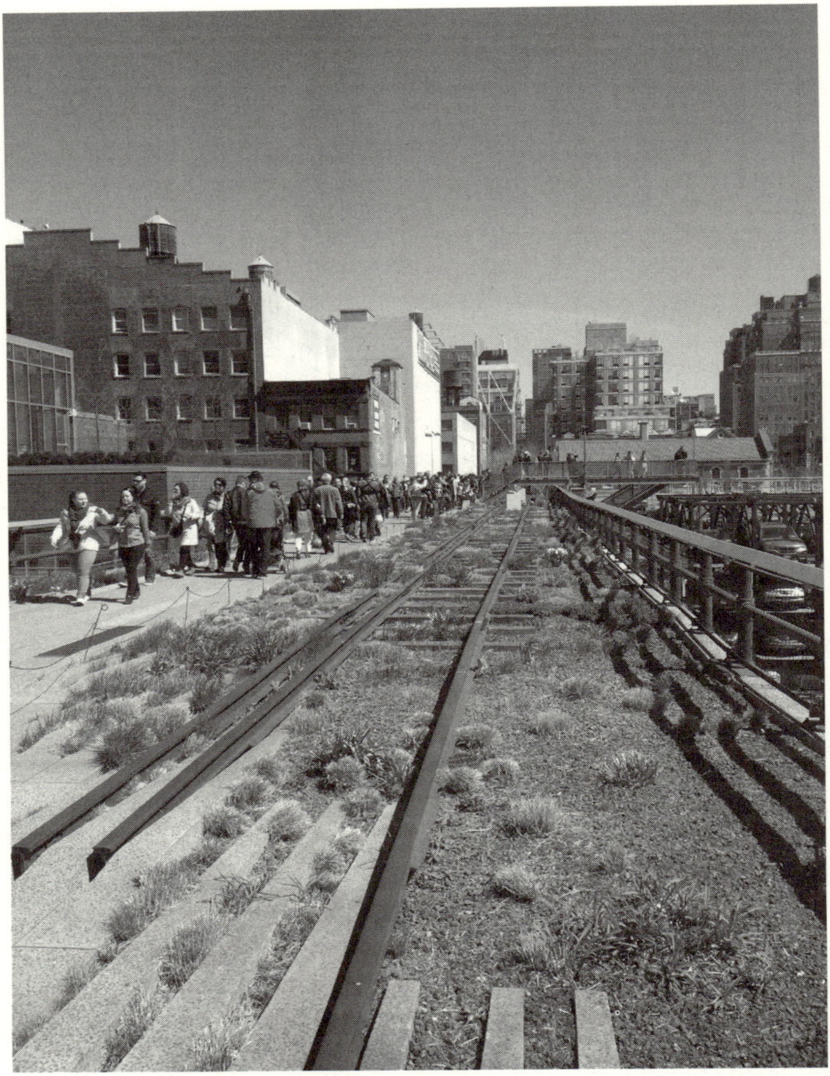

FIGURE 8.1. In the walkway, long concrete planks with tapered ends comb into the planting beds, giving visitors the sense of a wild, unkempt experience, as if nature is reclaiming the space. Photograph by the author.

a discursive-materialist examination of the landscape, where the material forms of nature are examined along with the sustainability discourse and the narrative of native ecologies.

In re-wilding this space, the design emphasized the evolution of the landscape. Recognizing that the draw for the FHL and those trying to preserve this space was the wild, unkempt landscape, Oudolf, the horticulturalist on the design team, noted that the new park was "still lush, still natural, but we used different trees and other species" (in Raver 2014). Oudolf's planting scheme used more than 350 species of trees, shrubs, grasses, perennials, vines, bulbs, and wetland plants to emphasize seasonal variety, various textures and colors, and hardiness (David and Hammond 2011: 266; Friends of the High Line 2012). The design highlighted planting patterns inspired by nature, pragmatic use of non-native plants, biodiversity, and the ecological fit to the conditions of the site (Oudolf and Kingsbury 2005). The design for the park claimed to emphasize the principles of ecological sustainability, urban regeneration, and adaptive reuse, in part, by paying attention to producing a "native ecology" (American Society of Landscape Architects 2010; Friends of the High Line 2014b).

The terms we use to describe park flora—"invasive," "exotic," "weeds," "native"—are heavily influenced by culture and politics, with native plants presented as better (more authentic) than others (Foster and Sandberg 2004: 178; Robbins 2004: 140; Warren 2007). Undercurrents of xenophobia run through our cultural preference for native plant species. In order to sidestep these uncomfortable connections, some designers and ecologists prefer to "use words like 'ecology' and 'ecological'" to describe their preferences for native landscapes, as if these terms "conferred moral authority" (Gröning and Wolschke-Bulmahn 1992: 116). Our cultural dislike of invasives emerges from the environmental imaginaries we create that privilege particular representations of nature. Environmental philosopher Neil Evernden argues that the spread of non-native species threatened our environmental imaginaries, since it was "not the environment at risk, but the very idea of the environment, the social *idea* of proper order" (Evernden 1992: 6, emphasis in original). The FHL and the designers used "native" in the broadest possible sense by privileging species native to North America. However, according to the Federal Native Plant Conservation Committee (1994), a native plant species is one that occurs naturally in a particular habitat, ecosystem, or region without direct or indirect human actions. Therefore, in order for the park on the High Line to be considered a *native landscape*, the plants found in the park must be *native to the region* (even if they are planted specifically through direct human action); but this is not the case.

Of the 359 plant species on the FHL plant list, 173 (48 percent) are not native to New York (Friends of the High Line 2012; United States Department of Agriculture 2015). Many of the species included ornamental cultivars bred for specific aesthetic qualities such as flower color, bloom length, and size (David and Hammond 2011: 94). A search of the USDA's Plant Database revealed that 39 of the 95 trees and shrubs, 53 of the 149 perennials, 12 of the 31 grasses, 9 of the 13 vines, 52 of the 52 bulbs, and 8 of the 19 wetland plants listed on the plant list are not native to New York. The planting list also identifies numerous hybrid species, which are not native to any region. These data stand in contrast to the FHL's stated planting design: "The species of perennials, grasses, shrubs and trees were chosen for their hardiness, sustainability, and textural and color variation, *with a focus on native species*" (Friends of the High Line 2014b, emphasis added). This dissonance can also be found in the "plant of the week" posts on the FHL (2015) blog:

- August 26, 2014—autumn moor grass (*Sesleria autumnalis*), a grass native to southern Europe and the Caucasus.
- November 10, 2014—mosquito grass (*Bouteloua gracilis*), a grass native to western North America from Alberta east to Manitoba and south through the Rocky Mountains, Great Plains, and Mexico.
- December 9, 2014—Winter Sun mahonia (*Mahonia × media*), is an interspecific hybrid evergreen shrub, its parent species are *Mahonia lomariifolia* and *Mahonia japonica*, both of which are native to Taiwan and China.
- December 30, 2014—Korean tassel fern (*Polystichum polyblepharum*), an evergreen fern native to Japan and Korea.
- January 12, 2015—pink astilbe (*Astilbe chinensis*), a rhizomatous perennial that is native to China.
- January 29, 2015—fragrant wintersweet (*Chimonanthus praecox*), a deciduous shrub native to the mountainous forests of China.

While almost half of all the plant species planted in the park are not native, many have been naturalized in the United States. The rationale for the profusion of non-native plants was to provide a prettier aesthetic throughout the changing of seasons. Since the native plants were mostly fallow and colorless in the winter, the design called for plants that would have more "textural and color variation" as well as "year-round interest and bloom" (Friends of the High Line 2014).

Despite the abundance of non-native plant species, the FHL have marketed the park's designed ecology as *native*. In doing so, they have implied that the flora was either: (a) naturally occurring without the intervention of human action; or, (b) that the human planting decisions and actions reflect the ecology that would have naturally occurred there, had humans not reworked it over centuries. This misleading claim goes to the heart of the notion of the conservancy park as an entrepreneurial tool for eco-gentrification. As part of the eco-gentrification process, postindustrial cities package green images of redeveloped spaces as sustainable and natural, in order to brand parks like the High Line as hip, trendy, and fashionable urban spaces.

CONSERVANCY PARKS AND THE URBAN SUSTAINABILITY FIX

By using parks and green spaces in the gentrification process, urban regimes use nature as a tool of social power. In controlling the transformation of the urban landscape, these regimes possess the ability to determine which environmental imaginaries dominate the discourse, and therefore, how the material landscape appears. The FHL set out to preserve an important part of New York City's industrial past by creating a park that they hoped would make the city more sustainable. While they do not actually define the word, they use "sustainability" as a term to brand the market by appealing to the public's environmental ethos. Interestingly, as Erik Swyngedouw and Nikolas Heynen note, "There is no such thing as an unsustainable city in general. Rather, there are a series of urban and environmental processes that negatively affect some social groups while benefiting others" (Swyngedouw and Heynen 2003: 901).

From the inception of the FHL, the regeneration of the neighborhood was a priority, and the creation of a new green space would act as a foundation on which future investment could be made. By most measures, the FHL have been very successful in this endeavor. The group used more than $140 million in city, state, and federal funding to help create a greenway that appeared to be re-wilding the industrial infrastructure, which in turn helped spur more than $2 billion in new developments, including 1,374 new housing units and four new hotels (New York City Department of City Planning 2013b: 19; New York City Economic Development Corporation 2014). The amount of commercial office space increased from 4 million square feet in 2005 to 5.6 million in 2008 and to 6.4 million in 2013 (New York City Department of City Planning 2013b: 18). There are also three new housing, commercial, retail, nonprofit, or gallery space projects under construction (New York City Economic Development Corporation 2014). Since the design was unveiled in 2005 and construction began, the High Line "has been the favorite cause of New York's rich and powerful. Celebrities attended fund-raisers on its deck. City officials endorsed it. Developers salivated over it, knowing it would raise land values" (Ourousoff 2009). Owing to the High Line's ability to generate value as an environmental amenity, some have dubbed it a "playground for plutocrats" (Jose 2010).

One way to understand how the High Line symbolizes a space of wealth and power is to examine the material day-to-day practices within the space. The new park helped revitalize the neighborhood through new residential developments, but it also served visitors from around the world coming to explore the High Line and the trendy new galleries, restaurants, and retail establishments in the neighborhood. In 2013, the High Line attracted 4.8 million people (half of whom were New York City residents), up from 3.7 million visits in 2011 and double the 2010 figure (Birnbaum 2014). As the High Line became more popular, it became what one blogger called "a tourist-clogged catwalk" and a "Disney World on the Hudson" (Moss 2012). In order to maintain safety and security as millions of visitors use the space, the City of New York allocated eleven park patrol officers to oversee the 7.08 acres of parkland on the High Line. In contrast, the city allocated just five park patrol officers to oversee all 6,970 acres of parkland in the Bronx (Calder 2009).

The processes of creating, restoring, or preserving an urban park are inherently political. Attention must be paid to both the urban sustainability discourses and the particular socio-natural urban conditions produced by urban regimes. Increasingly, cities come to rely on the work of private park conservancies to produce urban parks (and other forms of urban nature) as tools for urban entrepreneurialism and gentrification. Environmental amenities, such as parks, play significant roles in opening up spaces for reinvestment and in bringing the middle classes back to cities. In the case of the High Line, the FHL chose to imagine the space as a native ecology rewilding the industrial infrastructure, despite the fact that almost half of the plants species used in the design were not native to the region. This did not stop the FHL from branding the park as a sustainable form of green infrastructure. In the end, the success of the High Line is not so much about recreation or native plants, but rather about "the wider regeneration of the area and increase in property values to the point where the world's best-known architects are now seeking permissions, which can only further exaggerate the High Line as an oasis in city life" (Pollok-Morris 2014).

9 · OF SUCCESS AND SUCCESSION

A Queer Urban Ecology of the High Line

DARREN J. PATRICK

DURING NEARLY THREE decades of abandonment, the High Line grew into a queer urban ecology that was both invoked and displaced by the successful preservation-through-redevelopment effort led by the Friends of the High Line (FHL). This period of abandonment—perhaps more potently viewed as an era of unofficial self-management—allowed the space to become home to a successional, weedy ecosystem inhabited by more than seventy-five plant species (New York City Department of City Planning 2005, app. C), a bevy of urban animals (Foster 2010),[1] and a range of human uses, including queer sex and cruising, artistic production, encampment/squatting, and drug use. The park that replaced this landscape has been lauded as a landmark achievement of ecological design and civic activism, an ostensibly inexorable part of Manhattan's evolution into the world's leading leisure ground for finance capital. As many contributions to this volume witness, this success is increasingly being viewed through a critical lens, not least because of the ever more tangible effects it has had on both local and global scales. This chapter takes a queer, and perhaps melancholic, look at that success and its contradictory relationships to the successional landscape that preceded it. This backward view resists uncritical celebration, favoring instead a more nuanced valuation of the human and nonhuman relationships creatively destroyed along the way. Only by appreciating what was lost can we fully understand the cost of what has been saved.

In 1991, a five-block section of the High Line south of Gansevoort Street was torn down over the objection of community activists (first wave/pioneer gentrifiers; see Smith 1996) who had been moving into abandoned factories and lofts on the Far West Side and turning them into private homes. Despite promises to the contrary, Rockrose Development Corporation, which owns the sites, eventually sought and obtained zoning variances to develop high-rise residential properties on the formerly industrial lots freed by the elimination of the High Line overhead. The achievement of zoning variances sent a strong message to other High Line property owners that condemnation and demolition would be the best way to profit from otherwise very limited development opportunities for single-story lots located under the structure. Such development pressure encouraged the Chelsea Property Owners (CPO)—a vocal group led by Edison Properties CEO Jerry Gottesman—to push for condemnation and demolition at City Hall. Their justification for demolition was the apparent public safety threat posed by the decaying structure and its unsavory surroundings. Defeat, or victory, appeared inevitable when, in his last days in office in 2001, Mayor Rudy Giuliani signed a demolition order. This act set the bar for success.

Two years earlier, in 1999, Joshua David and Robert Hammond—two white, bourgeois, gay men—met at a Community Board meeting concerning the fate of the structure. The pair would soon cofound FHL, which is the only not-for-profit organization to license the right to operate a publicly owned park in New York City. Their success is measurable in multiple ways. For example, during his time as executive director of the organization, Hammond came to be better compensated than Adrian Benepe, former commissioner of the New York City Department of Parks and Recreation (Kovaleski 2009). By 2010, FHL had grown quite successfully, with an 84-person staff to manage and operate a 6.7-acre park (12.54 staff per acre). Compared with the Friends of Hudson River Park and the Hudson River Park Trust combined (17 staff for 550 acres = 0.03 staff per acre), the Central Park Conservancy (367 staff for 843 acres = 0.44 staff per acre), or the Prospect Park Alliance (263 staff for 585 acres = 0.45 staff per acre), the High

Line is the most highly staffed park per acre in New York City.[2] Beyond the costs of staffing, the park's per-square-foot operating costs are also the highest of any in New York City (Calder 2009). It is quite the growth engine.

On the other side of such cost-benefit analyses, project advocates claim that the redevelopment has spurred nearly $2 billion in real estate development through the zoning compromise crucial to the formation of the park (McGeehan 2011: n.p.). The New York City Economic Development Corporation indicates that, prior to the park's redevelopment, "surrounding residential properties were valued eight percent below the overall median for Manhattan." By 2011, the value of property within a five-minute walk of the park had increased by 103 percent (New York City Economic Development Corporation 2011: 2). Such statistics demonstrate how challenging it is for smaller-scale business owners, apartment renters, or residents of public housing near the High Line to maintain their position in the neighborhood, to say nothing of the fact that increased property values almost invariably bring increased ideological and material resistance to "unsavory" and "unruly" users, uses, and inhabitants of urban space.

THE HIGH LINE'S (SELF-)DEVELOPMENT

While these facts begin to bespeak the unevenness of resources and funding accorded to the High Line in comparison with other parks—which itself highlights some very basic environmental justice issues (see chapter 5, by Julian Brash)—they do not tell the whole story of how the High Line came into its own as a successful gentrifying force. For this, we need to look to alliances forged not only around the idea of preservation-through-redevelopment, but also with the very queer ecology of the High Line's postindustrial landscape itself. Related to the former, and owing to their confessed ignorance of urban spatial politics,[3] David and Hammond resourcefully assembled a group of pro-development experts, neoliberal consultants, powerful figures in real estate development, and a bevy of celebrities to aid in crafting and promoting their redevelopment strategy.[4] This glittering group easily overshadowed FHL's community-based supporters, though the latter remain an important source of funding and public relations support.[5] FHL's early efforts are too detailed to recount here,[6] but it is important to note that its emphasis on building high-level support through recruitment of powerful developers, politicians, and celebrities breaks with more "quaint" forms of Jane Jacobs–style community activism (Herman 2009), let alone radical or social justice–driven approaches to urban space. It is hardly surprising that such a coalition came to support the organization so quickly, in light of its avowedly pro-business disposition and professed political neutrality regarding gentrification (David and Hammond 2011: 10, 55).

But the High Line's success is not simply another New York tale of money, power, and prestige. As Hammond pointed out in a 2012 interview preceding an event called "Behind the Bushes: The Secret Homo History of the High Line,"[7] FHL relied on a strong connection to gay aspects of the project. "The High Line is totally gay," Hammond said in the interview (quoted in Pipenburg 2012). In addition to noting that the High Line runs through Chelsea, which, next to Hell's Kitchen, is Manhattan's most established gay neighborhood, he pointed out that "the core part of [FHL's] early supporters were gay people" (Pipenburg 2012). These were not just any gay people; they were people like legendary artist AA Bronson, lesbian city councilperson and future speaker of the City Council Christine Quinn, and the flamboyant and famed restaurateur Florent Morellet, whose eponymous diner ironically closed in 2008 as a result of, in part, rising rents and real estate values preceding the opening of the park. These supporters, many of whom already inhabited positions of political power and class, race, and/or gender privilege, were drawn on for their ability to fund the project or to provide political or cultural capital to FHL's effort. Their implication in a gentrifying process had far less impact on their material survival than on those in more tenuous circumstances.

When asked further about the connection between gays and redevelopment, Hammond offered the following explanation: "I believe gays have an ability to see beauty in places other people might find repellent or unattractive. It was easier for gays to see potential in the High Line. They were more willing to support a crazy dream. It goes back to Richard Florida and his concept of the creative class, this theory that gays are vital to neighborhoods because they see something special in them that real estate agents may not" (Pipenburg 2012: n.p.). By invoking the neoliberal avatar Richard Florida, Hammond opens up FHL to critiques of Florida's ignorance of the urban poor (Wilson and Keil 2008). In the fetishized and overdetermined world of the "creative city" we easily lose track of the socially and spatially exclusionary impacts of policies undertaken to lure the so-called creative class back to central-city neighborhoods. As we will see, Hammond's response also implicates FHL in critiques of homonormativity (Duggan 2003) and metronormativity (Halberstam 2005), in which white gay men are overrepresented in (urban) spatial politics, provided they are conversant in the depoliticizing discourses of good gay citizenship (see Bell and Binnie 2004). If we accept that "gays are vital to neighborhoods" such as the one rebranded by the High Line redevelopment, then we must also realize that bodies and practices marked as abject, excessive, or surplus—perhaps especially queer and trans people of color and the urban poor, cruising and public sex, or the production of anti-institutional art and culture—are all too frequently displaced in order for the "creative class" to claim success in their revitalization efforts.

FHL's deep entanglement with high-powered gay and lesbian New Yorkers in shaping the project in its early stages bypassed organizations such as the LGBTQ youth-of-color group Fabulous Independent Educated Radicals for Community Empowerment (FIERCE!), which has a long history of socio-spatial justice activism on Manhattan's West Side.[8] FIERCE! has been critical of the undemocratic, neoliberal approach to privately led public space development in which marginalized communities are often consulted, but less often positioned in key decision-making roles. Its long-standing work points to an enormous contradiction in the provision of tens of millions of public dollars to a gay-park-cum-speculative-real-estate-venture, even as queer and trans youth of color have been fighting for affordable housing, self-determined spaces, access to health care, and an end to state and police violence, all while resisting increased police profiling and everyday hostility that are endemic to and intensified by gentrification.

Indeed, while the High Line's gayness has been invoked as a cultural, economic, and sustainable "value added" according to the logic of the creative class, the reality of the project's uneven impact on the wider LGBTQ community, itself differentiated along racialized, classed, and gendered lines, is powerfully obscured by such statements as "The High Line is totally gay." This is to say nothing of the fact that the redevelopment of the High Line and subsequent influx of millions of tourists to the neighborhood has further commercialized, securitized, parodied, sanitized, and all but eliminated one of the few historically active and activist zones of public sexual (bio)diversity in Manhattan in the name of good, gay, and green development.[9] But, if you were to ask Hammond, as Piepenburg did, about the High Line's role in this transformation, you would receive a sanguine answer suggestive of the ostensibly organic nature of urban spatial transformation:

"The High Line gets too much credit and too much blame for the changes [in the neighborhood], which would have happened with or without it. . . . Young gay people go where the rents are cheaper" (in Piepenburg 2012). That is, of course, if they could afford the rent in the first place.

QUEERING ECOLOGY'S DISPLACEMENTS

With this empirical sketch on the table, the remainder of the chapter focuses on developing a queer ecological critique of gay and green gentrification by way of considering entanglements of human sexuality and more-than-human agencies, specifically those of plants. Building on a foundation of semistructured interviews with experts and archival research undertaken in 2010 (with a special attention to the entanglement of gay and environmental politics and history), I think relationally—and, I hope, provocatively—with one of the former botanical inhabitants of the space, *Ailanthus altissima,* also known as the "tree of heaven."[10] My wager is that *A. altissima*'s biological capacities, along with its reputation as a so-called nonnative invasive species, offer some crucial insights into the political and ethical possibilities of a queered urban ecology. *A. altissima* is an unruly actor, whose success as a species is inseparable from the continual anthropogenic production of waste spaces and successional ecological landscapes. What's more, *A. altissima*'s successional emergence in the abandoned ecology of the High Line and its subsequent erasure from the planned landscape that replaced that ecosystem are both metaphorically and literally entangled in the preservation-through-redevelopment effort spearheaded by FHL.

As FHL constructed an organization that ironically valorized the very queer urban ecology it would eventually displace, it became instrumental in driving a novel mode of homonormative gentrification. In analyzing the mainstreaming of metropolitan, white, bourgeois, and male gay sexuality in the neoliberal era,[11] Lisa Duggan elaborates homonormativity as "a politics that does not contest dominant heteronormative assumptions and institutions, but upholds and sustains them, while promising the possibility of a demobilized gay constituency and a privatized, depoliticized gay culture anchored in domesticity and consumption" (Duggan 2003: 50). Extending the critique of homonormativity to considering the queer urban ecology of the High Line suggests that the normalization of gay (that is, homonormative) gentrification as a mode of urban spatial capitalism not only powerfully obscures and displaces queer spatial histories, but also mystifies the process itself when it covers these spaces with well-designed, highly scripted, and nostalgically refurbished landscapes. In this context, the concept of homonormativity demonstrates the speciousness of FHL's claims to progress, success, and neutrality as a totally gay park.

Though FHL is not solely responsible here, its spatial and political strategy built on both gay territorialization and civic activism in New York's Lower West Side neighborhoods through a selective and naturalized narrative of succession between waves of gentrifiers, effectively blocking—even hopefully immunizing against—significant critiques and political opposition in crucial early phases of the project. FHL's claim to success might be better understood as a form of succession, which makes it difficult to hold the organization and its boosters politically accountable, precisely because this claim so often obscures or eliminates that which preceded and conditioned it by neutrally including it as a superficial element of the finished "product." Thus, not only does the preservation-through-redevelopment of the High Line embody classic neoliberal and gentrifying tactics, it also relies on an implicit appeal to homonormative urban ecologies in which possibilities for political and ethical linkages between sexuality and urban nature can only be expressed within the narrow limits set out by the exigencies of capitalist urban development. It is in this context that *A. altissima*'s own aggressive invasive capacities render it a spectral and highly suggestive figure, whose disappearance from the landscape of the High Line bespeaks an insidious tendency to obscure the project's negative impacts on marginal human communities. As for whether or not FHL's recently intensified steps toward taking responsibility as a *community* park are adequate to this task (see chapter 2, by Danya Sherman), much remains to be seen.

Here, queer ecological critique rooted in a notion of responsibility *to* and *for* abandoned urban spaces begins to speak more clearly to the complex entanglements that such spaces both enable and embody. Cate Sandilands draws our attention to the political work of queer ecologies when she calls us to "assume responsibility for a place by pressing ourselves to 'look both backward at the burden of its history and forward at our responsibility for those parts of its future that lie under human control'" (Sandilands 2005). Responding to this call in the context of the High Line redevelopment demands that we critically refuse to see the space as either gay-friendly or particularly green in the positive sense. Instead, we must focus on how the redevelopment of the High Line consolidated an increasingly insidious and naturalized urban homonormativity (see Andersson 2011), sidelining, silencing, or displacing the politics of race and racialization, class, and gender by way of normalizing white gayness as a crucial part of the survival of urban capitalism.

FROM GAY AND GREEN GENTRIFICATION TO PLANT GEOGRAPHY

For their part, critical geographers have examined gentrification—the process most highlighted in recent criticisms of the High Line—as an essential part of the (re)production of the late capitalist city. This well-developed conceptual terrain deals directly with questions of who inhabits and produces urban space, how they come to inhabit it, and under what conditions they displace others, in particular the urban poor and people of color, from spaces targeted for redevelopment. Literature on gentrification is traditionally divided according to emphasis on either production (Smith 1996, 2002) or consumption (Ley 1996, 2003; Zukin 1982, 1995, 2010). Production-focused accounts tend to emphasize the role of both the local and national state in securing the privately owned space for private-public development. Consumption-focused accounts highlight notions of authenticity, rebranding strategies, and cultural dimensions of the right to the city. Broadly, both sides of the critique identify the economic, social, and cultural mechanisms/drives that help to account for gentrification as a process by which the children of a generation who abandoned central city neighborhoods (in the United States, at least) during the historical era of white flight, come to destroy, rebuild, and reinhabit the very spaces left apparently unmanaged or in the hands of unruly inhabitants, human or otherwise. Without wading further into the details of the scholarly debate, it should be clear that the dynamics of abandonment and the resistant insistence on the right to self-determine, inhabit, and, if displaced, return to specific areas of the city form a core conceptual target of critiques of gentrification (Lefebvre 1996).

While I unequivocally share the political and scholarly commitment to naming, theorizing, and resisting gentrification, both mainstream and critical geographic literature do not leave much room to analyze the constitutive roles of either sexuality or urban ecology, both of which are central to the High Line's redevelopment in terms of both production and consumption.

In short, a queer ecological politics of gentrification is lacking. Nevertheless, in a classic piece by Jon Caulfield (1989), the author suggests the limitations of structuralist analyses of gentrification on both the production and consumption side, suggesting some interesting avenues for critique. Caulfield argues that the desires of gentrifiers must be considered a crucial force driving successive waves of gentrification. Where structuralist critics of gentrification are too bent on critiquing the "complicity" of gentrifiers with market forces, Caulfield suggests that it is perhaps more ironic, rather than complicit, when gentrifiers are displaced by the very process in which they are implicated (627). Further, Caulfield points to the role that erotic or spectacular excess plays in producing raw materials for uptake by more familiar, and undoubtedly more sinister, versions of gentrification:

> Deeply embedded in the landscape of gentrification is an immanent critique of modernist/capitalist city-building. . . . [T]he relationship among different groups of old city neighborhood resettlers may be best understood in the context of a model of entrepreneurial appropriation of marginal cultural practice. . . . [C]ultural forces may be vital in shaping urban landscapes. . . . [N]ot only economistic or "practical" factors matter. Crucial among these forces in the case of resettlement of old city neighborhoods is the desire of certain social actors to elude quotidian domination, whether by technique or by spectacle (or by the hegemony of heterosexualism). Their activity constitutes emancipatory practice of a kind that mainstream social science, serenely naturalizing existing structures, and Marxian political economy, finding in existing structures a monologic totality, are not always well situated to detect. (Caulfield 1989: 628)

Caulfield's intervention suggests that both market forces and more recent "creative city" arguments are inadequate to account for the (re)production of urban space and the displacement, direct or otherwise, of those who maintain, inhabit, or rely on the wasted spaces produced by deindustrialization. What's more, Caulfield's argument hints at the notion that landscape itself—or, in the case of the abandoned High Line, the plants, queers, and animals that bodied forth a queer urban ecology—is an important source of both the excess by which gentrification (and, by extension, urban capitalism) reproduces itself and the immanent critique by which the same process may be more thoroughly subverted. In light of more recent efforts to theorize both gay and green gentrification, Caulfield's prescient, if partial, invocation of notions of landscape and desire suggests a moment of the urban in which the perverse nature of a weedy ecology and the deviant sexuality of a queer cruising space come together to undercut the falsely creative homogeneity of even the most apparently progressive forms of gentrification.[12]

For this claim to carry weight in a queer ecological critique, it is important to situate our understanding of particular forms of desire, most notably a desire for gay and green neighborhoods and urban spaces, in terms of the critical scholarship on gentrification. Among many vibrant academic discussions of these topics, Larry Knopp's (2004, 2007b) work stands out not only as charting the evolution of such scholarship over time, but also for his more recent investigations of material and ontological concerns related to the more-than-human (see also Thrift 2005b, 2008; Whatmore 2002). Knopp remains strongly, if not centrally, concerned with "queer quests for identity" (Knopp 2004) even as queer theorists and feminists interested in many of the same ontological and biopolitical questions push for alternate framings of politics in terms of multispecies engagements (Giffney and Hird 2008), micropolitical/affective scales (Chisholm 2010), or imperceptibility (Grosz 2005), rather than emphasizing visibility or indulging in the taxonomic tendencies sometimes endemic to identity politics.

Knopp's hopeful forecast for the outcomes of these engagements is "a geography that is less arrogant and elitist, more hopeful than fear-driven, more possibilistic than deterministic, and more human (and humane) than inhuman (and inhumane)" (Knopp 2007: 27–28). And as for the nonhuman? While I am sympathetic to Knopp's vision,[13] I am perhaps most interested in his notion that, viewed through "ecologies of place,"[14] "queer quests for identity" suggest that queers have "ambivalent relationships to place and identity" and "affection for placelessness and movement" (Knopp 2004a: 129). With an eye in this direction, we must be careful to pay close attention to displacement as an *unwanted* or *enforced* (rather than a fetishized) mobility, readable through real material relationships and ecological configurations. While ecology does not provide a template that can easily be grafted onto either ethics or politics, it certainly lends itself to mobilizing unlikely relationships and modes of resistance in urban spatial politics. In other words, we should pay attention to how purportedly placeless or nomadic queers often reshape entire urban ecologies in the neighborhoods they eventually "settle."

Even as the High Line project grew from a well-heeled side-project into a multibillion-dollar real estate development effort, FHL self-consciously emphasized an approach that fused metropolitan sexuality with urban pastoralism in order to naturalize a hitherto unimaginable transformation of both the structure itself and the character and economics of the surrounding neighborhood. Recalling Caulfield, this evolution may be more ironic than complicit, but, in either case, a queer ecological approach suggests that we can—and even must—pay close attention to how the reconfigured ecology of the High Line played a central role in the process. If, as both the anecdotal and archival evidence suggests, metropolitan sexuality is a primary referent for the aesthetic of the space, what are the political and ethical implications of the particular landscape that emerges as a result of emphasizing this dimension of the structure's history? And what of its occlusions and erasures?

The displacement of an organically queer ecology by a designed homonormative ecology is related to, yet distinct from, the notion of ecological gentrification lately explored by critical geographers (Bunce 2009; Dooling 2009; Quastel 2009). These authors detail specifically ecological arguments and policies fashioned to drive gentrification, though they have so far avoided textured analyses of more-than-human ecologies. Sarah Dooling coined the term "ecological gentrification" to critique the displacement of homeless people in Seattle on the basis of ecological redesign of city green spaces (2009: 629–630). Dooling claims that "ecological gentrification relocates gentrification within the environmental discourses and in the discourses related to the exclusionary aspects of public spaces" (631). No doubt, the ecological argument for preserving the High Line *as* green space was sold as a win-win scenario, a framing that quelled potential opposition to the project's overall impact on affordable housing, policing, and commercial rents (to name but a few areas affected) on the basis that the project was a great leap forward for both ecological design and in the greening of a formerly industrial, gritty, and (c)overtly sexualized area of the city.

Critics focused on green gentrification hold a common understanding of urban environmentalism as a set of development, planning, and political problematics related to the ever more emphasized imperative for cities to grow sustainably. As Aidan While, Andrew Jonas, and David Gibbs (2004) have shown with their notion of the "sustainability fix," the ruling capitalist classes and urban gentry clearly find themselves under pressure to articulate pro-growth positions in terms ideologically immunized against environmental (and political) critique. Critics of ecological gentrification and capitalist proponents of green growth seem to agree, however, that urban environments must be adapted for a future laden with deep anxieties about environmental and social change. Nevertheless, when it comes to displacement, contributions to thinking sustainability, environment, and gentrification together remain fairly squarely focused on the human side of things. What might be gained by expanding our consideration to the nonhuman realm?

This question points toward key contributions to the scholarly literature of plant geography. Recent work by Cate Sandilands (2014) draws very important attention to the ways in which both the creation of parks and the notion of ecological "integrity" at stake in the management of invasive species reveal nuanced politics and power relations at the heart of urbanization and nation-building. The work of the plants themselves, to which Renate Sander-Regier attributes a form of agency expressed as activity or "by virtue of being alive" (2009: 69), has lately become the concern of a variety of authors writing under the umbrella of plant geography (Cloke and Jones 2002, 2003; Head and Atchison 2008; Heynen 2006; Hitchings 2003; Jones and Cloke 2008). Sander-Regier focuses on the production of abundance and excess as a strategy of survival for plants, eventually feeding a concept of the "ethics of partnership" based on Lorraine Johnson's notion of reciprocity, which is rooted in openness and mutual cultivation (2009: 80). Most interestingly, her understanding of weeds is sensitive to the irony that a weed often "initially serves a desirable purpose, yet with time and incessant activity, the plant becomes invasive and undesirable" (70). By emphasizing the recursive temporality of weediness, Sander-Regier reveals the process of dislocation that subtends the disjunction between an ecology of desire and a desirable ecology.

Extending these positions to a consideration of the queer urban ecology of the abandoned High Line, it is useful to distinguish an ecology of desire, which reflects relations of mutual benefit and attraction between human and more-than-human figures from a desirable ecology, which tips the relation toward the human, objectifying or instrumentalizing the vegetal as a component of the landscape that lends itself to management for human reproductive ends. As with Caulfield's description of pioneer gentrifiers, initial attraction to particular areas of the city suggests a desire to escape homogenization or an ability to survive with fewer resources than would be required in more well-established areas. The irony of appropriations of often "gritty" neighborhoods is that they clear the way for the same homogenizing forces that the settlers sought to escape in the first place. In this particular case, we witness the creative appropriation of abandoned and transitional space which was part garden, part gay pleasure ground, part neighborhood, part postindustrial zone, part public, part private, and, all the while, through-and-through political. Across time, this queer urban ecology shaped and was shaped by the actions and desires of cruisers, gentrifiers, and plants, each displacing and being displaced by the other in various modes of anomalous relation.

FROM CRITIQUES OF GENTRIFICATION TO QUEER URBAN ECOLOGIES

Queer ecological critique of both gay and green gentrification has important referents in the foregoing literature, specifically: an assumption of a consequential relationship between sexuality and regimes of urban spatial and ecological management, as well as a temporal understanding of place that takes seriously the "entanglements of relationality and consequent affective politics and ethics" (Jones and Cloke 2008: 87), and, relatedly, the need for specifically queer relational figures, such as particular plants, which trouble our accounts of agency, action, and responsibility *to* and *for* anthropogenic urban ecologies. Queer ecological critique builds on the foundational work of Cate Sandilands (2002, 2005, 2008; Sandilands and Erickson 2010) and borrows insights from the more recent and limited speculations of geographer Matthew Gandy (2012). While neither has invoked queer ecology to critique gentrification per se, Sandilands has developed a powerful analysis of the biopolitics of heteronormativity and reprocentricity in ecocriticism, while, in a more constrained effort, Gandy combines Foucault's and Lefebvre's notions of heterotopic alliance and heterotopy, respectively, in order to ground an interest in queer urban spaces understood as "unruly," "ruderal," and "anomalous" (Gandy 2012: 8). Queer ecology calls our attention to the urgent task of developing ethical and political concepts that can link sexuality and ecology as they operate in discursive strategies, human subjectivities, and ecological processes. Developing an ethics of responsibility is a necessary first step toward a queer urban ecology in which a proliferation of creative concepts and unlikely figures of resistance might prove useful to existing efforts to oppose spatial injustices of gentrification. For this to carry weight, we must traffic between the determinate and determining aspects of particular urban contexts, while not underestimating the transformative and indeterminate capacities of unconventional actors.

Bringing a notion of responsibility to bear on the redevelopment of the High Line invites a return to the abandoned ecology of the space. FHL's own initial attachment to the space was ironically predicated on the charismatic assemblage of queers and plants, now replaced by a highly managed, labor-intensive ecosystem in which basic interactions between humans and plants are circumscribed (figure 9.1). Whereas the abandoned ecology of the High Line offered a space for less scripted interspecies interactions—sex "behind the bushes," for example—FHL's emphasis on management, development, and economic success demands both more social and ecological control over the space. FHL rewrites the ecology of the High Line into dominant discourses and practices of gentrification and urban development, rendering plants as inert objects and queers as normative subjects whose "excessive" desires always risk capture by an urban capitalism incapable of producing its own surpluses.

In order to take more seriously the notion that the abandoned High Line's queer and vegetal inhabitants and activities might offer an immanent, if anachronistic, critique of homonormative gentrification, we need to look more closely at the ways in which plants were enrolled in the political, economic, and social discourses and practices of redevelopment. Here, we turn to the iconic photographs of the abandoned space taken by landscape photographer Joel Sternfeld (figures 9.2 and 9.3). Sternfeld's images of the High Line's abandoned ecology played a crucial, yet ambivalent, role in redeveloping the space as a park. These particular images depict *Ailanthus altissima*, which, with its reputation as an "aggressive" invasive species with a strong affinity for "disturbed" ecologies, suggests immanent vegetal critiques of the purified discourses of preservation and sustainability advocated by FHL. Encountering the High Line's abandoned[15] ecology through Sternfeld's photos transgresses FHL's narrative of success by emphasizing the extent to which the planned landscape performs material erasures of unruly species and activities from the High Line's past and present as it invokes their characteristics in its design. Of course, Sternfeld's photos also play a significant role in purifying the landscape of its animals and queer uses by depicting a space free of non-plant figures, a space without any overt human sexuality, or, indeed, any humans at all. Nothing seems to be going on behind these

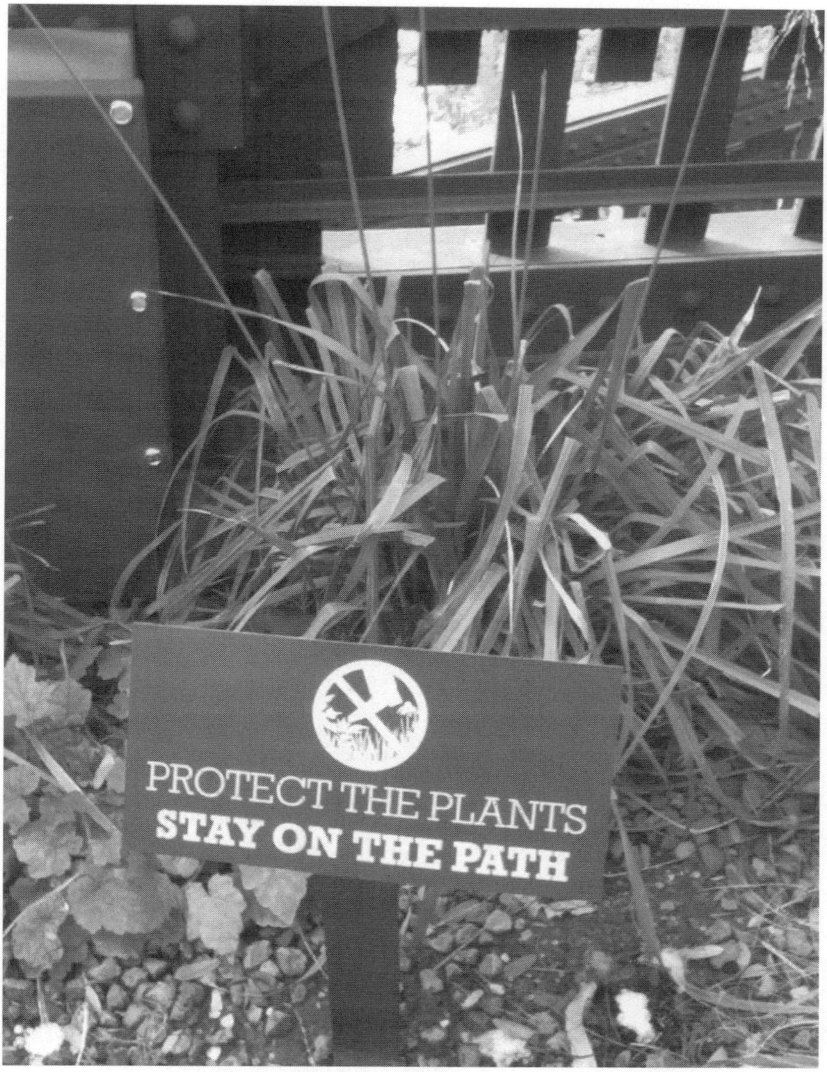

FIGURE 9.1. "Protect the Plants / Stay on the Path." Photograph by the author.

bushes. Sternfeld's aesthetic underscores the extent to which the park's carefully curated landscape invokes a queer attachment to the process of self-managed succession only to preclude any possibility of articulating, for instance, a political stance in defense of precisely the kinds of criminalized activities whose self-development precariously constituted the High Line's ecology in the first place. In this aesthetic, it is beyond imagination to argue

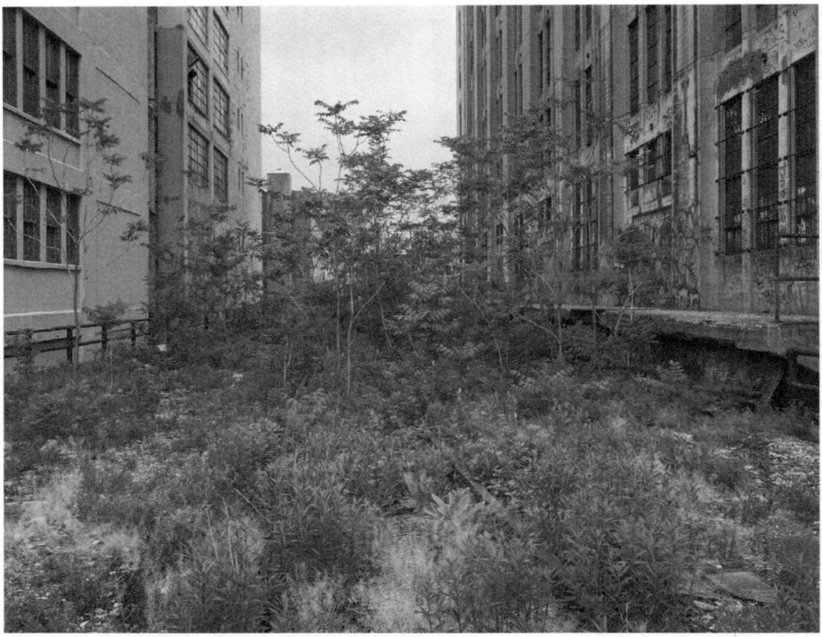

FIGURE 9.2. Joel Sternfeld, *Ailanthus Trees, 25th Street,* May 2000. © Joel Sternfeld. Courtesy of the artist and Luhring Augustine, New York.

for the provision of space in which such activities might have been undertaken safely—meaning without surveillance or the intervention of the police on the basis of quality of life—let alone with aesthetic enhancement.

As Michael Cataldi and his coauthors (2011) analyze in detail, Sternfeld's photographs have a complex and ambivalent relationship to the High Line redevelopment. On the one hand, they were crucial to galvanizing support for the project, despite the artist's preference for "maintaining the High Line in its 2000–2001 [abandoned] state" (2011: 362). On the other, they serve "as floating signifiers and design elements, divorced from the material conditions of maintenance labor, public and industrial transportation" (368). Focusing largely on the aestheticization of the space, Cataldi and coauthors offer a searing critique that points to many of the elements that I have discussed above, including the relationship of the High Line to gentrification, queer space, and post-9/11 security regimes (369–71). Picking up on the critique of landscape representation that they offer, we must still be careful to attend to the destruction of the High Line's abandoned landscape in terms that are sensitive not only to the human aspects of the ecosystem,

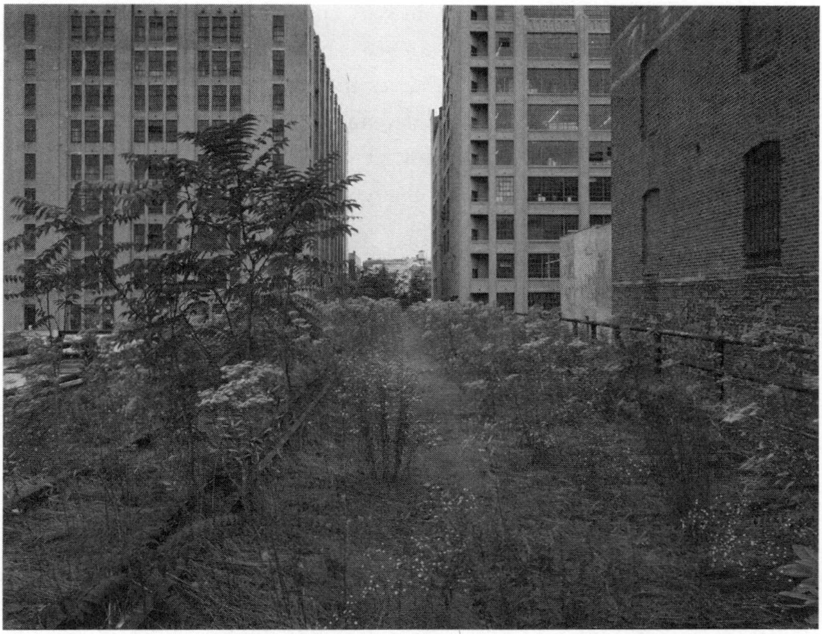

FIGURE 9.3. Joel Sternfeld, *Looking South at 27th Street,* September 2000. © Joel Sternfeld. Courtesy of the artist and Luhring Augustine, New York.

but also to the more-than-human. Even if problematically, Sternfeld's photos do afford us imaginative access to a charismatic landscape and some of its particular inhabitants in a moment when the apparently desirable and highly instrumentalized ecology of the redesigned High Line obscures and covers over the dynamics of the ecology of desire on which it is based.

As the now emeritus chair of FHL's board of directors recounted in a personal interview, Sternfeld's photos proved to be a "very powerful" tool for creating the High Line brand and for stimulating a "remarkably brilliant execution" of the designed landscape (Alschuler 2011). The official submission of the winning design team makes this explicit:

> Inspired by the melancholic, unruly beauty of the High Line, where nature has reclaimed a once-vital piece of urban infrastructure, the team retools this industrial conveyance into a postindustrial instrument of leisure, life, and growth. By changing the rules of engagement between plant life and pedestrians, our strategy of agri-tecture combines organic and building materials into a blend of changing proportions that accommodates the wild, the cultivated,

> the intimate, and the hyper-social. In stark contrast to the speed of Hudson River Park, this parallel linear experience is marked by slowness, distraction and an other-worldliness that preserves the strange character of the High Line. Providing flexibility and responsiveness to the changing needs, opportunities, and desires of the dynamic context, our proposal is designed to remain perpetually unfinished, sustaining emergent growth and change over time. (Friends of the High Line 2004)

The jury, which included FHL cofounder Robert Hammond, chose this design for its sensitivity to the High Line's plants and landscape (David and Hammond 2011: 75–77). Symbolic reverence for the original inhabitants again bespeaks a rather queer desire for maintaining melancholic attachments to disturbed urban ecologies of the bygone "gay ghetto" even as they are reworked, displaced, and sanitized. Yet, the design team's description leaves no ambiguity regarding the *proper* work to be performed by the figures populating the High Line's ecology. The team handily enfolds the queer ("unruly," "intimate," "strange character") with the vegetal ("nature," "wild," "cultivated," "plant life") in the context of neoliberal pressures for sustainable development ("flexibility and responsiveness," "perpetually unfinished, sustaining emergent growth and change over time"). The team makes the very condition of abandonment the basis for their design, embracing a mode of city building in which both unruly nature and deviant sexuality are perversely invoked to stimulate capitalist development. In this vision, the High Line's queers and plants (indeed, the animals seem to be lost in this narrative) carry more freight than the structure itself ever did. By seeking to "change the rules of engagement between plant life and pedestrians," the design team reveals a limited scope of acceptable modes of engagement with plant life in the park. Indeed, figuring all the park's users as "pedestrians" suggests that the redeveloped space is unfriendly, if not hostile, to the kinds of intimate and anomalous encounters enabled by the louche landscape of the abandoned High Line. Instead, the design puts the landscape as a whole into the ambiguous service of "sustaining emergent growth and change over time."

Accordingly, "plant selection [for the park] focuses on native, drought-tolerant, and low-maintenance species," which are arranged according to "naturally-created plant communities" that occurred in the self-seeded landscape. These choices are justified on the basis that they minimize resources necessary for maintenance (Friends of the High Line 2013b: n.p.). The role of plants as "native value added" belies FHL's claims of constructing the "world's longest greenroof," even as it obscures the reality that, prior to redevelopment, virtually no resources were required to maintain the space even as it provided valuable ecological services. While the continuation of unmanaged succession might have posed some measurable, but mitigable, risks to the stability of the structure itself,[16] it is clear that the exigencies of surplus value extraction took priority over any notion of responsibility *to* or *for* the existing ecology and the relations it already supported and enabled.

Sustainability is quite limited in this formulation, pertaining only to the "natural" elements of the space, while leaving the gentrifying impact of redevelopment on adjacent neighborhoods unaddressed as part of the project's eco-logic. Externalization of politically contentious impacts of the redevelopment deploys plants and queers in the construction of a desirable ecology, thereby naturalizing the displacement of both human and nonhuman inhabitants of the space under the guise of an eco-logic of succession. In other words, queers and plants, and eventually the public convened to befriend them, are permitted access on the condition that they yield to appropriately normative visions of redeveloping the space for the purposes of delimited growth and capitalist reproduction.

In light of its absence from the redesigned landscape, *A. altissima* offers an immanent potential for queer-cum-vegetal resistance to gentrification and redevelopment of postindustrial urban natures. Here it is useful to discuss some of *A. altissima*'s characteristics and entanglements with broader processes of urbanization. The tree of heaven was originally introduced to North America in 1784 by William Hamilton of Philadelphia (Shah 1997: 22). Native to central China, it is now found on every continent except Antarctica, a diffusion that has helped it earn a classification as a so-called exotic invasive species in many places, including parts of New York State.

British nature writer Richard Mabey points out, "In New York it's already clear that just a few months of neglect by city maintenance teams would lead to the streets becoming a burgeoning forest of Chinese tree-of-heaven seedlings" (2010: 237–238). Mabey goes on to describe how the sight of this charismatic tree on the High Line influenced desires to preserve the space as a park. What he does not discuss is that the very tree that populated the abandoned landscape would ironically be displaced by the very transformation in which it was implicated. Quite suggestively, Mabey follows his brief nod to the High Line with a passage on the proliferation of the tree in Detroit. There, in the paradigmatic epicenter of American postindustrial "decay" and "creative regeneration," Mabey suggests that "young people from all over America—musicians, Green activists, social pioneers—are flooding into the abandoned areas, keen to experiment with new patterns of urban living which accept nature—including its weedy frontiersmen—rather than attempting to drive it out" (239). *A. altissima* has a strong affinity for the same kinds of spaces that draw subjectivities frequently implicated in the gentrification of postindustrial urban areas. Invoked, but absent. Recalling Caulfield, we can begin to see a parallel attraction to specific ecological niches expressed by *A. altissima* and by urban gentrifiers, the latter being far more selective than the former. Here we can ask what would happen if we made more political room for the "succession" of the former rather than the "success" of the latter.

Turning to the behavioral ecology of *A. altissima* reveals some striking creative possibilities. Among the many qualities that make *A. altissima* a highly successful plant is allelopathy, or the production of so-called secondary metabolites that "have no apparent role in life processes or plant structure" (Heisey 1997: 28). While not fully understood, allelopathy is a plant capacity that, while unnecessary for reproduction, nonetheless plays a role in the profusion of the species. *A. altissima* produces a variety of chemicals that are believed to be capable of inhibiting the growth of other plants in areas immediately surrounding an *A. altissima* tree (Lawrence et al. 1991). Although this tactic is not uniformly successful, it has contributed to *A. altissima*'s localized success even as it has helped it earn a reputation as an unruly and unmanageable presence in urban ecosystems.

Allelopathy is too complex a process to describe in greater detail here, but we can already read *A. altissima*'s specific biological and ecological capacities as a differently temporalized process of displacement. *A. altissima* not only reproduces itself sexually, it also relies on territorializing tactics that transcend its strictly reproductive functions. Of course, these tactics have differential impacts on other aspirational species. What happens if we imagine queer human users of the space engaging in an analogous process through their transgressive patterns of use, like public sex and cruising? Is it possible to suggest a form of queer human/nonhuman alliance in which the anti-normative displacement of a scripted space of capital might support a politics of anti-gentrification? Is this an ecology worth saving? Is this a loss worth mourning?

Of course, we must distinguish between the form of displacement initiated by gentrification and the ongoing ontological reality of displacement wrought through the incessant relational interactivities of the material world. Instructively, Paul Cloke and Owain Jones advocate an understanding of tree agency, and, indeed, material agency more broadly, that is sensitive not only to "the very differing forms of beings and processes" in which such agencies are articulated, "but also the very differing velocities and rhythms they might be operating in" (Cloke and Jones 2002: 87). This suggests that a queer ecological critique of the High Line as gentrification should be at least as concerned with *time* as with *space*. Indeed, looking to the lost elements of the High Line's abandoned ecology helps us to understand the displacement of that ecology as a loss worthy of both ethical and political consideration. And, while the designers of the park embraced an ethos of "slow landscape," the park has nonetheless subjected the neighborhood to the velocities of touristic consumption.

What if the spatial tactics deployed by FHL had been countered by a temporal resistance? What would it have taken to advocate for a responsibility to allow ecologies that emerge in abandoned spaces to continuously determine the conditions of their own emergence, even as they are guided and shaped by those people who have cared for the space during such periods of so-called abandonment? These questions point to an ethic of non- or minimal intervention in abandoned spaces on specifically ecological grounds. Such arguments regarding the imperative to protect "fragile" ecologies in urbanized and anthropogenic environments are far from politically neutral, in light of more globalized discourses regarding sustainability and environmental protection in nonurban areas. Perhaps if critics of gentrification attended more closely to both the human and nonhuman sexuality, materiality, and symbolic production at the heart of gay and green gentrification, they might find alternative sources for disrupting the perverse logic of displacement. Rather than submitting the process to the overdetermined elements of dominant regimes of capitalist space making, queer ecological critique of gentrification foregrounds underdetermined elements as a source of potential tactics and terms for a renewed anti-gentrification politics as both queer and environmental politics.

ECOLOGIZING QUEER'S RELATIONS

With *A. altissima* as a guide, I have explored the ground on which political consideration of human-plant relationality might support challenges to dominant and normalizing modes of urban development. Of course, it is easy to exaggerate the radical potential of queer figures and derelict spaces as engines of difference and radical possibility. Let me be clear: I do not take queer ecologies or nonhuman elements to be inherently resistant to the vicissitudes of urban capitalism. Nevertheless, with all of the irony suggested by Caulfield, I do take FHL's desire to honor and preserve the High Line seriously enough to wonder whether it could have been more consciously mobilized against gentrifying ends. *A. altissima* is such an intriguing figure on account of its allelopathic capacity to relate to its environment and to create a space in which it can flourish despite severe limitations of vital resources. And yet, its impact on existing or "native" ecologies is far from neutral. Its success is deeply related to the ongoing tendency of humans to create highly disturbed ecologies in the midst of profoundly anthropogenic spaces. In other words, its natural success is linked in complex ways to our cultural failures.

In this natural-cultural paradox, we glimpse the outlines of queer resistance to gay and green gentrification. The High Line context is one in which non- or counternormative queer lives and forms of life are systematically undervalued, even attacked, because they are either not apparently (re)productive or are characterized as destructive, owing to their proximity to or inhabitation of the ruins of urban capitalism. Perhaps here we can begin to imagine a specifically queer resistance to homonormative gentrification on the basis of both more or less historically (bio)diverse communities, as well as nascent theories of urban ecology, which emphasize the material and symbolic exchanges that shape configurations of matter and energy in anthropogenic environments.

Rather than seeing the landscape as a passive ground, we must trace the movement and relational activity inherent in queer urban ecologies not simply to ogle multiple agencies, but also to learn and adapt tactics, if not strategies, for creating spaces in which the imperative of capitalist redevelopment is suspended long enough so that we might create and sustain justice-oriented, self-determining alternatives. If empowered and privileged metropolitan queers attended more closely to the socio-ecological specificity of the spaces so often ephemerally reclaimed for sociosexual purposes, they might be forced to confront compelling figures with whom there are possibilities to ally both politically and ethically. In so doing, they might denaturalize discourses of invasiveness associated with figures like

A. altissima, whose ability to thrive in disturbed ecologies is directly related to the political and ethical conditions in which such ecologies are coproduced by humans.

Perhaps our willingness to take queer urban ecologies seriously depends more on our ability as humans to imagine an ethics conditioned by the opportunity to appreciate, cultivate, or work with abandoned things and places as they are, than it does on the often unquestioned imperative to intervene or "improve" urban landscapes. Situating ourselves within dynamic ecologies, and valuing those that have been lost, begins to unsettle understandings of phenomena such as displacement. Far from naturalizing displacement—a move that would complicate any anti-gentrification politics—getting situated marks queer ecological awareness as a fundamental part of any such politic. Queerness displaces both hetero- and homonormative forms of identity and relationship (Sandilands 2014) whose reproduction is predicated on socionatural destructions and endless reproduction-of-same, associated with the homogenized landscapes of gentrification.

The goal of a queer ecological critique of gentrification is neither to pluralize nor to proliferate vogue queer identities *as such,* a process that, as we have seen, can too easily be co-opted and which too often fails to interrogate the intersections of race, class, and gender. Instead, queer ecological critique aims to consider the many contingent factors marshaled into position in order to sustain any apparently stable or reproducible form of identity. Rather than taking displacement to be an arrestable phenomenon, queer urban ecology asks what must be displaced in order to affirm the emergence of *any* particular space. The life that abounds in queer urban ecologies offers us a complex opportunity to consider the ethical and political intersections of queer and environmental politics. The challenge, then, is to hold space long enough to subvert incessant demands to reproduce "successfully," by developing tactics that enable our survival and flourishing here and now.

ACKNOWLEDGMENTS

I am grateful to have had the opportunity to present an earlier version of this chapter at the 2012 annual meeting of the Association of American Geographers in New York City as part of a series of panels on human-plant geographies organized by Dr. Jenny Atchison, Dr. Kathleen Buckingham, Dr. Lesley Head, and Dr. Catherine Phillips. This revised version of the original paper published from that presentation (Patrick 2014) benefited greatly from comments and discussion at a March 2015 authors meeting for *Deconstructing the High Line* held in New York City.

NOTES

1. I am grateful to Jennifer Foster for insisting on the role of urban animals in shaping the ecology of the High Line. Her work is an important foray into this aspect of the more-than-human inhabitation of the abandoned railway.

2. These figures are drawn from the websites and Internal Revenue Service Form 990 (nonprofit) filings of the respective organizations.

3. In the preface to their *High Line: The Inside Story of New York City's Park in the Sky* (2011), David and Hammond play into this mythology by describing themselves as "a pair of nobodies who undertook an impossible mission" (vii).

4. The list of supporters includes politicians Hillary Clinton and Christine Quinn; celebrities Edward Norton, Kevin Bacon, and Diane von Furstenburg; and less well-known figures like John Alschuler, chairman of the consulting firm HR&A and current president of the board of directors of FHL, and Phil Aarons, founding partner of the Millennium Partners, a billion-dollar real estate development corporation.

5. As the West Village, Chelsea, and the Meatpacking District have gentrified, any reference to "community" members must take account of the disproportionately high incomes increasingly required to live in these neighborhoods.

6. For an extended version, see David and Hammond (2011); also Patrick (2011), available at http://goo.gl/CcKw7.

7. The poster for the event can be viewed at https://www.dropbox.com/s/fzxioxlutq10yay/BehindTheBushes.jpeg?dl=0. The poster features a photo by Kevin McDermott in which a white, muscle-clad, able-bodied male stands naked (though creatively fig-leafed) atop the abandoned High Line.

8. For more on this, consult FIERCE!'s detailed archival website, http://www.fiercenyc.org. See also the work of the Parallel Lines collective, http://parallellinesproject.com, which has focused on the relationship between the Hudson River Park and the High Line development.

9. The use of the term *biodiversity* in this context is inspired by a particularly powerful presentation by Prof. Jin Haritaworn at a 2013 event called "Doing (and Being) Queer in Environmental Studies: Research and Visibility" held that Faculty of Environmental Studies, York University, Toronto. An exemplary popular critique can be found on Jeremiah Moss's blog, http://vanishingnewyork.blogspot.com. His work stands out both for its tone and for its exhaustive cataloging of the disappearing spaces of "old" New York.

10. My initial fieldwork involved sixteen interviews with experts and community activists and substantial archival and media research. Subsequently, I have continued archival and media research, paying particular attention to emergent popular critiques of the park's imbrication with ongoing gentrification of the surrounding neighborhoods.

In both endeavors, accounts of the power of landscape led me to considerations of the more-than-human aspects of the development of the park.

11. See also Stryker (2008) for more on the history and uses of this term.

12. See Wylie (2007) for important expansions on the influence of the concept of landscape.

13. A call richly expressed by recent works in queer theory. See Muñoz (2009) on concrete queer utopias and Halberstam (2011) on queer failure.

14. A term coined by Thrift (1999).

15. The term "abandoned" may also take a predicative form. To be *abandoned to* is to be "devoted or given up *to* an influence, passion, pursuit, etc.; (now *esp.*) devoted *to* something evil or immoral." Even a nonpredicative use, which reflects the attribution of a *quality* of abandonment, takes this moral tone: "Chiefly *attrib.* (without *to*). Uninhibited, unconstrained; devoted to an influence, passion, etc., *esp.* one which is evil or immoral; profligate" (*Oxford English Dictionary Online* 2012).

16. A possibility that was apparently never taken seriously enough to advocate for politically.

PART IV THE HIGH LINE EFFECT

10 ▪ A HIGH LINE FOR QUEENS

Celebrating Diversity or Displacing It?

SCOTT LARSON

On October 14, 2014, the New York City office of the Trust for Public Land (TPL), a national not-for-profit organization devoted to the development and preservation of public space, released a much-anticipated proposal for converting an abandoned rail right of way that cuts a 3.5-mile path through the borough of Queens into a forty-seven-acre linear park, to be called the QueensWay. Citing the popularity and success of the High Line (Larson 2013: 142–144; see also Krueger 2011; Taylor 2010; and chapter 4, by Kevin Loughran), the TPL and the Friends of the QueensWay (FQW), a private advocacy group founded to increase awareness and support for the proposed park, pointed to the potential of such an amenity to attract tourists, catalyze redevelopment investment, and enhance area property values.

In describing their plans, these groups also insisted that they were committed to preserving existing businesses and "the rich ethnic diversity of Queens." The project, they explained, would "be defined by the neighborhoods it passes through" rather than attempting to redefine or reshape them

(Foderaro 2013a). "It is the Friends of the QueensWay's intention to work closely with these diverse neighborhoods—both in the planning process and, ultimately in its operation—to celebrate the diverse cultural traditions that exist in the residents living in these neighborhoods," Travis Terry, a founding member of the FQW, said of the group's then still-emerging plans.

This raises a critical question: can a redevelopment initiative based on the High Line's model for neighborhood regeneration achieve both of these goals? This chapter explores the tensions inherent in the High Line model of repurposing disused urban infrastructure in general, and the QueensWay plan in particular, as a means of questioning the broader cultural, physical, and theoretical implications of such postindustrial redevelopment projects. It contends that while QueensWay proponents—much like their predecessors with the High Line—frame their project as a community-led initiative that enjoys broad local support and would enhance the quality of life for neighboring communities, their proposal is actually representative of a new notion of urban space, conceived and promoted by a privileged few, whose top-down emphasis on growth and economic development belies an ultimate goal of reshaping nearby neighborhoods to the desires of local elites and the logic of capital accumulation. Indeed, in spite of assurances that the QueensWay, were it to be built, would reflect and preserve the racial and ethnic mix of one of the most diverse neighborhoods in the country, the nature of the proposal emphasizes the development of an amenity aimed at attracting tourists and enhancing nearby property values. As a result, contrary to proponents' claims that the benefits of the QueensWay would flow to current residents and businesses, the experience of the High Line suggests such projects are far more likely to lead to the displacement of residents, small local businesses, and industry.

A HIGH LINE FOR QUEENS

Once a working commuter rail spur, the Rockaway Beach Branch of the Long Island Railroad (LIRR) connected the Rockaway peninsula off the southern coast of Queens to the LIRR's Main Line, with service on to Manhattan in the west and Long Island to the east. Along the way, it passed through the growing, mostly working-class Queens communities of South Ozone Park, Ozone Park, Richmond Hill, and Woodhaven. It then cut across 541-acre Forest Park and between the tonier residential neighborhoods of Glendale and Forest Hills, before merging with the LIRR Main Line in Rego Park.

Over time, rising operating costs led the LIRR to sell the line's right of way to the New York City Transit Authority, which, citing low ridership, suspended service in 1962. Only the southernmost portion of the right of way continues to be used for transit, with an arm of the Metropolitan Transportation Authority's A subway line traveling on an elevated trestle across Jamaica Bay to the Rockaways. For more than five decades, the northernmost 3.5 miles of the branch—which is still owned by the city and zoned for transportation—has sat abandoned, with washouts, crumbling structures, overgrown vegetation, and illegal dumping contributing to its dilapidated condition (fig. 10.1).

In 2011, a group of local residents led by Travis Terry, the CEO of the Manhattan-based strategic consulting firm Capalino + Company, formed FQW to advocate for the line's conversion to a linear park. Soon thereafter, FQW joined forces with TPL, and in January 2013, those two organizations received a $467,000 environmental protection grant from the New York State Department of Parks, Recreation, and Historic Preservation to assess the feasibility of transforming the right of way into a recreational and

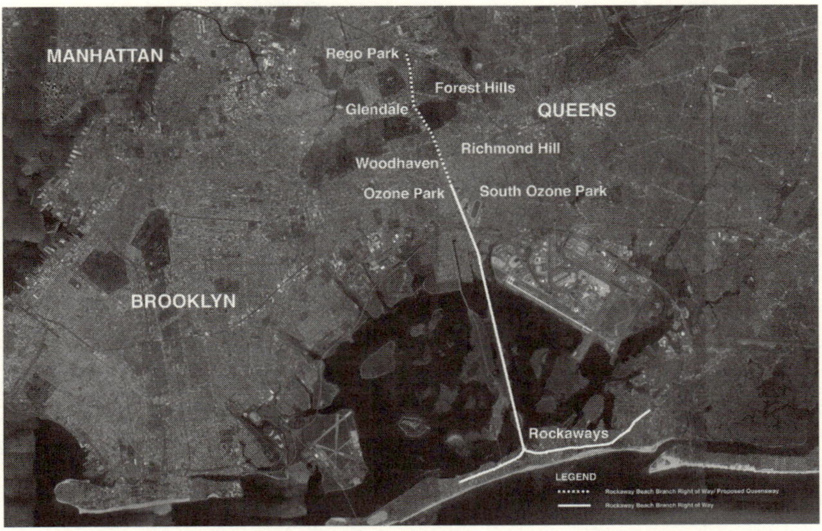

FIGURE 10.1. If built, the proposed QueensWay would convert a 3.5-mile section of the abandoned Rockaway Beach Branch right of way into a forty-seven-acre linear park stretching across central Queens. Photograph by the author.

"cultural greenway." Working with a team that included design firms WXY Architecture + Urban Design and dlandstudio, as well as economic and community outreach consultants and structural and transportation engineers, they spent the next eighteen months producing a detailed blueprint for the proposed QueensWay that was released to considerable media fanfare (see, e.g., Foderaro 2014a).

That plan, which proponents frame as a "community-led effort" that grew out of five "large" public design input sessions, "meetings with community groups," and "hundreds of stakeholder discussions," is oriented toward what advocates call six "themes that explain their vision for the QueensWay": Connections + Neighborhoods; Play + Health; Ecology + Education; Culture + Economic Development; Safety + Comfort; and Care + Stewardship (Friends of the QueensWay 2014). Describing the existing rail right of way as "blighted," with trash and "remnants of drug and alcohol use" littering the ground, the FQW and the TPL proposed a $121 million makeover that, from a physical design perspective, would create a park with six distinct sections with names like "The Clearing," "The Grove," and "The Metropolitan Hub," and proposed features such as event spaces, farmers' markets, street fairs, "iconic" overpasses and bridges, new cafés and mobile vendors, as well as cultural programming.

The resulting park, advocates contend, would improve access to other local parks, provide a safer and quicker route for commuting, and connect people and local businesses. From the outset, however, the FQW and the TPL insisted that the QueensWay would be far more than just a park. With the dramatic success of the High Line serving as the model, they argued for creating an "iconic" public space that would spark "economic and cultural development," enhance the value of residents' homes, and "improve 'the quality of life'" of surrounding communities (Friends of the QueensWay 2014).

If built as planned, proponents projected that the QueensWay would attract one million visits a year, a quarter of which would come from outside Queens. They further estimated that these day visitors and tourists would spend between $7 and $21 per visit and generate $2.2 million in annual spending in area restaurants and shops. To bolster claims about the proposed QueensWay's impact on area real estate, they referenced similar rail-to-park conversions—including the Capital Crescent Trail in Washington, DC, and London's Parkland Walk—and the fact that nearby home sellers advertise proximity to them. In addition, they provided links to two studies (Asabere and Huffman 2009; Racca and Dhanju 2006) that describe how trails and bike paths in cities in the United States have contributed to increases in nearby home prices and property values.

"The plan is beautiful, but highly functional," Adrian Benepe, director of city park development for the TPL and a former New York City parks commissioner during the Bloomberg administration, told the *New York Times*. "It's like the High Line on steroids. It's twice as long and seven times the acreage'" (Foderaro 2014). On the QueensWay plan's website, Joshua David, president and cofounder of the Friends of the High Line, offered his own endorsement of the plan, noting, "Completing a truly detailed plan driven by community interests . . . is a major milestone on the path to success" (Friends of the QueensWay 2014).

But does the QueensWay plan, with its orientation toward real estate values, economic development, and attractions such as trendy event spaces, food vendors, and shops, truly reflect nearby communities and their interests?

WHAT COMMUNITY? WHOSE INTERESTS?

As with the rest of Queens, which is the most ethnically and racially diverse county in the United States and where nearly one-half of all residents are foreign-born (New York City Department of City Planning 2013a), neighborhoods along the path of the proposed QueensWay are home to people of all races, multiple ethnic groups, and scores of national origins. According to the 2010 U.S. Census, 114,594 residents lived in forty-three census tracts completely or mostly within a half-mile of the proposed park, and of that total, 33.6 percent were non-Hispanic White, 31.3 percent Hispanic, 12 percent East Asian, 9.4 percent South Asian, 5.8 percent non-Hispanic Black, and the remaining 7.9 percent described themselves as something else (Office of Community Studies 2014). That diversity is not evenly distributed, however, and pockets of relative ethnic homogeneity create a distinct cultural patchwork. Along the right of way north of Forest Park, non-Hispanic whites predominate, making up more than 54.1 percent of the total population. South of Forest Park, however, a steady influx of immigrants over the past twenty-five years has given neighborhoods along the path of the proposed QueensWay a distinctly Indo-Caribbean and Hispanic character (New York City Department of City Planning 2013a: 59).

Questions of diversity, however, do not revolve solely around racial or ethnic identity. Diversity can also be expressed along economic and land use lines and be measured, for instance, in terms of home ownership rates, housing values and types, income, and relative poverty or wealth. Economically, households in the neighborhood of Forest Hills and in sections of Rego Park and Glendale at the northern end of the proposed park generally fare better than those in neighborhoods at the southern end, and significantly better than those in all of Queens and New York City as a whole. There, relatively high levels of employment in business, finance, and other professional occupations contribute to relatively high incomes (Office of Community Studies 2014). That economic well-being is reflected in terms of area housing and property values. These neighborhoods feature a mix of housing types, from mid-rise apartment buildings to large single-family homes on detached lots. Still, the vast majority of the area is zoned for one- and two-family residences, and in the wealthier sections of Forest Hills and Glendale, owners outnumber renters more than three to one, and median house values range from $600,000 to $951,000.

Richmond Hill and Woodhaven, meanwhile, historically have been known for their family-oriented, working- to middle-class character. Just over half of the 6,390 housing units in these two neighborhoods are owner occupied, and median house values reflect the area's more modest makeup, as do median family incomes, most of which fall in the range of $40,000–$60,000. Many of the local businesses are trade-related or specialty stores that serve the area's growing international communities. In Ozone Park and South Ozone Park, 59 percent of the 10,678 housing units are owner-occupied, and the vast majority of these are one- and two-family homes. Here, the neighborhood workforce is largely employed in service sector jobs, and median household incomes are even more modest. House values, as well, are lower than in other neighborhoods along the path of the proposed QueensWay, and during the mortgage-fueled financial crisis of 2007–2008 the area experienced an especially high rate of foreclosures.

Overall then, when viewed in racial/ethnic and economic terms, patterns of difference emerge along the path of the proposed QueensWay. Higher rates of home ownership, higher median household incomes, and higher home values tend to be in neighborhoods with higher percentages of white and, in some cases, Asian populations. More diverse neighborhoods and those where other racial/ethnic groups are relatively large or predominant tend to have lower incomes and house values, lower rates of

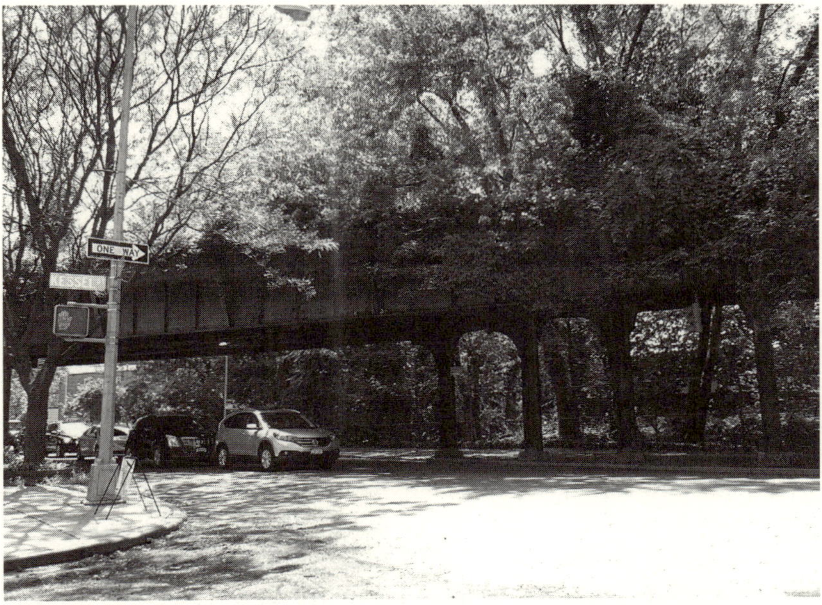

FIGURE 10.2. At its northern end, the proposed QueensWay would pass through the predominately white, single-family, residential neighborhood of Forest Hills. Photograph by the author.

home ownership, and higher rates of poverty (Office of Community Studies 2013: 22). Yet, neither the leadership of the Friends of the QueensWay nor the park they propose fully reflects that ethnic and economic diversity. In fact, despite proponents' portrayal of the project as community led and community inspired, it was the brainchild of a select group of individuals, who hatched the idea to convert the abandoned Rockaway Beach Branch right of way into a linear park long before they engaged in any meaningful dialogue with the broader community.

THE VENEER OF COMMUNITY SUPPORT

As the name suggests, the FQW was founded to advocate for what its founders hoped would be a High Line for Queens. At that point in 2011, the group's original members had already coalesced around the idea of transforming the rail right of way into a high-design, "world-class" amenity that would attract tourists and kick-start nearby economic development. Soon thereafter they formed an eight-person steering committee that, working closely with the TPL, established the project's basic perimeters and launched an ongoing campaign to line up the political and financial support needed to make their vision a reality.

However, while all but one of the steering committee's members are residents of the neighborhoods along the path of the proposed QueensWay, three live in the wealthier, whiter neighborhood of Forest Hills, and the group has a collective makeup that is hardly reflective of the social, economic, or racial diversity found elsewhere in Queens. Six of the eight members are non-Hispanic white—the other two are Hispanic and Guyanese (Friends of the QueensWay 2014). In addition, the committee is composed of three architects, the CEO of one strategic consulting firm and a principal partner in another, an attorney, a local entrepreneur/activist, and an employee of a health information technology startup in Manhattan. This gives it a distinctively design and professional services orientation that, while familiar in Forest Hills, is hardly reflective of the workforce in neighborhoods farther south. As such, the committee serves as a prime example of what Kevin Loughran describes as "the centrality of cultural elites to the neoliberal growth machine" (see chapter 4). Here, those with "high standing within socially constructed and intersecting hierarchies of gender, race, class, sexuality, and national origin" use their economic, cultural, and social capital to assert the right to make claims on public space and, through the creation of public-private partnerships, mobilize public funds to push market-friendly growth strategies that promote consumption, investment, and private development.

In the case of the QueensWay, this is reflected in efforts to secure the backing of other elites and raise funds for the proposed park's construction and ongoing operation. As of mid-December 2014, the FQW and the TPL had raised $1.2 million of the $121 million they estimated was needed to build and operate the park. That money came from a mix of public and private sources, including four private foundations, the most prominent of which is the Citi Foundation, as well as the Governor's Regional Economic Development Council and the New York City Department of Environmental Protection.

The proposed project's links to well-connected, capital-friendly voices also extend to a collection of thirteen local and citywide organizations listed as supporters on the project's website—including the Queens Chamber of Commerce and the Forest Hills Crescent Civic Association, a not-for-profit organization representing resident owners in the Forest View Crescent Cooperative—as well as online endorsements from five local, state, and national politicians, each of whom touted the QueensWay's potential to spur economic growth (Friends of the QueensWay 2014). Other high-profile early backers of the QueensWay included Ed Skyler, executive vice president of global public affairs at financial services giant Citigroup and a former deputy mayor in the Bloomberg administration, and Douglas Durst, a prominent New York City real estate developer and a member of the board of directors of the TPL.

Conspicuously missing, however, is any official representation of the dozens of organizations that speak for local ethnic and community groups and their interests, including the growing Hispanic and Indo-Caribbean communities. In fact, only one such organization—the Indo-Caribbean Alliance—is even listed among the QueensWay's supporters. In seeking community support, the FQW attempted to reach out to "as many broad and diverse organizations as possible," according to a representative of the Hester Street Collaborative (HSC), a community design and outreach consultancy that was part of the QueensWay team (2014, pers. comm.). However, that effort mainly "drew on existing networks of [FQW] partners for recommendations," focusing on the Indo-Caribbean community in Ozone Park and known organizations with well-developed infrastructures. Beyond that, HSC went "on the road" with informational "toolkits," visiting community meetings, schools, and church groups to spread information about the proposed park. In spite of this effort at outreach, a number of local community and ethnic organizations—including South Asians for the Empowerment of Richmond Hill, the Sikh Cultural Center of Richmond Hill, and the School Sisters of Notre Dame Educational Center and the Church of Saint Thomas the Apostle, both of which serve the area's growing Hispanic population—were never contacted by the FQW or the HSC, and said they had no knowledge of plans to redevelop the right of way into a park (2014, pers. comm.). In yet another example of how the FQW and the TPL privileged certain voices and communities over others, the presentations and materials used at public input workshops for the QueensWay were available only in English, and even though facilitators explained that a Spanish translator was available, that announcement, too, was in English.

Regardless, even when the FQW and the TPL engaged with local organizations, the focus of their outreach was on promoting the QueensWay, with the conversion of the Rockaway Beach Branch right of way into a linear park presented as the predetermined outcome. In reality, however, the right of way was—and remains—the site of intense debate over its best future use, with a number of competing ideas proposed by community members and interest groups. Those include its reactivation as a transit line that would reestablish service to the Rockaways—a section of Queens that has among the highest concentrations of public and elderly housing and the least access to public transportation in New York City—and leaving it as is.

In September 2012, for example, four months before the TPL and FQW received the grant to explore the feasibility of converting the right of way into a park, the Woodhaven Residents Block Association (WRBA), a civic organization whose membership includes dozens of homeowners on 98th Street whose houses abut the right of way, hosted a forum where the FQW's Terry and John Rozankowski, a Rockaways resident and leading advocate for reactivation of the line for rail service, presented their visions for the space. While Terry talked of the economic benefits of the QueensWay, including increased house values for homeowners and new development in adjacent neighborhoods, Rozankowski spoke of better access to jobs and shorter commute times for all residents along the right of way. In doing so, Rozankowski framed the debate as a battle of "haves," whose vision of the QueensWay would benefit a select few, versus "have nots" (Woodhaven Residents Block Association 2012). Reactivating rail service, Rozankowski argued, would have a more direct positive impact on the residents of southern and central Queens, where a lack of transportation options have combined with past public policy and a range of socioeconomic factors to create zones of economic hardship.

Ultimately, the WRBA expressed its opposition to both the QueensWay and rail reactivation plans, noting, "In light of the diverse—and sometimes conflicting—opinions we've received from our community, we believe that leaving the abandoned rail line alone is the best way to satisfy the needs and desires of as many residents as possible" (Rafter 2012). Among the concerns raised by WRBA members, particularly those whose back yards border the right of way, was the potential negative effect that either a park or a reactivated rail line would have on their privacy, safety, quality of life, and, ultimately, property values.

Needless to say, by framing the QueensWay as the preferred option for the right of way, the FQW and the TPL generated considerable animosity toward their plan. On November 13, 2013, at the second of the groups' public design input sessions, a dozen or so homeowners and a handful of rail

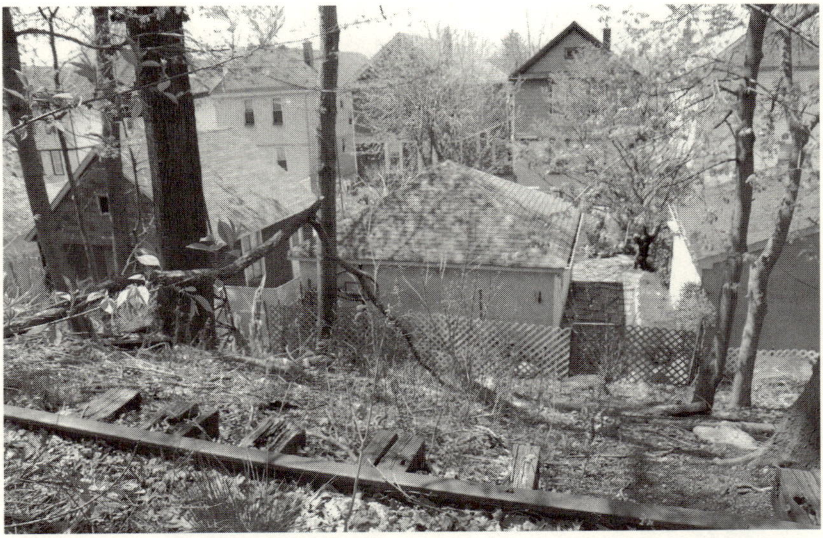

FIGURE 10.3. Residents on 98th Street in Woodhaven have voiced opposition to the proposed QueensWay because of its proximity to their homes. Photograph by the author.

reactivation advocates were among the fifty or so attendees. While representatives of the QueensWay design team opened the session by declaring, "We want to hear it all. What you're excited about, what you are concerned about," when they began describing their plans for a linear park, the meeting turned contentious (2013, author's personal account). "When you start talking about the QueensWay, in my mind it's inevitable it's going through, one way or another," one attendee angrily objected. "That's not what this should be all about. It should be about whether or not it should go through in the first place. What you're saying is ten months from now you're going to have a proposal, and that's what's going to happen." "And we don't have any say in it!" shouted another.

Workshop facilitators responded that their mission, as defined by the grant from the New York State Department of Parks, Recreation, and Historic Preservation, was to study the feasibility of a linear park, not to broker conversations about other redevelopment options. But as a result, what proponents described as "public input workshops" focused not on questions of whether the community wanted a linear park, but rather more narrowly on what that park would look like, how it would function, and how its design might address community concerns about issues like privacy and safety.

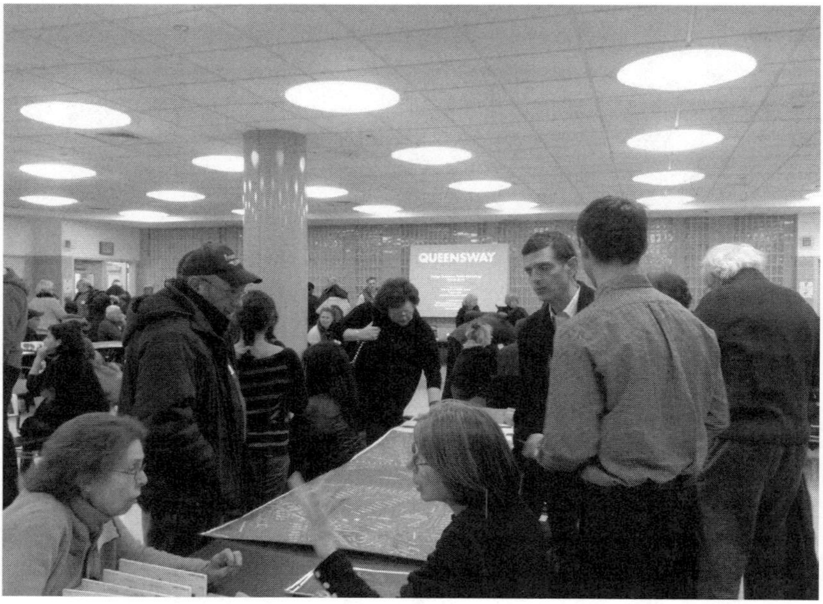

FIGURE 10.4. QueensWay workshop: QueensWay proponents frame their proposal as a "community-led" project that grew out of a series of public design-input sessions. Photograph by the author.

Certainly, such episodes test QueensWay proponents' claims that their plan is a reflection of broad community interests. They also raise questions about the timing and nature of meaningful public input. As Darren Patrick explores in chapter 9, among the issues raised by the High Line and, by extension, other redevelopment projects that use it as a model, are questions of who inhabits and produces urban space, how they come to inhabit it, and under what conditions they displace others—especially the urban poor and racialized communities. In terms of the QueensWay, the considerable social, economic, and cultural capital leveraged by the FQW and the TPL allowed them to preemptively assert, and then spend considerable energy promoting, their right to control the terms of future development of the Rockaway Beach Branch right of way. In turn, this self-granted power—or what Ryan Centner identifies as spatial capital—afforded them the "ability not only to win negotiations over the control of space, but also the capacity to shape the moments, sites, and terms of that jockeying" (Centner 2008: 198).

DEFINING CULTURE AS COMMODITY

Of course the physical manifestation of that spatial capital is the plan itself, and perhaps nowhere is the limited and selective nature of the design and community input process more clearly reflected than in the scheme's treatment of culture. Even as QueensWay proponents repeatedly expressed their commitment to respect and celebrate the diversity and character of communities along the right of way, their plan—as articulated in the Culture + Economic Development section, or "theme"—reduces a complex and potentially contested concept to ethnic food, then weds it to commerce and the opportunity to draw culinary adventurers to the area:

> You can ride a bike from Liberty Avenue, starting out with a roti at Trini Delight; bike to Jamaica Avenue for pollo a la brasa at El Anzuelo Fino; stop at the proposed Glendale ballfields concession area for food truck treats; check out Wafa's on Metropolitan for shawarma; and roll up Austin Street to Pahal Zan for falafels.
>
> Working with the Queens Chamber of Commerce, the QueensWay can host seasonal food festivals that will draw people to experience the borough's cuisines with special priority provided to neighborhood entrepreneurs. . . .
>
> The ethnic diversity of the surrounding neighborhoods, which includes New York's two most diverse community boards . . . are [*sic*] well-represented through local restaurants. (Friends of the QueensWay 2014)

Nowhere in the plan is there mention of the communities themselves, how their needs and desires might be met by the QueensWay, or how the park fits within their vision of what their neighborhood should be. Instead, by equating culture to food and conflating it with economic development, the QueensWay, as planned, is hardly an appreciation or celebration of diversity as defined and produced by the existing community, but more a superficial marketing ploy that translates those communities into products that can be performed, sold, and consumed, primarily by others.

Indeed, within the broader context of neoliberal urban development, the reframing of culture as a commodity has emerged as an important city-shaping tool, one that cities striving for a competitive edge on the global playing field increasingly employ "as a driver for urban economic growth" (Miles and Paddison 2005: 833). Here, the very meaning of "culture" has evolved to include practices that define established values and ways of life, which are then mobilized—often through the language of place making and place marketing—to promote cultural tourism and achieve social, economic, and political objectives. Centner, meanwhile, draws the connection between spatial capital and "practices of privileged consumption" (which he defines to include "expensive residences, high-end arts patronage, large nonpublic celebrations, usage of elite eating and drinking establishments") "as mechanisms for gentrification" (Centner 2008: 195).

"DESIGN AS CIVIC VIRTUE"

Ultimately, this combination of QueensWay proponents' spatial capital and the privileged consumption practices they espouse coalesces in a design scheme that is oriented toward encouraging certain activities and behavior, while actively designing out others. As Loughran notes, "the intentions of architects (and the elites who ultimately direct the production of space) do not wholly determine how people will use public space" (see chapter 4). Still, one of the fundamental features of the High Line, and by extension other parks created on its model, is the role of design in structuring and controlling how those spaces are experienced and used. Like the High Line, the proposed QueensWay is meant to be an "iconic" (Friends of the QueensWay 2014: n.p.), heavily scripted promenade, designed to appeal to users who will move along its length, stopping in designated places only long enough to experience programmed events—like farmers markets, exhibits, or street fairs—and consume products sold by select licensed vendors. Little to no room is given over to chance or the possibility of the type of spontaneous public and democratic interaction that is at the core of more traditional city parks. Contributing to this sense of control along the QueensWay are the limited number of entry and exit points, which combine with design features such as green fences and rows of newly planted trees to influence spatial interaction and enhance the privacy and security of nearby homeowners.

Such design features are also oriented toward the nebulous notion of improving the "quality of life" in neighborhoods along the path of the proposed park. As such, they are intentional mechanisms for driving up area real estate values and attracting new investment interest. On the QueensWay website, for instance, the plan's architects argue that among the greatest benefits of their proposed park, one that would lead to improved "quality of life for all Queens residents," is its potential to enhance property values (Friends of the QueensWay 2013): "Intuitively, creating beautiful public space along the abandoned LIRR corridor would add value to the area. Specifically, we believe that the creation of the QueensWay would provide a significant benefit to homeowners with property adjacent to, and near the trail. Research consistently demonstrates that *real estate values are positively impacted by the creation of urban greenways and trails*" (Friends of the QueensWay 2013, emphasis in the original).

Yet, while property owners along the path of the proposed QueensWay might benefit from increased property values, not all residents in the area own property or their homes. In fact, 15,295—or 54.5 percent—of the 28,575 residents living in census tracts all or mostly within a half-mile of the proposed park are renters (Office of Community Studies 2014). For those residents, and even low- or middle-income homeowners on tight budgets, a linear park designed to boost property values and appeal to speculative investment would undoubtedly put upward pressure on rents and property taxes. Given the diverse socioeconomic characteristics of the neighborhoods along the proposed QueensWay, any resulting benefits would be experienced unevenly. Residents in neighborhoods like largely white Forest Hills—with its higher homeownership rates and greater relative wealth—would reap most of the rewards, while residents of communities of color, with lower rates of homeownership, lower incomes, and higher rates of poverty, would confront newly energized forces of displacement.

In this way, the proposed QueensWay is illustrative of a new form of twenty-first-century urban park in which design is seen as a "civic virtue," a tool, in the words of Alexandros Washburn, former chief urban designer of the New York City Department of Urban Planning, for cultivating "habits important for the success of the community" and marketing the city (Washburn 2008). Indeed, the proposed QueensWay, like the High Line before it, is far less a public space in the traditional sense of the word, and more what former city planning director Amanda Burden has portrayed as "an amazing catalyst for private investment" (Larson 2013: 142–143).

In the end, then, in spite of QueensWay advocates' insistence that their plan reflects the desires and diversity of existing communities along its length, their primary goal appears to be the reshaping of the Rockaway Beach Branch right of way in their own image. By framing the right of way as both blighted and simultaneously worth celebrating, these privileged voices have asserted the right, as the owners of significant spatial capital, to create and control narratives about the value of that space, to determine its best and highest potential future use and, with the High Line serving as their blueprint, to direct its ultimate design. The result is a fetishization of space through design, a plan for a heavily programmed public space, of which the chief function is to encourage consumption and provide a foothold for other forms of capital accumulation. As such, the proposed Queens-Way is less a community-led project for celebrating the rich cultural and economic diversity of existing neighborhoods along its path, and more an effort to create the conditions for their gentrification.

11 • PROGRAMMING DIFFERENCE ON ROTTERDAM'S HOFBOGEN

DAAN WESSELMAN

As has been widely noted, the High Line has served as a touchstone for a spate of postindustrial urban redevelopment projects around the globe—one example of which is Rotterdam's Hofbogen project. The Hofbogen involves an ambitious plan to convert the 1.9-kilometer Hofplein viaduct running through Rotterdam, which lost its railway function in 2010, into a public space with a range of "creative-artisanal" enterprises in the vaulted spaces beneath the tracks. The Hofbogen project explicitly asks to be read in light of the High Line: proposals for the Rotterdam viaduct prominently feature the High Line among key international reference points for comparable redevelopments (Crimson Architectural Historians 2008: 67–70).

At the time of writing, Rotterdam's Hofbogen project is under way but far from completed. The Hofplein viaduct runs roughly northward out from Rotterdam's city center, with vaulted spaces under its 189 archways. The viaduct was first opened in 1907 and served as a railway connection between Rotterdam, The Hague, and other places until 2010. Since the completion of the viaduct, the vaulted spaces have been in continuous use in some form, and today many of the spaces remain occupied by a variety of small businesses, such as architectural design firms, printers, and furniture makers. (Figure 11.1 shows one vaulted space with the original 1905 facade largely intact, currently housing a furniture designer, and another space with graffiti of Muay Thai fighters.) In its use of reinforced concrete, the viaduct, which was also adorned with stone sculptures and stucco ornaments (figure 11.2), was a local marvel of civil engineering at the time of its construction. These elements contributed to the viaduct's classification as a listed monument in 2002, a status that safeguards it from demolition. In 2006, the viaduct was purchased by a conglomerate of social housing associations that owns a great deal of the housing stock in the surrounding neighborhoods. A cultural-historical study was commissioned, and a book-length vision for the future of the Hofbogen was published in 2008, which served as the basis for bringing together stakeholders in the project (at the time of writing there is no concrete design proposal for the viaduct as a whole). Small-scale redevelopment has been undertaken in the southern end of the viaduct, closest to the city center, with some success. With redesigned glass facades installed in a number of the vaulted spaces, this end of the viaduct is now made up of shops, bars, and restaurants and has become a venue for cultural events (figure 11.3).

However, further development of the project is currently uncertain, partly because of the general effects of the 2008 financial crisis, but more

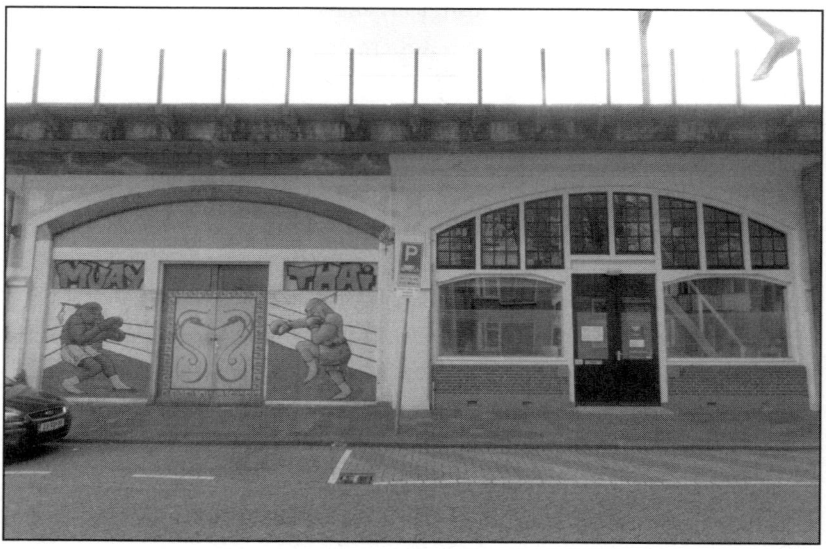

FIGURE 11.1. Two vaulted spaces of the Hofbogen. Photograph by the author.

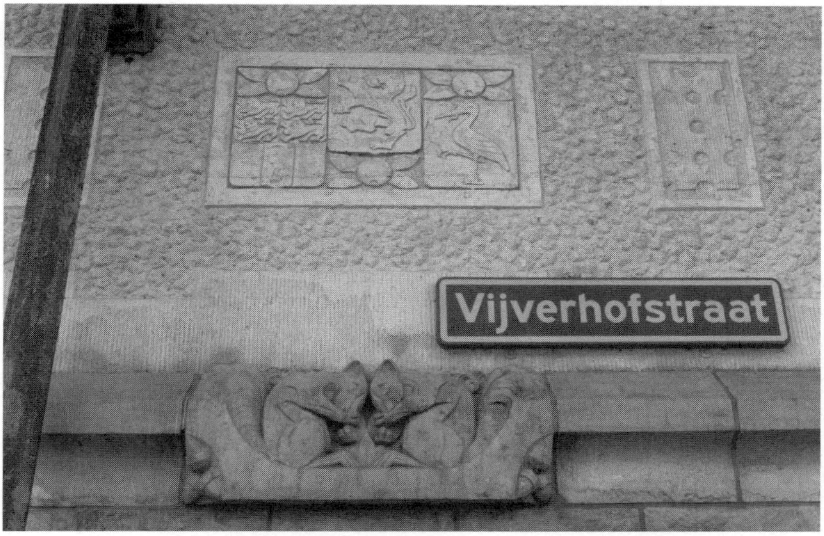

FIGURE 11.2. Ornamentation of the Hofplein viaduct. Photograph by the author.

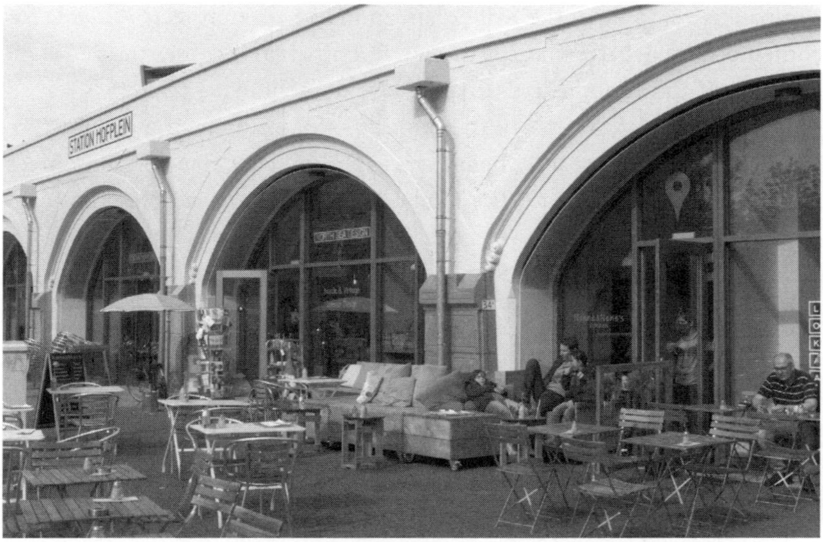

FIGURE 11.3. The new facades of the Hofbogen. Photograph by the author.

specifically because of difficulties for the housing associations that bought the viaduct. Recent government regulations have in principle restricted social housing associations to spending money on their primary task of providing housing, putting large investments in prestigious projects on hold. Moreover, one of the major associations involved, Vestia, has been involved in a financial scandal of its own, with billions of euros at stake. Along the way, the costs of the Hofbogen project have also been viewed with some reserve in the local media, drawing frequent comparisons to the recent large-scale renovation of the iconic steam liner SS *Rotterdam*, in which another housing association sustained astronomical losses (RTV Rijnmond 2014). The latest news at the moment of writing is that the necessary renovation of the viaduct's leaky roof will be carried out, financed by the owners, tenants, and the municipal government, while the current owners look to sell the building to a commercial party (Potters 2014). Consequently, the Hofbogen as a project that can be compared to the High Line currently exists only in the form of ideas and general proposals. A handful of the vaulted spaces closest to the center of Rotterdam have been successfully renovated, which resemble the Viaduc des Arts underneath the Promenade Plantée in Paris, but the linear public space on top of the viaduct has yet to be designed.

It is precisely the current status of the Hofbogen project that makes a comparative reading of the Rotterdam and New York projects valuable for contemporary debates on urban renewal. For when it comes to the "High Line effect" in postindustrial urban redevelopment, what matters is not so much the material features of the projects—for example, the architecture or the details of the spaces themselves—but the concepts and discourses involved. The proposals for the Hofbogen are illustrative here. The main ground for comparison between the Rotterdam viaduct and the High Line is clearly not spatial or architectural. Other than on the level of obvious spatial features—which we may almost call the park-atop-a-disused-railway formula—the "vision for the future" of the Hofbogen, commissioned in 2008, acknowledges that the similarities are limited: "The challenge for the High Line deviates from that for the Hofbogen in a number of ways. Contrary to the Hofplein viaduct, which is a closed building, the High Line is an open construction, so only the upper side of the roof is being redeveloped. Moreover, the dynamic and metropolitan urban context of the High Line is barely comparable to that of Rotterdam-North. Nevertheless, the project is significant for the Hofbogen. Particularly the design concept and the chosen program offer a number of points of reference for the Hofplein viaduct"

(Crimson Architectural Historians 2008: 67; all translations from Dutch by the author). Furthermore, the High Line had not yet opened in 2008, so "the execution of the design and its functioning cannot be assessed," but the text highlights instead that the "economic and cultural *spin-off* of the High Line is already noticeable in the surrounding neighborhoods" (70). Clearly, material and contextual incomparability between the projects is taken in stride.

In fact, there seems to be an active prioritizing of the conceptual level over material comparison. The discussion of the Promenade Plantée in the Hofbogen proposals is telling in this regard. The similarity of the Rotterdam viaduct to the Parisian park is acknowledged, and that park is presented in appreciative terms: "a simple, stylish urban park, which offers a point of rest in the busy, dynamic capital," which is "safe, clean and very well maintained. And successful, given the large number of people who use the green walkway daily" (Crimson Architectural Historians 2008: 79–80). Yet in spite of the architectural similarity and the fact that the positive effects in Paris had been actually observable for a decade, the comparison with the Promenade Plantée is made in order to provide an example to get away from:

> But while the 12th arrondissement in Paris needs rest and green spaces, a large part of Rotterdam-North needs more activities and public facilities in addition to rest and green spaces. A park alone would perhaps be too one-sided in Rotterdam and would not sufficiently connect to the existing urban context. The same reasoning applies to the activities that will need to be developed in the vaulted spaces. In the Viaduc des Arts, there was tight control over the question of which creative artisanal enterprises were and were not allowed in the vaulted spaces. Yet as a consequence, the range of shops and studios often makes an artificial and overly programmed impression. (Crimson Architectural Historians 2008: 80)

In this regard, the Hofbogen proposals illustrate a striking tendency whenever the High Line is referenced in urban redevelopment. Architectural similarity and actually observable effects, as in the Paris-Rotterdam comparison, go hand in hand with negatively oriented contrasts. In the New York-Rotterdam comparison, in contrast, noted dissimilarity goes hand in hand with a positive focus on the abstract "design concept and the chosen program." Simply put, the focus is not on the material particulars of the High Line but on the *idea* of an elevated space designed for different speeds, temporalities, and perspectives on the city below. This points to one way of thinking of the "High Line effect" generally: the park is taken as a point of reference to invoke the associated *discourses* of gentrification and the creative city. The elevated park can then be seen as a model for the neoliberal transformation of postindustrial cities (see chapter 4, by Kevin Loughran).

However, there is another reason why the High Line is relevant for projects such as the Hofbogen, which lies in the way the space fits in with its surrounding city. Above all, the High Line is a unique urban object with *difference* as one of its key features. What the Hofbogen shares with its reference point in New York is that at the core of both projects, the efforts of conservation hinge on cultivating the way in which the building stands out as a unique urban object. The elevation of the viaducts, for example, provides an unusual perspective on the city, and the linearity of the spaces contrasts with the customary ways of traversing the city. Moreover, the High Line depends for a large part on how it is *unlike* Central Park or how, as Christoph Lindner argues in chapter 6, it is designed for walking at a different speed. Close reading the Hofbogen and the High Line as spaces that are *other to* the surrounding city—in spatial and conceptual terms—brings out important contrasts that offer insights into the workings of contemporary urban redevelopment.

HETEROTOPIAN SPACES AND REPRESENTATION

The fact that difference is a key feature of the High Line and other similar projects is frequently acknowledged in explicit ways. For example, High Line designers James Corner and Ricardo Scofidio emphasize that the experience of the park is marked by "otherworldliness," which according to Scofidio "preserves the strange character of the High Line" (Friends of the High Line 2008b: 31). Such markedly different spaces invite an understanding of the phenomenon of the postindustrial elevated park in light of the concept of heterotopia (for more on this, see Dehaene and De Cauter 2008; Genocchio 1995; Johnson 2006, 2013). This idea, originally proposed for understanding spaces by French philosopher Michel Foucault, revolves around two key issues.

First, difference is obviously not an independent property of a space itself. As Kevin Hetherington emphasizes, heterotopian spaces "only exist in relation, that is, they are established by their difference in a relationship between sites rather than their Otherness deriving from a site itself" (1997:

43). One needs to consider such "otherworldly" or "strange" spaces in their particular urban contexts. The crux of heterotopia is thus the specificity of difference. The concept therefore steers one to consider both how a space is different and the dominant spatialities that surround it.

Second, the difference of heterotopias stems from the way that spatial and architectural features are intertwined with the meanings and ideas that make up that space. Spatially, both the High Line and the Hofbogen obviously stand out from their surroundings, but they equally depart from the dominant discourses of the city. For example, in the case of the High Line, cutting across the Manhattan grid also offers the possibility of an escape from the rationality and efficiency that are embodied in the city below. Furthermore, the park underscores a simultaneous (dis)connection to the streets below, perhaps exemplified best in its 10th Avenue loggia, where the amphitheater seating and glass windows overlooking the traffic turn the street below into a spectacle to be observed, providing an opportunity to reflect on the city from the unusual position of being suspended over the middle of the road. In the case of the Hofbogen, spatial otherness goes along with a doubleness of structural orders—for example, as a long, regular sequence of vaulted spaces with a highly irregular use and appearance, or as the preservation of a structure designed for transit in the form of a destination for leisure and consumption.

In addition, the *representational* character of the heterotopia needs to be emphasized (see Cenzatti 2008; Hetherington 1997). A characteristic of heterotopias that Foucault outlines is that they can "juxtapose in a single real place several spaces, several emplacements that are in themselves incompatible" ([1967] 2008: 19). His examples are oriental gardens, theaters, and cinemas: all spaces that revolve around representation, around the incorporation of other spatialities and orders within a clearly demarcated space. Foucault does not elaborate on this issue, but his concept can be supplemented with the work of Henri Lefebvre. Specifically, the concept of heterotopia can be linked to Lefebvre's idea of representational space, which is "directly *lived* through its associated images and symbols, and hence the space of 'inhabitants' and 'users'" (Lefebvre [1974] 1991: 39). For Marco Cenzatti, Lefebvre's notion of representational spaces helps to focus attention on how they "are produced by the presence of a set of specific social relations and their space," underscoring that "space is not an inert support of social action, but participates in the social action itself" (2008: 81). Since it depends on presence and usage, this representational space is at odds with being abstracted and turned into "the space of scientists, planners, urbanists, technocratic subdividers and social engineers," which is Lefebvre's description of "representations of space" ([1974] 1991: 38). Design and planning dominate these "representations of space," so these spaces only allow people to reproduce prescribed behavior.

Lefebvre helps us to recognize how the High Line and the Hofbogen are not, and cannot be, *totally* or *radically* different spaces. Each viaduct has points at which its difference encounters boundaries, for each space also represents and reproduces the dominant order. For example, for all its uniqueness, the High Line also resembles conventional parks, with places for sunbathing, ice cream carts, a list of forbidden activities to regulate behavior, attendants who close the park at night, and so on. Likewise, the Hofbogen may be an obstacle that is architecturally incongruent with the surrounding residential areas, but at some points where the vaulted spaces are publicly accessible (for example, in a space adapted into an espresso bar) or where a neighboring playground's murals continue on the archways' ceilings, the viaduct is woven into everyday life in Rotterdam. Moreover, both the New York and Rotterdam spaces are intricately bound to the local economies, for example, in the High Line's effect on surrounding real estate prices, or in the type of commercial use of the vaulted spaces in the Hofbogen. Both are also fully dependent on municipal cooperation and support for the redevelopment. Hence, while different orders are certainly at work in these spaces, these differences are neither total nor absolute. This is also how critique of the High Line can be situated: while not detracting from its qualities as a heterotopian space in my view, the High Line's story is "business as usual" to an important degree as well. In this light, one can view it as a story of gentrification and displacement from the perspective of queer ecology (see chapter 9, by Darren Patrick) or as a story of inequality that puts the *public* nature of an urban public space under pressure (see chapter 4, by Kevin Loughran).

Via Foucault and Lefebvre, one can also bring into view how representational mechanisms are at play in the High Line and the Hofbogen. These spaces are geared toward a different usage (for example, slow, leisurely walks on the High Line), which is reinforced by a range of signs and design elements that stimulate a reflection on urban change. In the Hofbogen, for instance, the renovated spaces at the site of the former Hofplein station (see figure 11.3) return the disused station to active public use with the upscale restaurants and boutiques located there. This renovation not only preserves the architecture of the building—the vaulted spaces, made very visible through the new glass facades—but also prominently features the name of the former station above one of the arches. Hence, the design and signage underscore the repurposing of a disused space, which foregrounds both the contemporaneity and the history of the site. Importantly, this foregrounding is a matter of practice and presence, of an embodied experience in space, of social relations. The new perspective on the city that one gets from the High Line, for example, is bound up with walking there (see chapter 6, by Christoph Lindner).

CONTRASTING HISTORIES OF DIFFERENCE

With the Hofbogen being a listed monument and the High Line doing its best to preserve its history through plant life and the remaining railway tracks, both spaces are geared toward an experience of different temporality. In short, the pivotal discourse in both spaces is that of history. The history of the Hofbogen differs from its New York reference point in a number of ways, one of which is the spatial relation of the viaduct to its urban environment. Whereas the High Line is suspended over the Manhattan grid, the Hofplein viaduct is woven into the fabric of the city of Rotterdam. When it was completed in 1907, only the southern half of the viaduct was surrounded by the built area of the city of Rotterdam. In order to build the southern end of the line and its art nouveau station, an area of Rotterdam had to be demolished. However, according to engineer and board member of the railway line N. J. Beversen in 1903, this area consisted only of "derelict housing for workers, slums and alleys, a dark London, the purchase of which has not been excessively expensive and the cleaning up of which can be called a great improvement for that part of Rotterdam" (cited in Crimson Architectural Historians 2008: 20). The northern half of the viaduct, in contrast, extended into the fields surrounding the city. It was built with rapid urban expansion in mind, with some archways already included in the design so that future streets could run underneath them. Hence, with the city developing and expanding around the viaduct, the Hofbogen has been a constituent part of the city since its construction, though with a notably double character: "Over the course of its existence the viaduct changed from an open structure into an elongated commercial building. On the one hand, by becoming increasingly closed, the object increasingly formed a barrier; on the other hand, the effect of the vaulted spaces, especially where semipublic functions are concerned (shops, businesses, etc.) has been that the viaduct has become more integrated in the urban environment and is experienced less as a strange element" (Crimson Architectural Historians 2007: 20). Essentially, the viaduct has worked as a heterotopian space throughout its history: an integral part of the urban fabric, with the vaulted spaces partly in use by people in their everyday life, yet also a strange obstacle in the city.

The Hofbogen's double nature is even more apparent in the usage of the vaulted spaces underneath the viaduct. The dominant function has always been the railway usage on top of the viaduct, with the archways designated as *residual* spaces (Rosa 2014), largely without a predetermined function. Yet the vaulted spaces have always been in use in some form. While the spaces were not initially conceived to be closed off with facades, this was quickly adopted as part of the design, so that some of them were rented out for commercial usage as early as 1905, even before the full viaduct was completed. Over the following decades, the spaces underneath the viaduct were used continuously, driven by shortages of space. In 1918, the remaining spaces in the southern part of the viaduct were considered for emergency housing but were deemed unsuitable, so they were rented out to small businesses. During World War II, the spaces were closed off haphazardly, and in the postwar decades, the remaining vaulted spaces were either rented out or closed off with a variety of facades. The process was frequently left to the tenants, resulting in an irregular outward appearance (see figure 11.1), described as "cacophonic" (Crimson Architectural Historians 2007: 43).

The use of these residual spaces has thus always been *adaptive*, based on practical considerations and without a dominant policy or design behind it. Since changes to the spaces were frequently driven by their users—the tenants—rather than the owners, one can see the use of the vaulted spaces as lived or representational, in Lefebvre's terms: whether considered for emergency housing, used for storage, or for small-scale businesses, the vaulted spaces have, in a way, always represented the social relations of their un-predetermined use. In fact, one might see the Hofbogen as an architectural manifestation of Lefebvre's distinction between representations of space and representational spaces: a lived space of social relations literally underneath a spatiality of functional use. The viaduct therefore has a notable history as a heterotopian space: its dominant railway use of the top, separated from the city streets, left residual space at ground level, the use of which led to the viaduct becoming a barrier in the city over time. Yet simultaneously entirely different usages were found for these residual spaces, according to what was needed or suitable in everyday urban life at the time. The viaduct itself juxtaposes the dominant order of the functional with the residual, with adaptation, and with complementarity to the city.

When contrasting this history of the Hofbogen with the High Line, the prominent role of representation in the New York park comes into view. Unlike the Hofbogen's history of double usage, the High Line's history is characterized by consecutive stages. Effectively, its story is that it was primarily used by trains, plants, and people, successively, with the current public usage being distinct from the earlier functional railway usage and the relatively "unregulated" plant phase. Even though today's park maintains some railway tracks and the landscape design partly features the types of plants that had previously sprung up spontaneously, the highly controlled and designed nature of the park environment turns these material elements into *signs* of previous stages, rather than authentically preserving them as persisting original elements. History in today's park thus hinges on a *representational strategy* to produce a sense of historicity, more than a space revolving around preservation or monumentality, for example.

Moreover, the experience of the High Line is bound up with representations that have shaped the park. For example, as Michael Cataldi and his coauthors convincingly argue, "the first push for its preservation was rhetorically organized by images of its ruin and rescue" (2011: 360) through the photography of Joel Sternfeld. Furthermore, it is not only the space, but especially its *story* that should be taken into account—a story subject to representational strategies of narrativizing, historicizing, and so forth. For example, as the *New York Times* reported in the article covering the park's opening, "The High Line project is something of a New York fairy tale" (Pogrebin 2009a), which, of course, is narrativized once again by key actors in that story themselves in David and Hammond's book *High Line: The Inside Story of New York's Park in the Sky* (2011). The representation of this history of the High Line in the park itself is thus the spatialization of this narrativized history.

Yet, one can also sense a tension here. Difference can be cultivated in design, signage, and landscaping, but of course there is the danger that this encroaches on the possibilities for being used as a "lived" space. One can argue, as Joern Langhorst does, that "the High Line provides a highly controlled, choreographed and pretexted experience, foregrounding the visual experience, much more akin to a promenade with a sequence of tableaus designed to be seen, but not otherwise interacted with" (2014: 1123). Likewise, Cataldi and coauthors make a connection between the representation of the High Line and the discursive aspects of the park, arguing that Sternfeld's photography presents an "elision of working-class, dirty and dangerous work" that "interpolates an upwardly mobile American middle class visiting the High Line for horticultural excursions" (2011: 368). This is in line with an "urban pastoral" discourse that translates to ways in which the space can be used, for, "contrary to its rhetoric of discovery, the park's lookout points direct camera-armed observers to specific positions within the park, prohibiting picture-taking in certain areas while encouraging it in others" (Cataldi et al. 2011: 370). While in my view this does not undo the heterotopian quality of the space in an analytical sense—difference, after all, remains a central feature—these analyses of the High Line demonstrate that the spatial and representational structures that constitute difference can be mobilized for economic and sociopolitical ends that call for critique.

This tension between representations of space and representational space, in Lefebvre's terms, is highly pertinent to the redevelopment of the Hofbogen as a different space. The Hofbogen proposal can be read as taking inspiration from the High Line precisely on the point of representing history, for example. Both publications by Crimson Architectural Historians effectively establish a narrative of recuperation of lost splendor: both feature descriptions of the original art nouveau terminus with its famous restaurant, all of which was destroyed in World War II and replaced with a modernist "oblong box" (2008: 52) in 1956, which in turn was demolished in 1990. Meanwhile, the facades closing off the archways have become "garish (and often poorly maintained)" and are in need of "thorough renovation, if the viaduct is to regain its original grandeur" (2007: 43). The history of user-driven adaptive use of the residual spaces does not really feature positively in this narrative, having led to a cacophony of badly maintained facades. One might also argue that this narrative of "original grandeur" incorporates the preservation of the building as a listed monument and the restoration of the ornamentation in the service of gentrification. In fact, one could even see gentrification *as* restoration in this narrative, since the line was originally targeted toward the middle class, to enable the wealthier people who had moved out of the city to commute to Rotterdam and to enable leisure trips to the seaside, with a terminus close to the beach in Scheveningen (Crimson Architectural Historians 2007: 8). The restaurant in the art nouveau terminus also reinforced the middle-class appeal of the viaduct, as did the benefits in terms of pollution and noise reduction, because it was the first electric railway in the Netherlands.

So just as the story of the High Line has emphasized the park's role as a vehicle for gentrification, the Hofbogen proposal seems to adopt the same discourse, for the same ends. Even explicitly recognizing that the model of "creative-artisanal" businesses in the vaulted spaces follows a popular trend in which "the creative industry as a stimulus is brought up whether appropriate or not" (Crimson Architectural Historians 2008: 101), the proposals seem to forgo possible points of criticism inherent in such policies and adopt them anyway. If taking the High Line as a reference point amounts to turning it into a Lefebvrian "representation of space"—or simply put, the park-atop-a-disused-railway formula for the sake of neoliberal urban renewal—this also leads to the problem of ignoring the specificity and uniqueness that underpin the differences of the High Line and the Hofbogen in the first place. In the case of the Hofbogen, this is all the more relevant, since there are several urban renewal projects—for example, the neighboring Zomerhof quarter and the Schieblock, a stone's throw away—that already follow the creative cities trend. The Hofbogen could successfully jump on the same bandwagon, but that would be likely to mean sacrificing difference as a feature.

The challenge for the Hofbogen is therefore to *maintain* its heterotopian character—unlike the High Line, which *produced* itself as one—which is why the project can be seen as situated at the intersection of current debates on urbanism and postindustrial renewal. While the proposals for redevelopment mobilize certain familiar discourses that call for reserve or critique, there are also possibilities for establishing guidelines in the redevelopment of this space that preserve its difference—possibilities that could go further than the High Line did, in terms of incorporating difference in the transformation of this viaduct into a public place. An obvious danger lies in the prioritizing of a representation of space. The Hofbogen studies emphasize unity as a guiding principle for any plans for the viaduct, calling for the building to "remain whole and indivisible as an urban object" (Crimson Architectural Historians 2007: 52) and for the "programmatic coherence between the top and bottom of the viaduct" (Crimson Architectural Historians 2008: 81), for example. While understandable from a designer's perspective, this emphasis on unity steers toward a focus on *totality* in the renovation of the building.

This is already proving impossible because of the above-mentioned financial difficulties, but it would also run counter to the history of adaptive and gradual change of the viaduct. A similar danger lies in the suggestions for usage of the vaulted spaces. The history of the residual spaces under the viaduct led to a usage that (self-)represents the social relations that are situated there. Implementing a program that seeks to locate "creative-artisanal" businesses in the renovated spaces would, on the one hand, not change much, since that type of business has been located there for a century, but it would, on the other hand, constitute a significant shift to a situation dominated by a representation of space—through policy and design, concretized in a redesigned uniform glass facade. Lastly, the proposals advocate turning the Hofbogen into an attraction, not only for residents of the city, but also for tourists (Crimson Architectural Historians 2008: 95), which seems to align with the success of the High Line, as well as with the critique that the park has become a spectacle of gentrification.

Yet the Hofbogen proposals also preserve the heterotopian character of the viaduct in important ways. On a general level, one can see the Hofbogen itself as a residual space within the larger urban context (while I would characterize the High Line as *supplementary*, as a newly developed public space superimposed on the city). This is not itself uncommon in the creative cities trend (the neighboring redevelopments in Rotterdam also reuse abandoned or derelict spaces), but the Hofbogen stands out in two regards. First, because it penetrates the center of Rotterdam and partly predates the built environment of the city, the scale of the viaduct and the degree to which it has always been woven into the urban fabric mean that other options, such as demolishing and replacing it with a new building, are not as straightforward as they could be with a disused office building, as in the neighboring Schieblock. The Hofbogen would leave a conspicuous trace or scar in the street pattern alone. While the Hofbogen proposals affectionately label the viaduct a "gift" to the city that requires a "careful and loving approach" (Crimson Architectural Historians 2008: 94), the viaduct could also be seen as a residue that comes with its own challenges, limitations, and demands. Second, even though it is mired in financial difficulties, the current development of the Hofbogen precisely mirrors its history of adaptive and gradual reuse of residual spaces. Bit by bit, starting at the southern end, the viaduct is being reused, with a varied program of commercial and cultural activities.

The proposed program for the viaduct also effectively preserves the viaduct as a heterotopia by highlighting *complementarity*. The proposals strongly emphasize not only a coherence between the top and bottom of the viaduct, but also the connection with the immediate neighborhoods, many of which are residential areas for which the creative-artisanal businesses and the "spectacle" of postindustrial urban renewal itself carry little weight. The proposals suggest that the park should cater to local residents, for instance, that schoolchildren should be able to take a slide from the top of the viaduct to street level—the conceptual approach for which is illustrated in figure 11.4 (Crimson Architectural Historians 2008: 94–95). On this front, the proposals express inspiration for future designs more than concrete possibilities, yet they emphasize diversity of users, inclusiveness, and complementarity to the urban surroundings. One could argue that in this regard the proposals align with the type of "complementary urbanism" that Nan Ellin advocates in the context of recent debates on landscape urbanism, which "looks at the whole environment including people," and "*complements* what is already there rather than attempt to replace it or compete with it. In the case of urbanism, what is already there may include existing buildings and infrastructure, market economies, and cultural traditions, as well as theories about which approach may be optimal" (2013: 283–84). In light of difference and representation, however, the Hofbogen proposals suggest an approach to redevelopment that engenders everyday usage connected to the social relations in the area. Crucially, this not only offers the possibility of maintaining the difference of the space by means of signifying strategies, as in the case of the High Line, but it could also be seen as aiming to preserve the double nature of the viaduct.

MAINTAINING DIFFERENCE

Of course it needs to be emphasized that the further development of the Hofbogen remains to be determined and that the proposals discussed here are aimed primarily at offering a direction for the further redevelopment process. While caution against the imposition of familiar discourses of urban renewal remains warranted, a positive emphasis on the uniqueness of the building remains paramount. Accordingly, maintaining the heterotopian character of the Hofplein viaduct requires continuing its history as a residual "lived" space, for which the Hofbogen proposals certainly offer possibilities, with a program that acknowledges how difference is constituted and can have its place in the postindustrial city. This is why the Hofbogen can already serve as a case study that underscores the importance

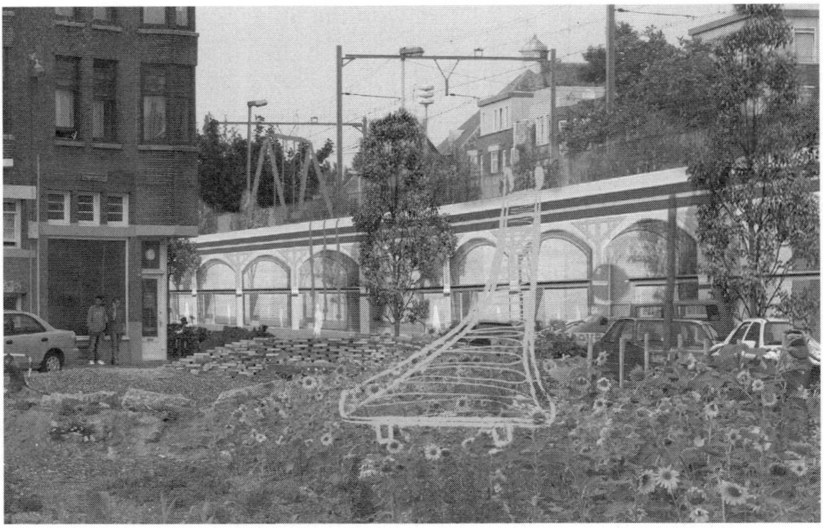

FIGURE 11.4. *Children's Playground,* by Crimson Architectural Historians/Joop Reijngoud, courtesy of Crimson Architectural Historians.

of considering *difference* in processes of urban redevelopment, calling for a focus on the specificity of a site in its relation to the surrounding city.

Reading the Hofbogen with the High Line as a reference point shows that, while both spaces involve disused railways that are repurposed as public space in the era of the postindustrial city, each project is built on different structural orders, which means that the projects display two different strategies in urban renewal. The design of the High Line uses the stages of its history to (re)present it as a narrative. This aligns with its separation from the ground and the grid, underscoring how the perspective from the High Line is *not* like the rest of the city through mechanisms of representation. In contrast, the Hofbogen has an alternative history of being different as a space: intrinsically double in nature and characterized by adaptive (re)use of its residual spaces. The Rotterdam viaduct has always catered to both a dominant functional order and to a (self-)representational everyday life at the same time. Spatially and discursively, then, the two spaces differ from each other in important ways. Accordingly, insofar as the proposals for the Hofbogen may claim to take inspiration from the High Line—and insofar as the Hofbogen is an illustrative case for projects that aim for the "High Line effect" generally—one should locate this inspiration in the way both projects develop their particular heterotopian features.

12 · PUBLIC SPACE AND *TERRAIN VAGUE* ON SÃO PAULO'S MINHOCÃO

The High Line in Translation

NATE MILLINGTON

COLLOQUIALLY KNOWN AS the Minhocão (Portuguese for "big earthworm"), São Paulo's Via Elevada Presidente Costa e Silva is an elevated highway that runs through the neighborhood of Santa Cecilia for roughly two miles (figure 12.1). Like other urban elevated highways that have led to neighborhood decline (Avila 2014; Berman 1983), the Minhocão is credited with the relative bad fortune of its surrounding neighborhoods owing to its out-of-scale intervention into a dense residential area. Anecdotally known as a kickback to developers, the Minhocão created a dank, dark space below and exposed the surrounding buildings to the unceasing noise and vibration of traffic. Built in 1971, during the mayoral administration of Paulo Maluf, the Minhocão is broadly described as a case of bad urban design—a model of engineer-driven urban development that prioritizes large-scale infrastructural investments over the micro-geographies of neighborhoods. It deeply scarred the landscape of its nearby neighborhoods, and

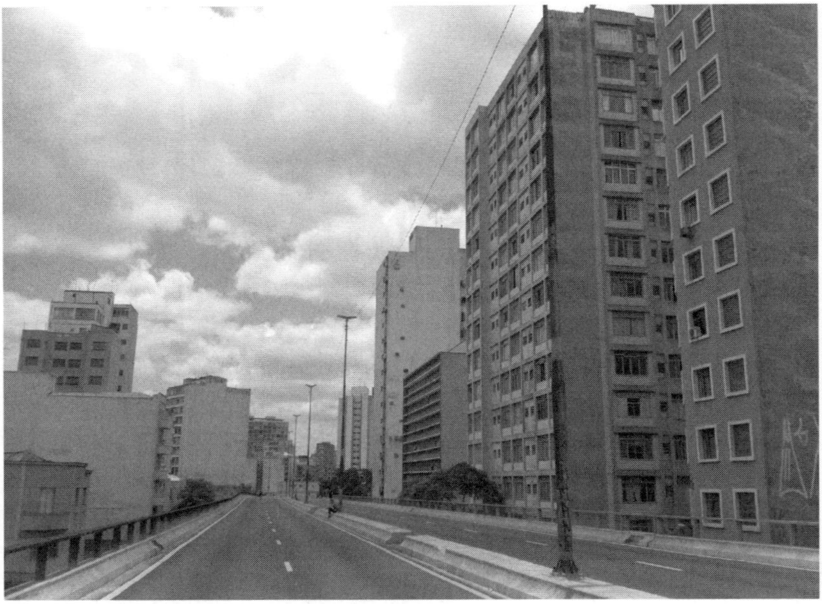

FIGURE 12.1. The Minhocão on a slow day. Photograph by the author.

given its relationship to the military dictatorship, demolition has long been seen as a potential future for the controversial highway.

Yet there is one particularity to the Minhocão that complicates its relationship to other urban elevated highways. On Sundays, Saturday afternoons, holidays, and after 9:30 P.M. on weekdays, the highway is closed to traffic and becomes an informal and wildly popular public space. When blocked to automobile traffic, the roadway immediately fills up with thousands of joggers, walkers, and lingerers eager for public space in a city underserved. Despite its total lack of landscaping and design, the car-free Minhocão is a transect through central São Paulo that allows for a variety of activities, ranging from informal soccer games to performance art.

As a result of the highway's popularity as a public space, the possibility of deactivating it and preserving it as an elevated urban park has become a potential option in recent years. The idea, in a sense, is to turn the Minhocão into São Paulo's High Line. The most visible of organizations interested in the site, the Associação Parque Minhocão [Minhocão Park Association, or MPA], stresses the ways that a renovated Minhocão could benefit the city through the provisioning of public space and the development of a more pedestrian- and bicycle-friendly metropolis. The organization is currently working toward developing a park at the site, and through a combination of grass-roots activism and political pressure, its members have worked with city council members to begin the legal process of deactivating the elevated road. Through the political support of eight city council members, the *elevado*'s gradual deactivation has been included in the city's strategic plan, a recently approved document that has the potential to dramatically rewrite São Paulo's socio-spatial inequality through a series of progressive policy interventions (Caldeira and Holston 2014; Pardue 2015).

Interestingly, though, this has been done with no guarantees that the viaduct itself will survive the highway's eventual deactivation. In keeping with the broadly participatory nature of São Paulo's strategic plan process, the text leaves the future of the site open, with the possibility of an elevated park existing alongside the possibility that the highway will be demolished with a new park built in its place, or that no park will be built at all. This uncertainty about the Minhocão's future is matched by the MPA's own unwillingness to dictate a design before adequate community input. The result is that over the next few years, the future of the Minhocão will be decided through a series of public meetings. These will coexist, presumably uneasily, with the traffic demands of the city and the desires of local developers and real estate speculators.

There are some risks to redeveloping the site. First, there is a concern that the Minhocão's accidental and largely indeterminate landscape will be lost if the site is formally redeveloped. Second, concerns have been raised that redeveloping the site will lead to displacement of low-income residents in the region, who have long been sheltered by the site's lowered real estate values. These concerns suggest that a renewed interest in public space in São Paulo, of which the broader interest in the Minhocão is only one expression, will yield a series of interventions that actually make the city less livable for a broader swath of the public. As proponents of the "just green enough approach" argue, urban sustainability initiatives may have "paradoxical results," as urban greening makes cities healthier and more livable while at the same time generating rounds of gentrification and displacement of low-income communities (Wolch et al. 2014: 239; see also Curran and Hamilton 2012).

These questions are suggestive of the broader politics of public space, a term whose normative or perhaps colloquial function can serve to obscure the distinct ways in which claims made in behalf of the public need to be understood as partial and particular (Crossa 2009; Hubbard 2004; Hunt 2009; Malone 2002; Massey 2005; Mitchell 1997; Wright 2004). Public space is a multifaceted concept, but its usage often disguises the ways it can be utilized to cleanse urban landscapes of seemingly out-of-place publics, such as sex workers, the homeless, or the urban poor. While contemporary designers highlight the importance of public space as part of a broader urban sustainability program, it is important that we be critical of the ways in which public space can serve to exclude particular publics. Specifically, residents who have long been sheltered by the Minhocão's effect on housing prices and values may be forced to leave if a park is built. The (possible) future of the Minhocão—which ties together public space provisioning with the potential for dislocation of low-income residents—raises significant questions about the politics of urban design in an era of neoliberal, financialized urbanism.

At the same time, inspiration can be found in the radical and equitable urban alternatives being articulated by Brazilian urbanists, activists, and housing movement members in the wake of the June 2013 protests (Takahashi 2015; see also Rolnik 2015). The extent to which advocates of the Minhocão's redevelopment can take inspiration from other public space organizations in the city—many of which tie together questions of environmental and social justice—will determine whether or not a solution to the Minhocão that does not end in wholesale dislocation can take place. While the ultimate outcome of the Minhocão remains to be seen, the fact that alternatives are at least on the radar is a rare feat in a contemporary policy moment in which urban questions are often reduced to instrumental questions of property development and speculation. This offers the possibility that São Paulo's High Line could take on its own distinctive shape.

DESIGNING THE MINHOCÃO

The history of the Minhocão is intimately tied to São Paulo's long-standing automobile-dependent conservatism, linked with a populist penchant toward public works projects and large-scale infrastructural interventions. This brand of infrastructure-centric politics is perhaps most directly exemplified by the mayoral administration of Paulo Maluf, who presided over the construction of the elevated highway while serving as mayor from 1969 to 1971. Inaugurated in 1971, the Minhocão echoed other infrastructural interventions by Maluf, including the extension of Avenida Brigadeiro Faria Lima and the construction of the Avenida dos Bandeirantes (as well as the broader expansion of the *marginais* [marginals], multi-lane highways that transport traffic east-west and north-south). Representing a focus on transportation and auto-centric modernity, the Minhocão was designed to move traffic east to west through the city's expanded center, but it would soon be seen as redundant in the face of the expansion of the Marginal-Tietê. A 1970 headline in *Estado de São Paulo,* for instance, referred to the Minhocão as the "sad future of the avenue," demonstrating the almost immediate controversy associated with its construction.

In 1976, only five years after its inauguration, the *elevado* began to be closed to traffic at night because of routine automobile accidents and concerns about noise. In 1989, during the mayoral administration of Luiza Erundina, the Minhocão's hours of traffic were further restricted. Instead of the previous midnight to 5:00 A.M. schedule, the Minhocão was now open to pedestrians and closed to cars from 9:30 P.M. until 6:30 A.M. The decision to close the highway was not linked to a broader project of public space provisioning but was instead a response to accidents and noise complaints. In this sense, the Minhocão is something of an accidental product, a result of concerns about traffic accidents, combined with some municipal accommodation and inklings of informal neighborhood management.

In closing the *elevado* to automobile traffic at night, São Paulo gained a peculiarly hybrid space, a unique amalgamation of traffic infrastructure with car-free public space. The Minhocão is a concrete High Line that offers the sorts of unexpected vistas that were so central to the High Line's initial popular appeal (Cataldi et al. 2011; David and Hammond 2011; chapter 9, by Darren Patrick). But unlike the pre-redevelopment High Line, accessible only via unsanctioned trespassing, the current Minhocão is broadly accessible to all, requiring nothing more than utilizing one of the road's on-ramps. With absolutely no landscape or design conventions—and no greenery—the Minhocão dramatically rewrites pedestrians' engagement with the urban fabric, while on some level drawing their attention to it and its material infrastructures. It offers new views of the buildings that run alongside it and a feeling of true urban mixture in a space that is not privatized. It is, to use Karen Franck and Quentin Stevens's phrasing, a "loose space," one that feels used, diverse, safe, and open to reinterpretation and reappropriation (Franck and Stevens 2006). As soon as it is closed to traffic, the road fills up, primarily with joggers, cyclists, skaters, and (dog) walkers, who take advantage of the site's uninterrupted landscape. Groups of teenagers huddle around cell phone speakers passing joints, couples sunbathe, and often the passage is interrupted by organized races featuring joggers, skateboarders, or cyclists (figure 12.2). And while the road's location in São

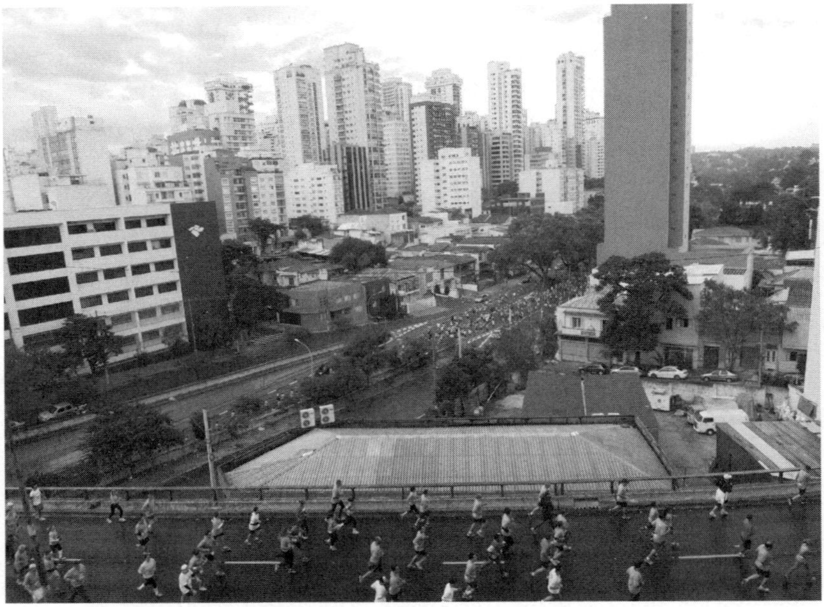

FIGURE 12.2. A race on the Minhocão. Photograph by the author.

Paulo's expanded center means that it is by no means easily accessible for those who live in the city's sprawling periphery, it nevertheless is suggestive of a kind of class mixture that is often missing in the city (Caldeira 2000).

In its fluctuation between providing space for vehicles and providing space for people, the Minhocão is a compelling demonstration of the temporality of place, the changing geographies of urban spaces between day and night, between workday and leisure, between light and dark. As an infrastructural space turned into a space for lingering, the Minhocão inverts the experience of being in the neighborhoods that surround it. And as a street whose meaning shifts dramatically depending on the hour of day, the Minhocão calls attention to the capacity of urban infrastructure to be reimagined and put to new use. Indeed, the constant modifications made to its signage by graffiti writers is suggestive of a flexible, playful engagement with the materiality of urban life that is given space by the Minhocão's particularly ephemeral existence.

In its in-betweenness, the Minhocão—like the pre-renovation High Line, perhaps—speaks to the possibilities offered by spaces that lack clear purpose or clear function. This is in part a result of the state's own unwillingness to regulate the site. For the municipality of São Paulo, the Minhocão exists in a kind of administrative indeterminacy. As Athos Comolatti, the president of the Minhocão Park Association, told me: "Today, on Sundays, the city [*prefeitura*] considers the Minhocão an elevated road. For them, at 9:30 at night when it closes, they understand that no one goes there. Sundays too. Bureaucratically, they're not responsible. . . . For the city, the Minhocão is simply a highway. The occupation of the Minhocão is spontaneous, public, and totally informal. No one asks permission to use it" (interview with the author, May 29, 2014, translation mine; see also Scruggs 2015). In its administrative indeterminacy as a functional highway whose public space dynamics are largely a product of the city looking the other way, the Minhocão is a counter to too many overly manicured public spaces that prescribe particular uses. As a result, it is a kind of accidental landscape or, in the language of contemporary architects and designers interested in overgrown or left-behind landscapes, a kind of *terrain vague*. First brought into scholarly conversations by Ignasi de Solà-Morales ([1993] 2014), *terrain vague* refers to indeterminate, vacant, or residual spaces, locations with an unclear relation to broader processes of development and design. Further defined by Manuela Mariani and Patrick Barron as a "collective term for a multitude of subtypes of marginal, leftover land, from 'derelict land' and 'brownfield' to 'void' and 'dead zone'"—the idea of *terrain vague* calls attention to the creative political possibilities offered by (urban) abandonment or reappropriation (Mariani and Barron 2013: xi; for broader work on indeterminate landscapes, see Brownlow 2006; DeSilvey 2006; DeSilvey and Edensor 2012; Franck and Stevens 2006; Gandy 2013; Garrett 2013; Rosa 2016).

Much of the literature on *terrain vague* has focused on forsaken and left-behind landscapes, but the Minhocão's indeterminacy is of a different sort. It is a highly utilized space, both by pedestrians and the thousands of cars that use it every day except Sunday. As such, it requires constant maintenance and repair, like all infrastructures (Graham and Thrift 2007; Thrift 2005). But its maintenance serves two purposes, resulting in a disjunction between the traffic infrastructures that exist alongside the dynamics of public space. As a result, its usage compels a feeling of dislocation, an ability to see traffic infrastructure as only one particular way of ordering and managing urban space. The result is that engagements with the Minhocão are suggestive of the broader work in urban cultural geography on the reappropriation of urban space by communities who use the urban landscape for diverse purposes (Borden 2001; de Certeau 1984; Fenton 2004; Lefebvre

1968; Mould 2009; Patrick 2014; Pinder 2000, 2011; Rosa 2014). This spirit of reappropriation, of a lack of clear regulation and determinacy, and of a popular and spontaneous engagement with the site made possible by its administrative indeterminacy, is suggestive of a political openness made possible by public space that is not relegated to banal encounters and regulated presence.

The possibility exists that this playful feeling of reappropriation will be lost if the site is redeveloped. In this sense, parallels can be made with the pre-renovation High Line, where critics have argued that an urban space of indeterminate political potentiality was traded for a much more public, but much more regulated park (Cataldi et al. 2011; Gandy 2013; chapter 4, by Patrick). The story of the High Line shows that the creation of public spaces can serve to obscure the decidedly political implications of (urban) design interventions in the form of gentrification and urban renewal (Dooling 2009; Ghertner 2010; Wolch et al. 2014). At the same time, urban social movements and others interested in the right to the city make clear that good public space—spaces that facilitate interaction, that lower urban heat island effects, that offer non-motorized transportation opportunities—are necessary components of a more just city. This tension between urban amenities and the dynamics of real estate speculation renders complex the provisioning of urban public space, which both improves the lives of urban residents while encouraging processes of speculation that can displace low-income residents.

BRINGING THE HIGH LINE TO SÃO PAULO

When discussing the High Line at a public event in São Paulo, High Line codesigner Charles Renfro (of the architecture firm Diller, Scofidio + Renfro) struck an ambivalent tone, noting, "High Lines are now happening around the world. It has become a cause, and I'm not saying that that is not a good thing nor a bad thing. I think it's an interesting thing. Can this, will this, or should this High Line phenomenon be exported to the rest of the world and what will it achieve?" (Renfro 2013). Renfro was not talking about the Minhocão (at least at that moment), but he could have been. Plans to develop the Minhocão into a park make many references to the High Line, and the founders of the Friends of the High Line visited the offices of the Minhocão Park Association in 2013. More generally, though, journalistic engagements with the possibility of renovating the Minhocão make constant reference to the site, both in English and Portuguese. Take, for instance, Greg Scruggs's recent piece for *Next City*, titled "Brazil May Be Getting Its Own High Line" (2015).

In campaigning for the redevelopment of the Minhocão into a public park, the MPA echoes many of the sentiments that were initially brought to bear on the development of the High Line, but within a register specifically attuned to the contemporary visibility of public space movements in São Paulo. These movements emerged as a result of explosive political manifestations in June 2013, but also as a response to more long-standing engagements with urban public space in the city. They showcase new relationships to the urban landscape being articulated by activists in the wake of decades of fortification, violence, and neglect. While some of these interventions are state-led, including the provisioning of wireless Internet in public squares, a variety of subsidized concerts and events, and twenty-four-hour programming at some of the city's parks, many public spaces in the city are currently marked by interventions and playful occupations produced by a variety of activist groups. Echoing contemporary articulations of tactical urbanism (Lydon and Garcia 2015), many of these occupations or interventions are lighthearted or small-scale, like the community mobilizations in the Largo de Batata, a square in the neighborhood of Pinheiros. Frustrated by the lengthy conclusion to a revitalization project of a square that yielded a broad slab of concrete with almost no landscaping, nearby residents began organizing events and intervening by building outside furniture and planting trees. Other examples of these sorts of small-scale initiatives abound, from the Ocupe e Abrace [Occupy and Embrace] collective in the neighborhood of Pompeia to the Movimento Boa Praça [Good Square Movement] in Lapa to the environmental organization Rios e Ruas [Rivers and Roads]. The Minhocão bears the stamp of this renewed interest in lively and community-minded occupation through an explosive sense of ownership over the site by activists, artists, and residents. Street signs and directives are constantly modified by graffiti writers, plays are performed from windows, and carnival *blocos* bring drums and dancers to the space regularly (figures 12.3 and 12.4).

The MPA calls attention to this spirit of (re)appropriation and occupation in its desire to develop an elevated urban park: "Since the passing of the law that closes the highway to cars at night and on Sundays, the city is bearing witness to the surge of new spontaneous appropriations of this

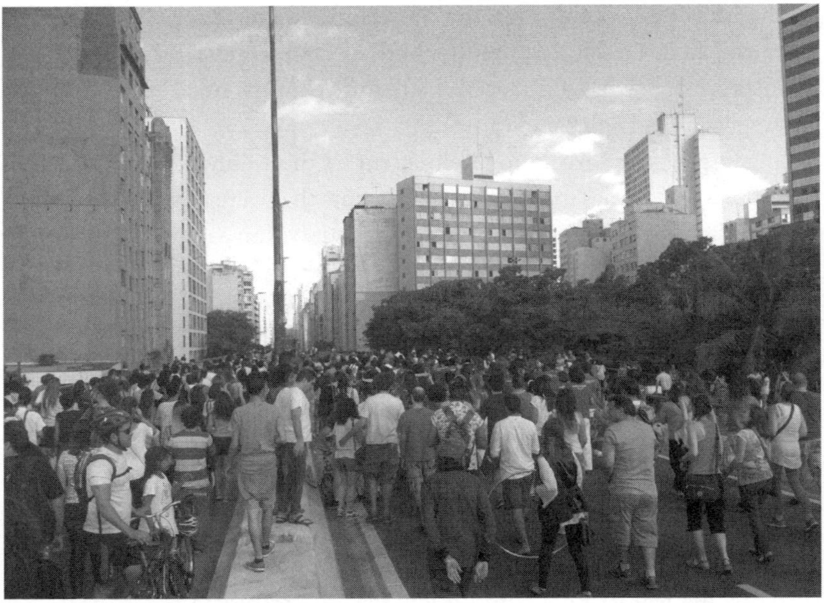

FIGURE 12.3. A carnival *bloco* practicing on the Minhocão. Photograph by the author.

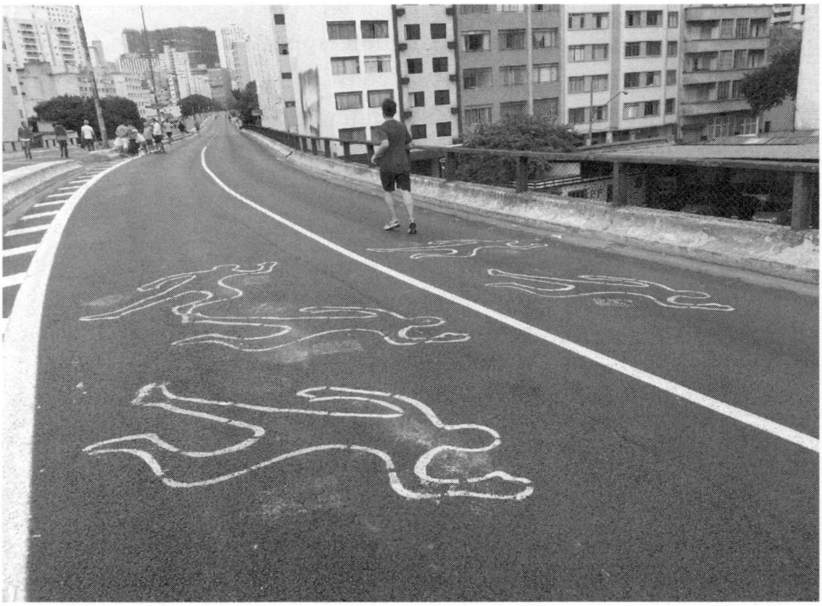

FIGURE 12.4. Artistic interventions on the Minhocão. Photograph by the author.

symbol of São Paulo: the Minhocão as a space for leisure for residents, of encounters, of cultural and artistic expression, and of sport. . . . We want to transform the Minhocão into an elevated park with a bike lane, creating a public leisure space that reaffirms and impels even more the appropriation and resignification of place for the population, from the conviction that we should live in a 'city for people'" (Associacão Parque Minhocão n.d., translation mine). In this articulation, the Minhocão becomes a symbol of a new São Paulo, a city that, in the language of contemporary urban boosterism, is *para pessoas* ("for people") (Gehl 2010). The idea of a "city for people" is an increasingly common idea in São Paulo (and beyond), part of a contemporary interest in sustainability and resiliency that is being voiced by many in the design profession. And while what a "city for people" looks like is different in São Paulo than in other cities, the kinds of visions espoused by theorists like Gehl are global in scale, reflective of a contemporary "policy ecology" (Peck 2011) attuned to sustainability, pedestrian life, and public space.

However, the dynamics of public space in São Paulo are complex, tying together a vital and vibrant street life with the scars of a violent and unequal city. As such, normative pronouncements about public space can ignore the ways that its provision can serve to cleanse the urban landscape of particular publics. Furthermore, to assume that public life only happens in parks, squares, and sidewalks ignores the broader social geography of urban street life and public space in São Paulo (Caldeira 2000). This can be seen through an analysis of the *rolezinho* phenomenon that occurred in 2013 and 2014 (Vargas 2014). Organized via social media by young people in the urban periphery, *rolezinhos* (translated in Vargas [2014] as "cruises" or "little strolls") brought hundreds of young, often dark-skinned teenagers to São Paulo's shopping malls (referred to as *shoppings*). *Shoppings*, which began to emerge in Brazilian cities in the 1980s in response to the rise of violent crime, allow wealthier urban residents to drive to these locations, park their cars under the watchful eye of surveillance, and shop, eat, and socialize in controlled environments (Caldeira 2000). The sudden appearance of hundreds of young people who were seen not to belong because of their class, age, and race caused a public outcry, and commentators fumed over the invasion of shopping malls by supposed criminals. Echoing a broader engagement with urban space formulated by residents of the urban periphery, *rolezinhos* and their cultural counterparts in the form of funk, hip hop, and poetry are suggestive of the ways in which residents of the urban periphery have laid claim to the urban landscape and made extensive claims on the city's political and cultural life in recent decades (Caldeira 2000, 2012; Pardue 2007, 2010). In response to the *rolezinhos,* city administrators requested and demanded that they occur in more functional public spaces, specifically parks.

By laying claim to spaces that are decidedly not public but sometimes function as such, *rolezinhos* called attention to the slippery, indeterminate nature of public space in São Paulo. While claims that the city lacks public space are often repeated and constitutes a kind of rallying cry for many public space activists or urban designers in the city, public street life is undeniable in the neighborhoods that have yet to become completely securitized. Furthermore, demanding that teenagers do their socializing in parks instead of shopping malls ignores the ways in which malls have functioned as de facto public spaces for those able to afford them in the past two decades. Juxtaposing parks and other formal spaces with shopping malls ignores the dynamic ways in which street life and public space in São Paulo are related. Public space in the city is often not strictly or formally public, but instead functions in an administrative or bureaucratic indeterminacy (as with the Minhocão). Laying claim to shopping malls, then, is about more than just having access to adequate public spaces. It is about the capacity of peripheral urban residents to enter the classed and racialized spaces of leisure and consumption in the city and the broader dynamics of inequality and the policing of who belongs where. As such, engaging with public space in São Paulo requires a broader interest in the contours of inequality that shape the city. Efforts to construct public space that borrow from European and North American perspectives run the risk of missing out on the complex, overlapping ways in which public space in São Paulo is often much more about the lack of regulation than the existence of formally regulated or codified public spaces.

In a sense, this is a point made by Teresa Caldeira in her canonical 2000 monograph, *City of Walls.* In it, Caldeira highlights the tense and conflicting dynamics of public space in São Paulo, in which an insurgent democratization process unhappily coexists with a broader walling off and securitizing of the city's urban landscape. For Caldeira, São Paulo's streetscape bears the wounds of the city's enduring inequalities, but she notes that its formal public spaces like parks retain a democratic and dynamic public life that appeals to residents of varying class positions. Nevertheless, she notes that the tension between an insurgent democratization led by the city's poor and a retrenchment into securitized enclaves has resulted in an apprehensive public life that threatens the dynamics of citizenship and belonging that are necessary to the broader project of creating democratic cities and societies.

In order to examine São Paulo's conflictual public space dynamics, Caldeira focuses not on the Minhocão but on Praça da Sé, a public square located next to the historic Sé Cathedral (*sé* is translated into English as "see" or "seat," both references to Catholic authority). Given its symbolic and religious location, Praça da Sé is a site deeply linked to Brazil's transition to democracy in the 1980s, functioning as the location for mass mobilizations against the military dictatorship. Yet while Sé retains a symbolic dimension, it is also representative of the changing contours of São Paulo's downtown, where wealth and capital have continued to move southward toward increasingly isolated communities that rely on cars for transportation. The result is that Sé has become, in many respects, a non-elite space, bringing together evangelical preachers who share the square with many homeless people and the occasional tourist. For Caldeira, Praça da Sé represents "the political reappropriation of public space by citizens in the transition to democracy," while also representing "the deterioration of public space, danger, crime, anxieties about downward mobility, and the impoverishment of the workers who continue to use it for commuting, working in the informal market, and consuming its cheap products." In her view, Sé "symbolizes both the strength and deterioration of public space and, therefore, the disjunctive character of Brazilian democracy" (Caldeira 2000: 321). The result is that Sé and other parts of the historic core have long been subject to attempts at revitalization that have sought to purge the core of its reputation for violence and criminality (Frúgoli 2006; Jose 2010). That these attempts have largely failed is not only a testament to the political capacity of urban social movements, but also a result of the broader geographies of capital and real estate speculation that continue to push into new territorial frontiers.

Praça da Sé makes clear that, in many respects, public space in São Paulo retains a distinctly popular feel, and it raises concerns that the current vogue of public space activism in the city will only serve to further gentrify and encourage large-scale urban redevelopment (regardless of whether or not that is the goal of public space activists). As such, projects that aim to encourage street life in the urban center need to be engaged with tentatively, as their relationship to a broader process of urban renewal is still being determined. Efforts to provide public space need to be understood as potentially elite interventions into the city's landscape that may foreshadow a broader process of revitalization that writes out the urban poor from what have been effectively their spaces. That the Minhocão will become such a space is a cause for considerable concern.

The experience of the High Line is consequently illustrative. Critics of the High Line have focused on its disproportionate resource use and role in the gentrification of its surrounding neighborhoods, calling attention to a kind of ecological or green gentrification that forces urban residents to choose between affordability and urban amenities (Cataldi et al. 2011; Wolch et al. 2014). These critiques are attuned to the ways in which urban parks are vectors for further neoliberalization of urban space, both through the relationships between developers and green space but also through the sorts of innovative public/private initiatives encouraged by the spectacular financial success of the High Line. As a result, the most worrisome dimension of any efforts to redevelop the Minhocão is not just that a playful spirit of reappropriation will be lost if the site is redesigned, but that low-income residents who reside alongside the *elevado* will be displaced. It is the perversity of its violent disruption of the surrounding urban landscape that has preserved the affordability of its surrounding neighborhoods, a rarity in a city where the vast majority of the population is forced to live in far-flung suburbs because of the disproportionately high cost of living (Whittaker 2014). The possibility that its redesign could fuel development that would undoubtedly raise rents and ultimately displace residents is thus a serious cause for concern.

As Brazilian urbanist João Sette Whittaker notes, a legitimate plan to manage low-income residents in the region is needed before anything happens to the Minhocão. He argues:

> [B]efore discussing whether or not to transform the Minhocão into a park, the demand should be different: the presentation of a plan, on the part of the mayor, of price regulation and protection for low-income residents that live there. This should be the struggle at the moment. The risk is that, if we don't do this, we will carry the blame for having defended the creation of something that could turn into one of the most gentrifying projects the city has ever had. . . . There are many ways of doing this, which require political victories in a city council that will probably be extremely disinterested: a law of tenancy specific to the Minhocão to protect the residents who live there, reduced taxation for real estate negotiations that affect residents who have been there

> for years, the designation of zones of special interest in buildings where the majority of residents are low-income, and so on. (Whittaker 2014: n.p., translation mine)

A similar critique is made by Raquel Rolnik (2015), who sees efforts to redesign the Minhocão as irresponsible when other potential park spaces linger in disuse (see chapter 5, by Julian Brash). Rather than engaging with what is sure to be a complex and long process of remodeling the highway, Rolnik highlights spaces like Parque Augusta [Augusta Park], a swath of green space in central São Paulo that has been a site of considerable conflict between activist-residents, developers, and the mayor's office in recent years (Rigby 2015). For Rolnik, efforts to redesign the Minhocão are inherently complex, owing to the site's continued functionality as a traffic corridor. Parque Augusta, and other municipal parks like it, offers green space without requiring complicated urbanization plans that will drag on for years, if not decades. Instead of intervening into the convoluted legal conversations that will accompany the development of the Minhocão, Rolnik is calling for the city to honor its commitment to Parque Augusta made in 2014 (Rigby 2015).

In a sense, Rolnik calls attention to the degree to which the Minhocão functions more as a symbolic intervention than a necessary piece of urban public space. This, perhaps, is where the Minhocão and the High Line match up most particularly. Spaces of indeterminate and creative possibility before being integrated into broader development regimes, both the Minhocão and the High Line are deeply compromised by their relationship to the broader contours of urban development. Indeed, the property speculation that is already occurring along the Minhocão is a clear demonstration that future park plans are even now generating real estate activity in the region (Scruggs 2015).

Ultimately, the possibility that turning the Minhocão into a park could entail the removal and pricing out of nearby communities makes clear that the real tragedy of the contemporary moment is that good urban spaces—ones that facilitate interaction, that offer reprieve from noise and concrete, that make clear that the urban and the natural are intimately linked—cannot be disentangled from the processes of real estate speculation and development that continue to rewrite cities in profound ways. As Whittaker explains, good design requires infrastructures of aid that are less politically visible and less attuned to broadly neoliberal approaches to the city. The danger of the Minhocão's redesign—and this is a danger that faces the current vogue of occupation that is present in urban landscapes in São Paulo and beyond, too—is that public space will function as a means of excluding particular publics. Socially and ecologically just urbanism demands good public spaces that allow for just the sorts of things the MPA is advocating: encounter, connection, non-motorized transportation. But the real estate boom that is sure to accompany the development of the Minhocão into a park forces urban residents to choose between quality of life and affordability (see Wolch et al. 2014). Ultimately, the High Line, and the tentative Minhocão, force a reckoning between good public space and the realities of a financialized, neoliberalized urban dynamic that forecloses alternative visions and possibilities.

But while this may seem like cause for pessimism, some inspiration can be taken from the myriad examples of radical, politically progressive public space movements currently operating in São Paulo. In recent years, occupations of abandoned skyscrapers organized by social movements have ramped up dramatically, visibly marking the urban landscape, and housing thousands of low-income families. These occupations are a product of the increasingly unaffordable cost of living in São Paulo and the broader financialization of housing in the city and beyond, but they also speak to a broader understanding that urban space can be appropriated by those in need (Boulos 2014; Harvey 2012; Lefebvre 1996). Housing occupations are not public in the sense that a park is public; as a result, they raise questions about the broader politics of urban space and alternative ways that it can be collectively managed. In this sense, housing takeovers can be matched by ongoing occupations of urban green spaces that offer another alternative reference for the Minhocão. Take, for instance, the activists in the Organismo Parque Augusta [Augusta Park Organism]. Referenced by Rolnik in her piece on the Minhocão, the Organismo Parque Augusta has used the failure of the city to develop a park in a piece of green space into a broader critique of an urbanism attuned too closely to the provisioning of elite housing. Or take the Estelita occupation in Recife, which has carved out a compelling critique of urban redevelopment in that city, using an abandoned factory space slated for urban renewal.

As these examples demonstrate, activists interested in the Minhocão need not look to the High Line for inspiration, but rather to the myriad examples of collective occupation and appropriation happening in Brazil and around the world. These occupations and public space interventions are suggestive of new approaches to urban space that are being developed, not just by architects or urbanists, but by residents in need of housing, environmentalists committed to more and better green space, and artists interested in creative engagements with the cityscape. Most important, contemporary movements interested in occupation tie together environmental critiques with a broader pushback against a city bent to the will of financial capital. While these movements are sometimes atomized and fractured, they make clear that the vision of a city that does not trade quality of life for affordability remains present. Occupations demonstrate that the provisioning of green space cannot be separated from the broader political economy of housing and inequality, meaning that proponents of urban public space need to take seriously the political ecologies of urban parks. That public space remains a vital and radical possibility in São Paulo is cause for tentative hope, and this should provide creative inspiration for the designing and implementing of public space there and in other cities.

NEXT STEPS

In the case of the Minhocão, probably not much will happen anytime soon. The road is still heavily used and will remain so for the immediate future, as São Paulo continues to grapple with intractable traffic. A poll in September 2014 found that only 7 percent of São Paulo's population wanted the road demolished, while 53 percent would prefer for it to stay as it is, and 23 percent were in favor of a park (DataFolha 2014). This makes clear that any project to preserve the Minhocão as an urban park will be an uphill battle, but the legal provisions passed in 2014 suggest that the process is at least beginning.

In any case, the issues raised by the possibility of the park get at much of what is currently at stake within contemporary urban governance, even without commenting on the deep relationships in São Paulo between habitation, inequality, and open space. Good public space is an urban right, and cities need more green space, more ways to reduce the rise of heat levels that are already occurring as a result of climate change, and more spaces that open up the possibility of cross-class conversation and encounter. But urban environmentalism does not happen in a vacuum, and a sustainable city only makes sense if coupled with affordable housing, democratic and participatory decision making, and limits on the power of development and real estate speculation. In São Paulo, there are glimmers of hope in the city's current rewriting of its strategic plan, but legal sanction does not always yield progressive effects (Caldeira and Holston 2014; Pardue 2015).

A conversation is currently ongoing in São Paulo about the relationship between urban development, real estate speculation, and design, and this is a necessary discussion if this problematic but extremely vital city loses the abundant and unpretentious street life that makes it so compelling. Public space in São Paulo cannot be disconnected from the broader processes through which urban housing is increasingly financialized, which drives up the prices of rental apartments and leaves many who are in search of housing with no choice but to occupy public land. Any attempt to improve the quality and quantity of public spaces in São Paulo needs to be tied to forceful measures both to limit real estate development and to ensure mechanisms for providing affordable housing. That these mechanisms already exist but are underutilized, if not completely ignored, is cause for both optimism and pessimism, but the visible presence of active urban social movements in both the center and the urban periphery suggests that the vision of an affordable, livable city remains alive in São Paulo. To what extent these movements can find ways of productively engaging with the Minhocão will determine if São Paulo's High Line can escape that historical reference.

ACKNOWLEDGMENTS

This book is the result of a wonderfully collaborative effort. It started with a conversation about landscape architecture, urban infrastructure, and wastelands in June 2014. From a casual lunchtime chat during a break from a conference on global garbage—occurring in the incongruous landscape of a manicured Parisian park—our conversation rapidly evolved into an extended, transatlantic discussion about the impact of the High Line on New York City. We began considering the effects of the elevated linear park at a variety of scales, from the neighborhood level, to New York City as a whole, to the numerous other cities seeking to implement similar projects worldwide. From there, we started working with authors and solidifying a collection of essays bringing together urban scholars and practitioners from a range of disciplinary backgrounds. We are immensely grateful to the authors in this volume for being part of the ongoing discussion and for contributing their work. For hosting an author meeting and a public symposium on the High Line at the New School in New York City, we would like to thank Joseph Heathcott and the Milano School of International Affairs. This event was co-sponsored by the Amsterdam Center for Globalization Studies and the Department of Urban Studies at Queens College, CUNY, and we are grateful for their involvement and support. Tijmen Klous in Amsterdam has been an indispensable editorial and research assistant without whom this book would have taken much longer to complete. Finally, our sincere thanks to Leslie Mitchner at Rutgers University Press for her enthusiasm, attention, and feedback.

Christoph Lindner and Brian Rosa

BIBLIOGRAPHY

Adorno, T., and M. Horkheimer (1944) "The Culture Industry: Enlightenment as Mass Deception." In T. Adorno and M. Horkheimer, *Dialectic of Enlightenment*. New York: Social Studies Association.

Allen, S. (1999) "Infrastructural Urbanism." In S. Allen (ed.), *Points + Lines: Diagrams and Projects for the City*. New York: Princeton Architectural Press.

Alpers, P. (1996) *What Is Pastoral?* Chicago: University of Chicago Press.

Alschuler, J. (2011) Chairman of the board of directors of the Friends of the High Line. Interview with D. Patrick, 18 April.

Amateau, A. (2007) "Talk in Cutting-Edge Building on Cutting-Edge Park." *Villager* 76 (53/May 30–June 5). http:/www.thevillager.com/villager_213/talkincuttingedge .html (accessed 9 June 2011).

American Society of Landscape Architects (2010) "2010 ASLA Professional Awards." http://www.asla.org/2010awards/173.html (accessed 20 May 2016).

Anderson, E. (2012) *The Cosmopolitan Canopy: Race and Civility in Everyday Life*. New York: W. W. Norton.

Anderson, K. (2005) "The Little Abandoned Train Line That Could, Did." *New York Magazine*, 21 May.

Andersson, J. (2011) "Heritage Discourse and the Desexualization of Public Space: The 'Historical Restorations' of Bloomsbury's Squares." *Antipode* 44(4): 1081–1098.

Angelo, H., and D. Wachsmuth (2014) "Urbanizing Urban Political Ecology: A Critique of Methodological Cityism." *International Journal of Urban and Regional Research* 39(1): 16–27.

Antrop, M. (2005) "Why Landscapes of the Past Are Important for the Future." *Landscape and Urban Planning* 70(1–2): 21–34.

Arnstein, S. (1969) "A Ladder of Citizen Participation." *Journal of the American Institute of Planners* 35(4): 216–224.

Asabere, P., and F. Huffman (2009) "The Relative Impacts of Trails and Greenbelts on Home Price." *Journal of Real Estate Finance and Economics* 38: 408–419.

Associacão Parque Minhocão (n.d.) http://www.minhocao.org (accessed 16 May 2016).

Avila, E. (2014) *The Folklore of the Freeway: Race and Revolt in the Modernist City*. Minneapolis: University of Minnesota Press.

Ayer, A. (2009) "The High Line: Think, Reuse, Grow Up." *Huffington Post*, 28 June. http://www.huffingtonpost.com/%20anjuliayer/the-high-line-think-reuse_b _220793.html (accessed 20 June 2011).

Azzarito, L., P. Munro, and M. A. Solomon (2004) "Unsettling the Body: The Institutionalization of Physical Activity at the Turn of the 20th Century." *Quest* 56(4): 377–397.

Bachin, R. F. (2003) "Cultivating Unity: The Changing Role of Parks in Urban America." *Places* 15(3): 12–17.

Bagli, C. V. (2012) "Olympic Bid, though Unsuccessful, Brought Benefits to the City, Its Champion Says." *New York Times*, 4 August, A14.

Bagli, C. V., and R. Pogrebin (2014) "With Bold Park Plan, Mogul Hopes to Leave Mark on New York's West Side." *New York Times*, 17 November.

Bathurst, M. (2012) "A 'Low Line' for London?" *Design Week*, 9 October. http://www.designweek.co.uk/news/a-low-line-for-london/3035377.article (accessed 27 December 2014).

Baudrillard, J. (1982) "The Beaubourg-Effect: Implosion and Deterrence." *October* 20 (Spring): 3–13.

Beckett, K., and A. Godoy (2010) "A Tale of Two Cities: A Comparative Analysis of Quality of Life Initiatives in New York and Bogotá." *Urban Studies* 47(2): 277–301.

Bedoya, R. (2013) "Placemaking and the Politics of Belonging and Dis-belonging." *GIA Reader* 24(1). http://www.giarts.org/article/placemaking-and-politics-belonging-and-dis-belonging (accessed 20 May 2016).

Bell, D., and J. Binnie (2004) "Authenticating Queer Space: Citizenship, Urbanism and Governance." *Urban Studies* 41(9): 1807–1820.

Bell, D., and G. Valentine (eds.) (1995) *Mapping Desire: Geographies of Sexualities*. London: Routledge.

Bender, T. (2002) *The Unfinished City: New York and the Metropolitan Idea*. New York: New Press.

Berman, M. (1983) *All That Is Solid Melts into Air: The Experience of Modernity*. London: Verso.

Birge-Liberman, P. (2010) "(Re)Greening the City: Urban Park Restoration as a Spatial Fix." *Geography Compass* 4(9): 1392–1407.

Birnbaum, C. (2014) "Is the MoMA Sculpture Garden Doomed?" http://www.architectmagazine.com/architecture/museum-of-modern-art-sculpture-garden-doomed-cultural-landscape-foundation_o.aspx?dfpzone=news (accessed 20 May 2016).

Bloomberg, M. R. (2002) "Foreword." In *Reclaiming the High Line*. New York: Design Trust for Public Space, Friends of the High Line.

Bloomberg News (2015) "Art Galleries Are Leaving Chelsea." *Crain's New York Business*, 28 August.

Boone, C. G., G. L. Buckley, J. M. Grove, and C. Sister (2009) "Parks and People: An Environmental Justice Inquiry in Baltimore, Maryland." *Annals of the Association of American Geographers* 99(4): 767–787.

Borden, I. (2001) *Skateboarding, Space and the City: Architecture and the Body*. London: Berg.

Boulos, G. (2014) *Por que ocupamos? Uma introdução à luta dos sem-teto*. São Paulo: Scortecci.

Bourne, M. (2012) "The High Line: New York's Monument to Gentrification." http://www.themillions.com/2012/06/the-high-line-new-yorks-monument-to-gentrification.html (accessed 20 May 2016).

Boyer, M. C. (1992) "Cities for Sale: Merchandising History at South Street Seaport." In M. Sorkin (ed.), *Variations on a Theme Park: The New American City and the End of Public Space*. New York: Hill and Wang, 181–204.

———. (1996) *CyberCities: Visual Perception in the Age of Electronic Communication*. New York: Princeton Architectural Press.

———. (2001) "Twice-Told Stories: The Double Erasure of Times Square." In I. Borden, J. Kerr, J. Rendell, and A. Pivaro (eds.), *The Unknown City: Contesting Architecture and Social Space*. Cambridge, MA: MIT Press, 30–53.

Brash, J. (2011) *Bloomberg's New York: Class and Governance in the Luxury City*. Athens: University of Georgia Press.

———. (2012) "Downtown as Brand, Downtown as Land: Urban Elites and Neoliberal Development in Contemporary New York City." In G. McDonogh and M. Peterson (eds.), *Global Downtowns*. Philadelphia: University of Pennsylvania Press, 253–271.

Brenner, N. (2009) "What Is Critical Urban Theory?" *City* 13(2–3): 198–207.

———. (2013) "Open City or Right to the City?" *TOPOS: The International Review of Landscape Architecture and Urban Design* 85: 42–45.

Brenner, N., and N. Theodore (eds.) (2002) *Spaces of Neoliberalism: Urban Restructuring in North America and Western Europe*. Malden, MA: Blackwell.

Brooks, M. L. (1997) *Subway City: Riding the Trains, Reading New York*. New Brunswick, NJ: Rutgers University Press.

Brown, A., J. Novak-Leonard, and S. Gilbride (2011) "Getting in on the Act: How Arts Groups Are Creating Opportunities for Active Participation." James Irvine Foundation. https://www.irvine.org/arts/what-were-learning/getting-in-on-the-act (accessed 20 May 2016).

Brown Wilson, B., and L. Ogbu (2015) "When Good Intentions Aren't Enough: Linking Intent to Impact." Impact Design Hub. http://www.impactdesignhub.org/2015/04/15/linking-intent-to-impact (accessed 20 May 2016).

Browne, K., J. Lim, and G. Brown (2007) *Geographies of Sexualities*. Aldershot, UK: Ashgate.

Brownlow, A. (2006) "An Archaeology of Fear and Environmental Change in Philadelphia." *Geoforum* 37(2): 227–245.

Bryson, J. (2013) "The Nature of Gentrification." *Geography Compass* 7(8): 578–587.

Bunce, S. (2009) "Developing Sustainability: Sustainability Policy and Gentrification on Toronto's Waterfront." *Local Environment* 14(7): 651–667.

Burden, A. (2014) "How Public Spaces Make Cities Work." *TED*, March 2014. http://www.ted.com/talks/amanda_burden_how_public_spaces_make_cities_work?language=en#t-762849 (accessed 20 May 2016).

Caldeira, T. P. (2000) *City of Walls: Crime, Segregation, and Citizenship in São Paulo*. Berkeley: University of California Press.

———. (2012) "Imprinting and Moving Around: New Visibilities and Configurations of Public Space in São Paulo." *Public Culture* 24(2): 385–419.

Caldeira, T. P., and J. Holston (2014) "Participatory Urban Planning in Brazil." *Urban Studies* 52(11): 2001–2017.

Calder, R. (2009) "Sky 'High' Costs: Tax-Seeking New Park Already NY's Priciest." *New York Post.* http://www.nypost.com/p/news/regional/item_jWqyN168fwWJ3YVGVNlOhL (accessed 19 July 2013).

Cardwell, D. (2009) "For High Line Visitors, Park Is a Railway out of Manhattan." *New York Times,* 21 July. http://www.nytimes.com/2009/07/22/nyregion/22highline.html (accessed 20 May 2016).

Caro, R. (1975) *The Power Broker: Robert Moses and the Fall of New York.* New York: Vintage Books.

Castells, M. (1983) *The City and the Grassroots: A Cross-Cultural Theory of Urban Social Movements.* Berkeley: University of California Press.

Cataldi, M., D. Kelley, H. Kuzmich, J. Maier-Rothe, and J. Tang (2011) "Residues of a Dream World: The High Line." *Theory, Culture and Society* 28(7–8): 358–389.

Caulfield, J. (1989) "'Gentrification' and Desire." *Canadian Review of Sociology/Revue Canadienne de Sociologie* 26(4): 617–632.

Centner, R. (2008) "Places of Privileged Consumption Practice: Spatial Capital, the Dot-Com Habitus, and San Francisco's Internet Boom." *City & Community* 7(3): 193–223.

Central Park Conservancy (2014) "The History of Central Park." http://www.centralparknyc.org/visit/history (accessed 20 May 2016).

Cenzatti, M. (2008) "Heterotopias of Difference." In M. Dehaene and L. de Cauter (eds.), *Heterotopia and the City: Public Space in a Postcivil Society.* Milton Park, UK: Routledge, 75–85.

Chan, E. C. (2009) "What Roles for Ruins? Meaning and Narrative of Industrial Ruins in Contemporary Parks." *Journal of Landscape Architecture* 4(2): 20–31.

Chan, S. (2009) "Thompson Criticizes Deal for High Line Food and Merchandise." *New York Times,* 9 July. http://cityroom.blogs.nytimes.com/2009/07/09/thompson-criticizes-deal-for-high-line-food-and-merchandise (accessed 10 April 2014).

Cheape, C. W. (1980) *Moving the Masses: Urban Public Transit in New York, Boston, and Philadelphia, 1880–1912.* Cambridge, MA: Harvard University Press.

Checker, M. (2011) "Wiped Out by the 'Greenwave': Environmental Gentrification and the Paradoxical Politics of Urban Sustainability." *City & Society* 23(2): 210–229.

———. (2015) "Green Is the New Brown: 'Old School Toxics' and Environmental Gentrification on a New York City Waterfront." In C. Isenhour, G. McDonogh, and M. Checker (eds.), *Sustainability in the Global City: Myth and Practice.* New York: Cambridge University Press.

Chisholm, D. (2010) "Biophilia, Creative Involution, and the Ecological Future of Queer Desire." In C. Sandilands and B. Erickson (eds.), *Queer Ecologies: Sex, Nature, Politics, Desire.* Bloomington: Indiana University Press.

City of New York (1873) "Third General Report of the Board of Commissioners of the Department of Public Parks for the Period of Twenty Months, from May 1st, 1872, to December 31st, 1873." New York: William C. Bryant & Co.

———. (2009) "Press Release—Mayor Bloomberg, Speaker Quinn, and Friends of the High Line Announce Opening of the First Section of New York City's Newest Park." 8 June, PR-257–09.

Clarke, J. (2004a) *Changing Welfare, Changing States: New Directions in Social Policy*. London: Sage.

———. (2004b) "Dissolving the Public Realm? The Logics and Limits of Neoliberalism." *Journal of Social Policy* 33(1): 27–48.

Cloke, P., and O. Jones (2002) *Tree Cultures: The Place of Trees and Trees in Their Place*. Oxford: Berg Press.

———. (2003) "Grounding Ethical Mindfulness for/in Nature: Trees in Their Places." *Ethics, Place & Environment* 6(3): 195–213.

Collins, G. (2008) "In Winds of Winter, Midair Park Takes Shape." *New York Times*, 2 January. http://www.nytimes.com/2008/01/02/nyregion/02highline.html?scp=1&sq=In+Winds+of+Winter%2C+Mid (accessed 9 June 2011).

Committee on Parks and Recreation (2014) "Equity in Parks: Do Disparities Exist in the Care of the City's Open Space?" New York: New York City Council.

Corner, J. (2006) "Terra Fluxus." In C. Waldheim (ed.), *The Landscape Urbanism Reader*. New York: Princeton Architectural Press, 21–33.

———. (2014) "Hunt's Haunts." In J. Corner and A. Bick Hirsch (eds.), *The Landscape Imagination: The Collected Essays of James Corner, 1990–2010*. New York: Princeton Architectural Press, 340–349.

Crain's New York Business (2014) "Cannibalizing Conservancies." *Crain's New York Business*, 28 April.

Cranz, G. (1978) "Changing Roles of Urban Parks: From Pleasure Garden to Open-Space System." *Landscape* 22(3): 9–18.

———. (1989) *The Politics of Park Design: A History of Urban Parks in America*. Cambridge, MA: MIT Press.

Crimson Architectural Historians (2007) "De Hofbogen: Cultuurhistorische Verkenning." http://www.hofbogen.nl/IMG/pdf/Hofbogen-spread.pdf (accessed 2 May 2016).

———. (2008) "Toekomstvisie De Hofbogen: Het Langste Gebouw van Rotterdam." http://www.hofbogen.nl/IMG/pdf/Toekomstvisie.pdf (accessed 2 May 2016).

Crossa, V. (2009) "Resisting the Entrepreneurial City: Street Vendors' Struggle in Mexico City's Historic Center." *International Journal of Urban and Regional Research* 33(1): 43–63.

Cunningham, M. (2001) "One Street at a Time: Gansevoort Street." *New York Times*, 16 September. http://www.nytimes.com/2001/09/16/magazine/one-street-at-a-time-gansevoort-street.html (accessed 31 August 2011).

Curran, W., and T. Hamilton (2012) "Just Green Enough: Contesting Environmental Gentrification in Greenpoint, Brooklyn." *Local Environment* 17(9): 1027–1042.

Dasgupta, S. (2013) "Permanent Transiency, Tele-visual Spectacle, and the Slum at Postcolonial Monument." *South Asian Studies* 29(1): 147–157.

DataFolha Institute of Research (2014) "Termômetro Paulistano—Elevado Costa e Silva." 16 and 27 September. http://media.folha.uol.com.br/datafolha/2014/09/23/termometro-elevado-costa-e-silva.pdf (accessed 15 March 2016).

David, J. (2002) *Reclaiming the High Line*. New York: Design Trust for Public Space with Friends of the High Line.

David, J., and R. Hammond (2011) *High Line: The Inside Story of New York City's Park in the Sky*. New York: Farrar, Straus and Giroux.

Davidson, J. (2009) "Elevated: The Twin Pleasures of the High Line: A Petite New Park, and a District of Lively Architecture." *New York*, 7 June. http://nymag.com/arts/architecture/features/57176 (accessed 20 May 2016).

Debord, G. (2008) "Introduction to a Critique of Urban Geography." In H. Bauder and S. Engel-Di Mauro (eds.), *Critical Geographies: A Collection of Readings*. Kelowna, BC: Praxis (e)Press, 23–27.

Debucquoy-Dodley, D. (2012) "New York's High Line Goes from Train Tracks to Elevated City Park." CNN, http://www.cnn.com/2012/09/28/travel/high-line-new-york-grows/index.html (accessed 26 November 2012).

de Certeau, M. (1984) *The Practice of Everyday Life*. Berkeley: University of California Press.

———. (2000) "Walking in the City." In G. Ward (ed.), *The Certeau Reader*. London: Blackwell, 101–119.

Dehaene, M., and L. De Cauter (eds.) (2008) *Heterotopia and the City: Public Space in a Postcivil Society*. Milton Park, UK: Routledge.

De Monchaux, T. (2005) "How Everyone Jumped Aboard a Railroad to Nowhere." *New York Times*, 8 May, A6.

Dennis, R. (2008) *Cities in Modernity: Representations and Productions of Metropolitan Space, 1840–1930*. Cambridge Studies in Historical Geography. Cambridge: Cambridge University Press.

Design Trust for Public Space (n.d.) "Reclaiming the High Line: 1999–2002."

Design Trust for Public Space and Friends of the High Line (2002) *Reclaiming the High Line*. New York: Design Trust for Public Space.

DeSilvey, C. (2006) "Observed Decay: Telling Stories with Mutable Things." *Journal of Material Culture* 11(3): 318–338.

DeSilvey, C., and T. Edensor (2012) "Reckoning with Ruins." *Progress in Human Geography* 37(4): 465–485.

De Solà-Morales, I. ([1993] 2014) "Terrain Vague." In P. Barron and M. Mariani (eds.), *Terrain Vague: Interstices at the Edge of the Pale*. London: Routledge, 24–30.

Donald, B., et al. (2014) "Austerity in the City: Economic Crisis and Urban Service Decline?" *Cambridge Journal of Regions, Economy and Society* 7: 3–15.

Dooling, S. (2009) "Ecological Gentrification: A Research Agenda Exploring Justice in the City." *International Journal of Urban and Regional Research* 33(3): 621–639.

———. (2012) "Sustainability Planning, Ecological Gentrification, and the Production of Urban Vulnerabilities." In S. Dooling and G. Simon (eds.), *Cities, Nature, and Development: The Politics and Production of Urban Vulnerabilities*. Burlington, VT: Ashgate, 101–119.

Draper, J. (1996) "The Art and Science of Park Planning in the United States: Chicago's Small Parks." In M. Sies and C. Silver (eds.), *Planning the Twentieth Century American City*. Baltimore, MD: Johns Hopkins University Press, 98–119.

Duany, A., and E. Talen (2013) *Landscape Urbanism and Its Discontents: Dissimulating the Sustainable City*. Gabriola Island, BC: New Society Publishers.

Duggan, L. (2003) *The Twilight of Equality? Neoliberalism, Cultural Politics, and the Attack on Democracy*. Boston: Beacon Press.

Duneier, M. (1999) *Sidewalk*. New York: Farrar, Straus and Giroux.

Dunlap, D. W. (1991) "Elevated Freight Line Being Razed amid Protests." *New York Times*, 15 January, B1.

———. (1999) "In West Village, a Developers' Gold Rush." *New York Times*, 29 August, 11.

Edensor, T. (2005) *Industrial Ruins: Space, Aesthetics and Materiality*. Oxford: Berg.

Eizenberg, E. (2012) "Actually Existing Commons: Three Moments of Space of Community Gardens in New York City." *Antipode* 44: 764–782.

11th Street Bridge Park (2015) *Equitable Development Plan*. https://indd.adobe.com/view/f22c1340-3bc2-4fff-94da-cde1395bef99 (accessed 16 May 2016).

Ellin, N. (2013) "Urbanism—New, Landscape, or Otherwise: The Case for Complementarity." In A. Duany and E. Talen (eds.), *Landscape Urbanism and Its Discontents: Dissimulation the Sustainable City*. Gabriola Island, BC: New Society, 281–292.

Empson, W. (1974) *Some Versions of Pastoral*. New York: New Directions.

Estado de São Paulo (1970) "Elevado, o Triste Futuro da Avenida." 1 December.

Evernden, N. (1992) *The Social Creation of Nature*. Baltimore, MD: Johns Hopkins University Press.

Fainstein, S. (2010) *The Just City*. Ithaca, NY: Cornell University Press.

Federal Native Plant Conservation Committee (1994) "Memorandum of Understanding Establishing the Federal Native Plant Conservation Committee." http://www.blm.gov/wo/st/en/prog/more/fish_wildlife_and/plants/pca/pca_mou.html (accessed 20 August 2015).

Fehrenbacher, J. (2014) "Interview: Landscape Architect James Corner on NYC's High Line Park." Inhabit.com. http://inhabitat.com/interview-architect-james-corner-on-the-design-of-high-line (accessed 4 October 2013).

Fenton, J. (2004) "A World Where Action Is the Sister of Dream: Surrealism and Anticapitalism in Contemporary Paris." *Antipode* 36: 942–962.

Filler, M. (2009) "Up in the Park." *New York Review of Books*, 13 August.

Fisher, M. (2011) Informal interview with T. Baker, 5 July.

Florida, R. (2002) *The Rise of the Creative Class: And How It's Transforming Work, Leisure, Community, and Everyday Life*. New York: Basic Books.

Flusty, S. (1994) *Building Paranoia: The Proliferation of Interdictory Space and the Erosion of Spatial Justice*. Los Angeles: Los Angeles Forum for Architecture and Urban Design.

Foderaro, L. (2011) "Record $20 Million Gift to Help Finish High Line." *New York Times*, 26 October. http://www.nytimes.com/2011/10/27/nyregion/20-million-gift-to-high-line-park.html (accessed 20 May 2016).

———. (2013a) "In Queens, Taking the High Line as a Model." *New York Times*, 7 January. http://www.nytimes.com/2013/01/08/nyregion/queens-wants-to-transform-an-abandoned-railway-into-a-park.html (accessed 20 May 2016).

———. (2013b) "New York Parks in Less Affluent Areas Lack Big Gifts." *New York Times,* 17 February.

———. (2014a) "A Plan to Turn a Queens Railway into a Park." *New York Times,* 14 October. http://www.nytimes.com/2014/10/14/nyregion/a-plan-to-turn-a-queens-railway-into-a-park.html?emc=eta1 (accessed 20 May 2016).

———. (2014b) "With Training Program, Central Park Conservancy Spreads Its Wealth." *New York Times,* 19 October.

———. (2014c) "At a Bronx Park, Dreams of Greener Landscapes." *New York Times,* 2 November.

Foster, J. (2010) "Off Track, in Nature: Constructing Ecology on Old Rail Lines in Paris and New York." *Nature and Culture* 5(3): 316–337.

Foster, J., and L. A. Sandberg (2004) "Friend or Foe? Invasive Species in Public Green Space in Toronto." *Geographical Review* 94(2): 178–198.

Foucault, M. ([1967] 2008) "Of Other Spaces." In M. Dehaene and L. de Cauter (eds. and trans.), *Heterotopia and the City: Public Space in a Postcivil Society.* Milton Park, UK: Routledge: 13–29.

Foundation Consortium (n.d.) "Framework for Inclusive Governance." http://racialequitytools.org/resourcefiles/foundationconsortium.pdf (accessed 20 May 2016).

Fox, T. (1990) *Urban Open Space: An Investment That Pays.* New York: Neighborhood Open Space Coalition.

Franck, K., and Q. Stevens (2006) *Loose Space: Possibility and Diversity in Urban Life.* London: Routledge.

Friedmann, J., and G. Wolff (1982) "World City Formation: An Agenda for Research and Action." *International Journal of Urban and Regional Research* 6(3): 309–344.

Friends of the High Line (2004) "James Corner Field Operations and Diller Scofidio + Renfro." http://www.thehighline.org/design/design-team-selection/field-operations-diller-scofidio-renfro (accessed 26 November 2012).

———. (2005) "Major Federal Authorization for High Line Project." 13 June. http://www.thehighline.org (accessed 11 April 2011).

———. (2008a) "Friends of the High Line and City Unveil New Images, Plans for Park Now under Construction." 25 June. http://www.thehighline.org (accessed 11 April 2011).

———. (2008b). *Designing the High Line: From Gansevoort Street to 30th Street.* New York: Friends of the High Line.

———. (2009) "High Line Improvement District FAQs." http://assets.thehighline.org/pdf/id_faq.pdf (accessed 11 April 2011).

———. (2010–2012) "IRS Form 990 Return of Organization Exempt from Income Tax."

———. (2012) "High Line Plant List." http://assets.thehighline.org/pdf/12_High%20Line%20Plant%20List.pdf (accessed 20 May 2016).

———. (2013a) "Beyond the High Line: Building Equitable Cities and Public Spaces." https://www.youtube.com/watch?v=dywxsvp1bua (accessed 20 May 2016).

———. (2013b) "Sustainability." http://www.thehighline.org/sustainability (accessed 31 January 2013).

———. (2014a) "2014 Corporate Membership." January. http://assets.thehighline.org/pdf/2014-corporate-membership-brochure.pdf (accessed 17 January 2015).

———. (2014b) "The High Line." http://www.thehighline.org.

———. (2015) "Plant of the Week." http://www.thehighline.org/blog/tagged/plant-of-the-week (accessed 20 May 2016).

———. (n.d.) "About Friends of the High Line." http://www.thehighline.org/about/friends-of-the-high-line (accessed 4 October 2014).

Friends of the QueensWay (2013) "QueensWay & the Case for Enhanced Property Values." 10 July. http://thequeensway.org/queensway-the-case-for-enhanced-property-values (accessed 20 May 2016).

———. (2014) "Plan Overview." http://thequeensway.org/the-plan/plan-overview (accessed 20 May 2016).

———. (n.d.) "About Us." http://www.thequeensway.org/about-us (accessed 6 October 2013).

Frisby, D. (2001) *Cityscapes of Modernity*. Cambridge: Polity Press.

Frúgoli, H., Jr. (2006) *Centralidade em São Paulo: Trajetórias, Conflitos e Negociações na Metrópole*. São Paulo: Edusp.

Fullilove, M. (2013) *Urban Alchemy: Restoring Joy in America's Sorted-Out Cities*. New York: New Village Press.

Fung, A., and E. Olin Wright (2003) *Deepening Democracy: Institutional Innovations in Empowered Participatory Governance*. New York: Verso.

Gabriel, N. (2014) "Urban Political Ecology: Environmental Imaginary, Governance, and the Non-human." *Geography Compass* 8(1): 38–48.

Gandy, M. (2003) *Concrete and Clay: Reworking Nature in New York City*. Cambridge, MA: MIT Press.

———. (2012) "Queer Ecology: Nature, Sexuality, and Heterotopic Alliances." *Environment and Planning D: Society and Space* 30(4): 727–747.

———. (2013) "Marginalia: Aesthetics, Ecology, and Urban Wastelands." *Annals of the Association of American Geographers* 103(6): 1301–1316.

Garcia, R. (2012) "High Bridge, High Line, and High Brow: Green Justice from New York to Los Angeles." http://www.kcet.org/socal/departures/columns/green-justice/high-bridge-high-line-and-high-brow-green-justice-from-new-york-to-los-angeles.html (accessed 7 April 2015).

Garrett, B. (2013) *Explore Everything: Place-Hacking the City*. London: Verso.

Gay, T. (2004) "Bring Back the Beefcake, and Add Some Flowers Too." *Villager* 74 (11/July 14–20). http://www.thevillager.com/villager_63/bringbackthebeefcake.html (accessed 31 August 2011).

Gehl, J. (2010) *Cities for People*. New York: Island Press.

Genocchio, B. (1995). "Discourse, Discontinuity, Difference: The Question of 'Other' Spaces." In S. Watson and K. Gibson (eds.), *Postmodern Cities and Spaces*. Oxford: Blackwell, 35–46.

Ghertner, D. A. (2010) "Calculating without Numbers: Aesthetic Governmentality in Delhi's Slums." *Economy and Society* 39(2): 185–217.

Gibbs, D., and A.E.G. Jonas (2000) "Governance and Regulation in Local Environmental Policy: The Utility of a Regime Approach." *Geoforum* 31(3): 299–313.

Gibson, D. W. (2015) *The Edge Becomes the Center: An Oral History of Gentrification in the 21st Century* (Kindle version). New York: Overlook Press.

Giffney, N., and M. J. Hird (eds.) (2008) *Queering the Non/Human*. Aldershot, UK: Ashgate.

Gilbertson, A. (2009) "Up over Chelsea, Something Saved, Something Lost." *New York Times*, 3 September. http://www.nytimes.com/2009/09/06/nyregion/06album.html (accessed 14 June 2011).

Gobster, P. H. (2007) "Urban Park Restoration and the 'Museumification' of Nature." *Nature and Culture* 2(2): 95–114.

Goldberger, P. (2011) "Miracle above Manhattan." *National Geographic*, April. http://ngm.nationalgeographic.com/2011/04/ny-high-line/goldberger-text (accessed 10 June 2015).

———. (2014) "The Final Segment of the High Line Is Stunningly Refreshing." *Vanity Fair*, September. http://www.vanityfair.com/unchanged/2014/09/high-line-final-segment-new-york (accessed 21 May 2016).

Gopnik, A. (2001) "A Walk on the High Line / The Allure of a Derelict Railroad Track in Spring." In J. Sternfeld, *Walking the High Line*. New York: Steidl/Pace/MacGill Gallery, 44–47.

Gottlieb, M. (1984) "Rail Fan Finds Rusting Dream of West Side." *New York Times*, 16 January, B1.

Gould, K., and T. Lewis (2009) "The Environmental Injustice of Green Gentrification: Socio-ecological Change in the Neighborhoods of Brooklyn." Paper presented at the annual meeting of the American Sociological Association, Hilton San Francisco, 7 August.

Graham, S., and N. Thrift (2007) "Out of Order: Understanding Repair and Maintenance Theory." *Culture and Society* 24(3): 1–25.

Greenberg, M. (2008) *Branding New York: How a City in Crisis Was Sold to the World*. New York: Routledge.

Gröning, G., and J. Wolschke-Bulmahn (1992) "Some Notes on the Mania for Native Plants in Germany." *Landscape Journal* 11(2): 116–126.

Grosz, E. (2005) *Time Travels: Feminism, Nature, Power*. Durham, NC: Duke University Press.

Grynbaum, B. (2014) "High Line Draws Millions, but de Blasio Isn't One." *New York Times*, 1 October.

Hackworth, J. (2002) "Postrecession Gentrification in New York City." *Urban Affairs Review* 37(6): 815–843.

———. (2007) *The Neoliberal City: Governance, Ideology, and Development in American Urbanism*. Ithaca, NY: Cornell University Press.

Hackworth, J., and N. Smith (2001) "The Changing State of Gentrification." *Tijdschrift voor Economische en Sociale Geografie* 92(4): 464–477.

Halberstam, J. (2005) *In a Queer Time and Place: Transgender Bodies, Subcultural Lives*. New York: New York University Press.

———. (2011) *The Queer Art of Failure*. Durham, NC: Duke University Press.

Hall, T., and P. Hubbard (1996) "The Entrepreneurial City: New Urban Politics, New Urban Geographies?" *Progress in Human Geography* 20(2): 153–174.

Halle, D., and E. Tiso (2014) *New York's New Edge: Contemporary Art, the High Line, and Urban Megaprojects on the Far West Side*. Chicago: University of Chicago Press.

Hamilton, W. (2006) "A Fence with More Beauty, Fewer Barbs." *New York Times*, 18 June.

Hammond, R. (2011) Interview with T. Baker, 1 July.

Harvey, D. (1981) "The Spatial Fix: Hegel, von Thunen, and Marx." *Antipode* 13(3): 1–12.

———. (1989a) *The Condition of Postmodernity*. Malden, MA: Blackwell.

———. (1989b) "From Managerialism to Entrepreneurialism: The Transformation of Urban Politics in Late Capitalism." *Geografiska Annaler* 71B(1): 3–17.

———. (1990) *The Condition of Postmodernity: An Enquiry into the Origins of Cultural Change*. Cambridge, MA: Blackwell.

———. (1999) *The Limits to Capital*. London: Verso.

———. (2001) "Globalization and the 'Spatial Fix.'" *Geographische Revue* 2: 23–30.

———. (2002) *Spaces of Capital: Towards a Critical Geography*. New York: Routledge.

———. (2005) *A Brief History of Neoliberalism*. New York: Oxford University Press.

———. (2012) *Rebel Cities: From the Right to the City to the Urban Revolution*. London: Verso.

Hauck, T., R. Keller, and V. Kleinekort (eds.) (2011) *Infrastructural Urbanism: Addressing the In-Between*. Rotterdam: DOM Publishers.

Head, L., and J. Atchison (2008) "Cultural Ecology: Emerging Human-Plant Geographies." *Progress in Human Geography* 33(2): 236–245.

Heathcott, J. (2013) "The Promenade Plantée: Politics, Planning, and Urban Design in Postindustrial Paris." *Journal of Planning Education and Research* 33(3): 280–291.

Heins, S. (2016) "Here's What the High Line's Upcoming 'Spur' Expansion Will Look Like." *Gothamist*. http://gothamist.com/2016/02/18/high_line_expansion_spur.php#photo-1 (accessed 16 May 2016).

Heisey, R. M. (1997) "Allelopathy and the Secret Life of *Ailanthus altissima*." *Arnoldia* 57(3): 28–36.

Hell, J., and A. Schönle (eds.) (2010) *Ruins of Modernity*. Durham, NC: Duke University Press.

Herman, M. (2009) "Fighting to Save the High Line, before It Was Chic." *Villager*. http://www.thevillager.com/villager_328/talkingpoint.html (accessed 22 February 2013).

Hetherington, K. (1997) *The Badlands of Modernity: Heterotopia and Social Ordering*. London: Routledge.

Heynen, N. (2006) "The Political Ecology of Uneven Urban Green Space: The Impact of Political Economy on Race and Ethnicity in Producing Environmental Inequality in Milwaukee." *Urban Affairs Review* 42(1): 3–25.

———. (2013). "Urban Political Ecology I: The Urban Century." *Progress in Human Geography* 38(4): 598–604.

Heynen, N., M. Kaika, and E. Swyngedouw (eds.) (2006). *In the Nature of Cities: Urban Political Ecology and the Politics of Urban Metabolism*. London: Routledge.

Hitchings, R. (2003) "People, Plants, and Performance: On Actor Network Theory and the Material Pleasures of the Private Garden." *Social & Cultural Geography* 4(1): 99–114.

Hitchings, R., and V. Jones (2004) "Living with Plants and the Exploration of Botanical Encounter within Human Geographic Research Practice." *Ethics, Place & Environment* 7(1–2): 3–18.

Hubbard, P. (2004) "Cleansing the Metropolis: Sex Work and the Politics of Zero Tolerance." *Urban Studies* 41(9): 1687–1702.

Hunt, J. D. (1992) *Gardens and the Picturesque: Studies in the History of Landscape Architecture.* Cambridge, MA: MIT Press.

———. (2000) *Greater Perfections: The Practice of Garden Theory.* Philadelphia: University of Pennsylvania Press.

———. (2004) *The Afterlife of Gardens.* Philadelphia: University of Pennsylvania Press.

Hunt, S. (2009) "Citizenship's Place: The State's Creation of Public Space and Street Vendors' Culture of Informality in Bogota, Colombia." *Environment and Planning D* 27(2): 331–351.

Husock, H. (2013) "Bill de Blasio's Philanthropy Fallacies." *Forbes,* 31 October. http://www.forbes.com/sites/howardhusock/2013/10/31/bill-de-blasios-philanthropy-fallacies (accessed 20 May 2016).

———. (2014) "NYC Parks and the Politics of Envy." *New York Post,* 3 December.

Inam, A. (2014) "Should We Love or Hate the High Line?" http://trulab.org/blog/2014/9/26/should-we-love-or-hate-the-high-line (accessed 20 May 2016).

Ingram, G. B. (2010) "Fragments, Edges, Matrices: Retheorizing the Formation of a So-called Gay Ghetto through Queering Landscape Ecology." In C. Sandilands and B. Erickson (eds.), *Queer Ecologies: Sex, Nature, Desire, Politics.* Bloomington: Indiana University Press, 254–282.

Ingram, G. B., A.-M. Bouthillette, and Y. Retter (eds.) (1997) *Queers in Space: Communities | Public Places | Sites of Resistance.* Seattle: Bay Press.

Iovine, J. V. (2004) "Elevated Visions." *New York Times,* 11 July. http//www.nytimes.com/2004/07/11/arts/architecture-elevated-visions.html (accessed 31 May 2011).

Jacobs, J. (1961) *The Death and Life of Great American Cities.* New York: Random House.

Jacobs, K. (2009) "Beyond the Hype." *Metropolis,* 17 June. http://www.metropolismag.com/story/20090617/beyond-the-hype (accessed 20 June 2011).

Johnson, P. (2006) "Unravelling Foucault's 'Different Spaces.'" *History of the Human Sciences* 19(4): 75–90.

———. (2013) "The Geographies of Heterotopia." *Geography Compass* 7(11): 790–803.

Jones, G. A. (2011) "Slumming About." *City: Analysis of Urban Trends, Culture, Theory, Policy, Action* 16(6): 696–708.

Jones, O., and P. Cloke (2008) "Non-Human Agencies: Trees in Place and Time." In C. Knappett and L. Malafouris (eds.), *Material Agency.* Boston: Springer, 79–96.

Jordan, S., and C. Lindner (eds.) (2016) *Cities Interrupted: Visual Culture and Urban Space.* London: Bloomsbury.

Jose, K. (2010) "Playgrounds for Plutocrats: Who Pays for Parks?" http://www.capitalnewyork.com/article/politics/2010/12/1015139/playgrounds-plutocrats-who-pays-parks (accessed 3 April 2013).

Jubas, K. (2007) "Conceptual Con/fusion in Democratic Societies: Understandings and Limitations of Consumer-Citizenship." *Journal of Consumer Culture* 7(2): 231–254.

Kaminer, T., M. Robles-Duran, and H. Sohn (eds.) (2011) *Urban Asymetries: Studies and Projects in Neoliberal Urbanization.* Delft School of Design Series on Architecture and Urbanism. Rotterdam: 010 Publishers.

Katz, C. (1998) "Whose Nature, Whose Culture? Private Productions of Space and the 'Preservation' of Nature." In B. Braun and N. Castree (eds.), *Remaking Reality: Nature at the Millennium*. London: Routledge, 45–62.

Kilgannon, C. (1999) "Fight over Unused Rail Line." *New York Times*, 16 May, 8.

———. (2010) "High Line's Next Phase: Less Glitz, More Glamour." *New York Times*, 19 December. http://cityroom.blogs.nytimes.com/2010/12/19/high-lines-next-phase-less-glitz-more-intimacy/?ref=highlinenyc (accessed 16 June 2011).

Kimmelman, M. (2014) "Mayor de Blasio's Plan for Parks Needs to Grow." *New York Times*, 28 October.

Kirkwood, N. (ed.) (2001) *Manufactured Sites: Rethinking the Post-Industrial Landscape*. London: Spoon Press.

Klingle, M. (2007) *Emerald City: An Environmental History of Seattle*. New Haven, CT: Yale University Press.

Knopp, L. (2004) "Ontologies of Place, Placelessness, and Movement: Queer Quests for Identity and Their Impacts on Contemporary Geographic Thought." *Gender, Place, and Culture: A Journal of Feminist Geography* 11(1): 121–134.

———. (2007a) "From Lesbian and Gay to Queer Geographies: Pasts, Prospects, and Possibilities." In K. Browne, J. Lim, and G. Brown (eds.), *Geographies of Sexualities: Theories, Practices, and Politics*. Aldershot, UK: Ashgate, 21–28.

———. (2007b) "On the Relationship between Queer and Feminist Geographies." *Professional Geographer* 59(1): 47–55.

Koolhaas, R. (1972) *Exodus, or the Voluntary Prisoners of Architecture*. London: Architectural Association.

———. (1978) *Delirious New York: A Retroactive Manifesto for Manhattan*. London: Thames & Hudson.

Kotz, L. (2001) "Post-Cagean Aesthetics and the 'Event' Score." *October* 95: 54–89.

Kovaleski, S. (2009) "With High Line's Success, Rewards for Robert Hammond." *New York Times*, 25 August. http://www.nytimes.com/2009/08/26/nyregion/26hiline.html?pagewanted=all&_r=0 (accessed 28 January 2013).

Krinke, R. (2001) "Overview: Design Practice and Manufactured Sites." In N. Kirkwood (ed.), *Manufactured Sites: Rethinking the Post-Industrial Landscape*. London: Spoon Press, 125–148.

Krueger, R. (2011) "Amanda Burden on Creating Value with Urban Open Space." *Urban Land*, 23 November. http://urbanland.uli.org/Aritcles/2011/Fa1111/KruegerBurdenVid (accessed 24 November 2015).

Lacayo, R. (2007) "Walk on the Wild Side." *Time*, 18 January. http://www.time.com/time/magazine/article/0,9171,1580397,00.html (accessed 22 May 2016).

LaFarge, A. (2014) *On the High Line: Exploring America's Most Original Urban Park*. New York: Thames & Hudson.

Langhorst, J. (2014) "Re-presenting Transgressive Ecologies: Post-industrial Sites as Contested Terrains." *Local Environment* 19(10): 1110–1133.

Larson, S. (2013) *Building like Moses with Jacobs in Mind: Contemporary Planning in New York City*. Philadelphia: Temple University Press.

Lawhon, M., H. Ernstson, and J. Silver (2014) "Provincializing Urban Political Ecology: Towards a Situated UPE through African Urbanism." *Antipode* 46: 497–516.

Lawrence, J. G., A. Colwell, and O. J. Sexton (1991) "The Ecological Impact of Allelopathy in *Ailanthus altissima* (Simaroubaceae)." *American Journal of Botany* 78(7): 948–958.

Le, V. (2015) "Are You or Your Organization Guilty of Trickle Down Community Engagement?" *Non Profit with Balls* (blog). http://nonprofitwithballs.com/2015/01/are-you-or-your-org-guilty-of-trickle-down-community-engagement/#more-1933 (accessed 6 April 2016).

Lee, L. (2004) "Glamour Rides the Rail." *New York Times*, 18 July, ST4.

Lees, L. (2003) "Super-gentrification: The Case of Brooklyn Heights, New York City." *Urban Studies* 40(12): 2487–2509.

Lees, L., T. Slater, and E. Wyly (2008) *Gentrification*. New York: Routledge.

Lefebvre, H. (1968) *Le droit de la ville*. Paris: Anthopos.

———. ([1974] 1991) *The Production of Space*. D. Nicholson-Smith (trans.). Oxford: Blackwell.

———. (1996) *Writings on Cities*. E. Kofman and E. Lebas (eds. and trans.). London: Blackwell.

Levere, M. (2014) *The Highline Park and Timing of Capitalization of Public Goods*. San Diego: University of California, San Diego.

Levine, M. (2014) "New York City Needs a Parks System Which Is Both Fair and Fabulous." http://www.huffingtonpost.com/mark-d-levine/new-york-city-parks-system_b_5002092.html (accessed 20 May 2016).

Ley, D. (1996) *The New Middle Class and the Remaking of the Central City*. Oxford: Oxford University Press.

———. (2003) "Artists, Aestheticisation, and the Field of Gentrification." *Urban Studies* 40(12): 2527–2544.

Lindner, C. (2008) "New York Undead: Globalization, Landscape Urbanism, and the Afterlife of the Twin Towers." *Journal of American Culture* 31(3): 302–314.

———. (2013) "Smart Cities and Slowness." *Urban Pamphleteer* 1: 14–16.

———. (2015) *Imagining New York City: Literature, Urbanism, and the Visual Arts, 1890–1940*. New York: Oxford University Press.

Lindner, C., and M. Meissner (2015) "Slow Art in the Creative City: Amsterdam, Street Photography, and Urban Renewal." *Space and Culture* 18(1): 4–24.

Lindquist, K. (2012) "Community Perspective: Letters from Supporters." http://www.thehighline.org/blog/2012/08/30/community-perspective-letters-from-supporters (accessed 20 May 2016).

Littke, H., R. Locke, and T. Haas (2015) "Taking the High Line: Elevated Parks, Transforming Neighbourhoods, and the Ever-Changing Relationship between the Urban and Nature." *Journal of Urbanism: International Research on Placemaking and Urban Sustainability*, (9 July): 1–19, doi:10.1080/17549175.2015.1063532.

Loftus, A. (2012) *Everyday Environmentalism: Creating an Urban Political Ecology*. Minneapolis: University of Minnesota Press.

Logan, J., and H. Molotch (1998) *Urban Fortunes: The Political Economy of Place*. Berkeley: University of California Press.

Loughran, K. (2014) "Parks for Profit: The High Line, Growth Machines, and the Uneven Development of Urban Public Spaces." *City and Community* 13(1): 49–68.

Low, S., and N. Smith (eds.) (2006) *The Politics of Public Space*. New York: Routledge.

Low, S., D. Taplin, and S. Scheld (2005) *Rethinking Urban Parks: Public Space and Cultural Diversity*. Austin: University of Texas Press.

Lydon, M., and A. Garcia (2015) *Tactical Urbanism: Short-Term Action for Long-Term Change*. Washington, DC: Island Press.

Lynch, K. (1960) *The Image of the City*. Cambridge, MA: MIT Press.

Mabey, R. (2010) *Weeds: In Defense of Nature's Most Unloved Plants*. New York: HarperCollins.

Machor, J. L. (1987) *Pastoral Cities: Urban Ideals and the Symbolic Landscape of America*. Madison: University of Wisconsin Press.

MacLeod, G. (2011) "Urban Politics Reconsidered: Growth Machine to Post-democratic City?" *Urban Studies* 48(12): 2629–2660.

Madden, D. J. (2010) "Revisiting the End of Public Space: Assembling the Public in an Urban Park." *City & Community* 9(2): 187–207.

Malone, K. (2002) "Street Life: Youth, Culture and Competing Uses of Public Space." *Environment and Urbanization* 14(2): 157–168.

Marchand, Y., and R. Meffre (2010) *The Ruins of Detroit*. Gottingen, DE: Steidl.

Mariani, M., and P. Barron (eds.) (2013) *Terrain Vague: Interstices at the Edge of the Pale*. London: Routledge.

Martinez, M. J. (2010) *Power at the Roots: Gentrification, Community Gardens, and the Puerto Ricans of the Lower East Side*. Plymouth, UK: Lexington Books.

Marx, L. (1964) *The Machine in the Garden: Technology and the Pastoral Ideal in America*. New York: Oxford University Press.

Maskovsky, J., and J. Brash (2014) "Governance: Beyond the Neoliberal City." In D. Nonini (ed.), *A Companion to Urban Anthropology*. New York: Wiley, 255–270.

Massey, D. (2005) *For Space*. New York: Sage.

Mattern, S. (2016) "Instrumental City: The View from Hudson Yards, circa 2019." *Places Journal* (April). https://placesjournal.org/article/instrumental-city-new-york-hudson-yards (accessed 16 May 2016).

McCann, E. (2004) "Best Places: Interurban Competition, Quality of Life, and Popular Media Discourse." *Urban Studies* 41(10): 1909–1929.

McCann, E., and K. Ward (eds.) (2011) *Mobile Urbanism: Cities and Policymaking in the Global Age*. Minneapolis: University of Minnesota Press.

McGeehan, P. (2011) "The High Line Isn't Just a Sight to See; It's also an Economic Dynamo." *New York Times*, 5 June, A18. http://www.nytimes.com/2011/06/06/nyregion/with-next-phase-ready-area-around-high-line-is-flourishing.html (accessed 26 November 2012).

McGinn, D. (2014) "The High Line Effect: Why Cities around the World (Including Toronto) Are Building Parks in the Sky." *Toronto Globe and Mail*, 1 October.

McKinney, C. (2011) Interview by T. Baker, 21 June.

McPeck, E., K. Morgan, and C. Zaitzevsky (1983) *Olmsted in Massachusetts: The Public Legacy*. Brookline: Massachusetts Association for Olmsted Parks.

Menking, W. (2011) Interview by T. Baker, 21 June.

Miles, S., and R. Paddison (2005) "Introduction: The Rise and Rise of Culture-Led Urban Regeneration." *Urban Studies* 43(5/6): 833–839.

Miller, K. (2007) *Designs on the Public: The Private Lives of New York's Public Spaces*. Minneapolis: University of Minnesota Press.

Millington, N. (2015) "From Urban Scar to 'Park in the Sky': Terrain Vague, Urban Design, and the Remaking of New York City's High Line Park." *Environment and Planning A* 47: 1–15.

Mitchell, D. (1995) "The End of Public Space? People's Park, Definitions of the Public and Democracy." *Annals of the Association of American Geographers* 85(1): 108–133.

———. (1997) "The Annihilation of Space by Law: The Roots and Implications of Anti-homeless Laws in the United States." *Antipode* 29(3): 303–335.

Molotch, H. (1976) "The City as Growth Machine: Toward a Political Economy of Place." *American Journal of Sociology* 82(2): 309–332.

Morris, K. (2014) "New Entry in Meatpacking District: Building Is Being Redeveloped as Restoration Hardware Store." *Wall Street Journal*, 13 October. http://www.wsj.com/articles/new-entry-in-meatpacking-district-1413251657 (accessed 15 October 2015).

Moss, J. (2012) "Op-Ed: Disney World on the Hudson." *New York Times*, 21 August. http://www.nytimes.com/2012/08/22/opinion/in-the-shadows-of-the-high-line.html?_r=1& (accessed 20 May 2016).

———. (2013) "Blue-Collar High Line." *Jeremiah's Vanishing New York*, 2 July.

Mossberger, K., and G. Stoker (2001) "The Evolution of Urban Regime Theory: The Challenge of Conceptualization." *Urban Affairs Review* 36(6): 810–835.

Mould, O. (2009) "Parkour, the City, the Event." *Environment and Planning D* 27(4): 738–750.

Muñoz, J. E. (2009) *Cruising Utopia: The Then and There of Queer Futurity*. New York: New York University Press.

New York City Department of City Planning (2005) "Final Environmental Impact Statement for the West Chelsea Zoning Proposal." New York: Department of City Planning.

———. (2013a) "The Newest New Yorkers." http://www1.nyc.gov/site/planning/data-maps/nyc-population/newest-new-yorkers-2013.page (accessed 6 September 2016).

———. (2013b) "Study for the Potential Expansion of the Special West Chelsea District." http://www1.nyc.gov/site/planning/plans/special-west-chelsea/special-west-chelsea.page (accessed 6 September 2016).

New York City Department of Parks and Recreation (2009) "The Daily Plant: First Section of the High Line Park Opens to the Public." https://www.nycgovparks.org/news/daily-plant?id=21962 (accessed 6 September 2016).

New York City Economic Development Corporation (2011) "Economic Snapshot: A Summary of New York City's Economy." August. http://www.nycedc.com/sites/default/files/files/economic-snapshot/EconomicSnapshotAugust2011_0.pdf (accessed 22 February 2013).

———. (2014) "High Line." http://www.nycedc.com/project/high-line.

New York Voices. "Joel Sternfeld" (2002) Thirteen/WNET, New York. http://archived.thehighline.org/content/new-york-voices-joel-sternfeld (accessed 27 April 2015).

Nickeas, P., and J. Gorner (2013) "Shooting of 13 at Park Puts Chicago Back in the Spotlight." *Chicago Tribune*, 20 September. http://www.chicagotribune.com/news/local/breaking/chi-multiple-people-including-3yearold-shot-in-south-side-attack-20130919.0.4108485.full.story (accessed 20 May 2016).

O'Connell, J. (2016) "Can D.C. Build a $45 Million Park for Anacostia without Pushing People Out?" *Washington Post*, 21 January. https://www.washingtonpost.com/lifestyle/magazine/can-dc-build-a-45-million-park-for-anacostia-without-pushing-people-out/2016/01/20/d96e9cde-a03c-11e5-8728-1af6af208198_story.html?utm_term=.622a3e837e55 (accessed 16 May 2016).

Office of Community Studies (2013) "QueensWay Diversity." http://qcurban.org/office-of-community-studies/our-work.

———. (2014) "A Community Impact Study of Proposed Uses of the Rockaway Beach Branch Right of Way." http://qcurban.org/office-of-community-studies/our-work/ (accessed 16 May 2016).

Oudolf, P., and N. Kingsbury (2005) *Planting Design: Gardens in Time and Space*. Portland, OR: Timber Press.

Ourousoff, N. (2009) "On High, a Fresh Outlook." *New York Times*, 10 June. http://www.nytimes.com/2009/06/10/arts/design/10high.html?pagewanted=all&_r=0.

Oxford English Dictionary Online (2012) "Abandoned, adj." Oxford University Press. http://www.oed.com.ezproxy.library.yorku.ca/view/Entry/74?redirectedFrom=abandoned (accessed 27 November 2012).

Pagano, M., C. Hoene, and C. McFarland (2012) "City Fiscal Conditions in 2012." National League of Cities. http://www.nlc.org/Documents/Find%20City%20Solutions/Research%20Innovation/Finance/city-fiscal-conditions-research-brief-rpt-sep12.pdf.

Page, M. (1999) *The Creative Destruction of Manhattan, 1900–1940*. Chicago: University of Chicago Press.

Pardue, D. (2007) "Hip Hop as Pedagogy: A Look into 'Heaven' and 'Soul' in São Paulo, Brazil." *Anthropological Quarterly* 80(3): 673–709.

———. (2010) "Making Territorial Claims: Brazilian Hip Hop and the Socio-Geographical Dynamics of Periferia." *City and Society* 22(1): 48–71.

———. (2015) "Lessons from São Paulo: A Deserved Shift in Urbanization Policy." *Postcolonialist*, 2 October. http://postcolonialist.com/civil-discourse/lessons-São-paulo-deserved-shift-urbanization-policy (accessed 16 May 2016).

Parker, B. (2009) "High Line Called Out for Using Amazon Wood." *Gothamist*, 24 September. http://gothamist.com/2009/09/24/high_line_called_out_for_using_amaz.php (accessed 16 May 2016).

Patrick, D. (2011) "The Politics of Urban Sustainability: Preservation, Redevelopment, and Landscape on the High Line." MA thesis, Central European University.

———. (2014) "The Matter of Displacement: A Queer Urban Ecology of New York City's High Line." *Social and Cultural Geography* 15(8): 920–941.

Pearsall, H. (2010) "From Brown to Green? Assessing Social Vulnerability to Environmental Gentrification in New York City." *Environment and Planning C: Government and Policy* 28(5): 872–886.

Peck, J. (2011) "Creative Moments: Working Culture, through Municipal Socialism and Neoliberal Urbanism." In E. McCann and K. Ward (eds.), *Mobile Urbanism: Cities and Policymaking in the Global Age*. Minneapolis: University of Minnesota Press, 41–70.

———. (2013) "Explaining (with) Neoliberalism." *Territory, Politics, Governance* 1(2): 132–157.

Peck, J., N. Theodore, and N. Brenner (2009) "Neoliberal Urbanism: Models, Moments, Mutations." *SAIS Review* 29(1): 49–66.

Peck, J., and A. Tickell (2002) "Neoliberalizing Space." *Antipode* 34(3): 380–404.

Pereira, I. (2014) "High Line's Third and Final Section Is Finished." *AM New York*, 18 September, http://www.amny.com/news/high-line-final-section-finished-1.9349965 (accessed 16 May 2016).

Perkins, H. (2009a) "Out from the (Green) Shadow? Neoliberal Hegemony through the Market Logic of Shared Urban Environmental Governance." *Political Geography* 28(7): 395–405.

———. (2009b) "Turning Feral Spaces into Trendy Places: A Coffee House in Every Park?" *Environment and Planning A* 41(11): 2615–2632.

———. (2010) "Green Spaces of Self-Interest within Shared Urban Governance." *Geography Compass* 4(3): 255–268.

———. (2013) "Consent to Neoliberal Hegemony through Coercive Urban Environmental Governance." *International Journal of Urban and Regional Research* 37(1): 311–327.

Piepenburg, E. (2012) "Under the High Line, a Gay Past." *New York Times*, 3 February. http://artsbeat.blogs.nytimes.com/2012/02/03/under-the-high-line-a-gay-past (accessed 22 February 2013).

Pincetl, S. (2003) "Nonprofits and Park Provision in Los Angeles: An Exploration of the Rise of Governance Approaches to the Provision of Local Services." *Social Science Quarterly* 84(4): 979–1001.

Pinder, D. (2000) "'Old Paris Is No More': Geographies of Spectacle and Anti-Spectacle." *Antipode* 32(4): 357–386.

———. (2011) "Errant Paths: The Poetics and Politics of Walking." *Environment and Planning D: Society and Space* 29(4): 672–692.

Pinkowitz, E. (2014) "The Power of Programming." *High Line Blog*. http://www.thehighline.org/blog/2014/06/13/the-power-of-programming (accessed 16 May 2016).

Pogrebin, R. (2004). "An Aesthetic Watchdog in the City Planning Office." *New York Times*, December 29, E1.

———. (2009a) "Renovated High Line Now Open for Strolling." *New York Times*, 8 June, C3. http://www.nytimes.com/2009/06/09/arts/design/09highline-RO.html (accessed 14 June 2011).

———. (2009b) "Philanthropist with a Sense of Timing Raises Her Profile." *New York Times*, 29 June. http://www.nytimes.com/2009/06/30/arts/30falcone.html (accessed 20 May 2016).

PolicyLink (2012) "The Community Engagement Guide for Sustainable Communities." http://www.policylink.org/sites/default/files/COMMUNITYENGAGEMENTGUIDE_LY_FINAL%20%281%29.pdf (accessed 20 May 2016).

Pollok-Morris, A. (2014) "Yard Meets Garden in High Line Phase 3." http://dirt.asla.org/2014/10/02/yard-meets-garden-in-high-line-phase-3/ (accessed 16 May 2016).

Polsky, S. (2009) "Arrested Artist Plans to Challenge High Line Art Selling Rules." *Gothamist,* December 7, Available at: http://ny.curbed.com/archives/2009/12/07/arrested_artist_plans_to_challenge_high_line_art_selling_rules.php (accessed 2 January 2011).

Potters, M. (2014) "Miljoenenimpuls voor verpauperde Hofbogen." *A.D.,* 9 October.

Powell, J. (2012) *Racing to Justice: Transforming Our Conceptions of Self and Other to Build an Inclusive Society.* Bloomington: Indiana University Press.

Powell, M. (2013a) "Park Deals Chip Away at City's Gems." *New York Times,* 29 April, A15.

———. (2013b) "Reducing Some City Parks to the Status of Beggars." *New York Times,* 27 May.

———. (2014) "Parks Department Takes a Seat behind Nonprofit Conservancies." *New York Times,* 3 February.

Quastel, N. (2009) "Political Ecologies of Gentrification." *Urban Geography* 30(7): 694–725.

Racca, D., and A. Dhanju (2006) "Property Value/Desirability Effects of Bike Paths Adjacent to Residential Areas." Project report prepared for Delaware Center for Transportation and the State of Delaware Department of Transportation. http://128.175.63.72/projects/DOCUMENTS/bikepathfinal.pdf (accessed 9 June 2012).

Rafter, D. (2012) "'Queens High Line' Faces Woodhaven Opposition." *Queens Chronicle,* 25 October. http://www.qchron.com/editions/south/queens-high-line-faces-woodhaven-opposition/article_aa628cc8-baee-500d-bb70-7bb3a82e3522.html (accessed 20 May 2016).

Raver, A. (2014) "Upstairs, a Walk on the Wild Side." *New York Times,* 3 September. http://www.nytimes.com/2014/09/07/arts/design/fall-arts-preview-unruly-final-section-of-high-line-to-open.html (accessed 18 August 2015).

Renfro, C. (2013) "Contingent City." Talk given as part of IDEAS CITY conference, São Paulo. 25–27 October. http://www.newmuseum.org/ideascity/global/view/sao-paulo.

Rice, J. L. (2014) "An Urban Political Ecology of Climate Change Governance." *Geography Compass* 8: 381–394.

Rigby, C. (2015) "Developers and Activists Battle over One of São Paulo's Few Remaining Green Spaces." *Vice News,* 28 January. https://news.vice.com/article/developers-and-activists-battle-over-one-of-so-paulos-few-remaining-green-spaces (accessed 20 May 2016).

Rios, M. (2014) "Learning from Informal Practices: Implications for Urban Design." In V. Mukhija and A. Loukaitou-Sideris (eds.), *The Informal American City: Beyond Taco Trucks and Day Labor.* Cambridge, MA: MIT Press, 173–192.

Robbins, P. (2004) "Comparing Invasive Networks: Cultural and Political Biographies of Invasive Species." *Geographical Review* 94(2): 139–156.

Rogers, E. B. (1987) *Rebuilding Central Park: A Management and Restoration Plan.* Cambridge, MA: MIT Press.

Rolnik, R. (2014) "Sobre Minhocão e Parques: Folha de São Paulo." 6 October. http://www1.folha.uol.com.br/colunas/raquelrolnik/2014/10/1527725-sobre-minhocao-e-parques.shtml (accessed 25 June 2015).

Rosa, B. (2014). "Beneath the Arches: Re-appropriating the Spaces of Infrastructure in Manchester." PhD diss., University of Manchester.

———. (2016) "Waste and Value in Urban Transformation: Reflections on a Post-Industrial 'Wasteland' in Manchester." In C. Lindner and M. Meissner (eds.), *Global Garbage: Urban Imaginaries of Waste, Excess, and Abandonment*. New York: Routledge, 242–271.

Rose, G. (2007) *Visual Methodologies: An Introduction to the Interpretation of Visual Methodologies*. 2nd ed. London: Sage.

Rosenberg, Z. (2014) "Ambitious Harlem 'High Line' Pitch Includes Affordable Housing." http://ny.curbed.com/archives/2014/10/16/ambitious_harlem_high_line_pitch_includes_affordable_housing.php (accessed 5 December 2015).

Rosenzweig, R., and E. Blackmar (1992) *The Park and the People: A History of Central Park*. Ithaca, NY: Cornell University Press.

Ross, L. (2011) Interview by T. Baker, 22 June.

Rothenberg, J., and S. Lang. (2015) "Repurposing the High Line: Aesthetic Experience and Contradiction in West Chelsea." *City, Culture, and Society*, October. doi:10.1016/j.ccs.2015.10.001.

RTV Rijnmond (2014) "Het is Nu of Nooit voor de Hofbogen in Rotterdam-Noord." 20 February. http://www.rijnmond.nl/nieuws/112683/Het-is-nu-of-nooit-voor-de-Hofbogen-in-Rotterdam-Noord (accessed 18 September 2015).

Rubin, V. (2008) "The Roots of the Urban Greening Movement." In E. Birch and S. Wachter (eds.), *Growing Greener Cities*. Philadelphia: University of Pennsylvania Press, 187–206.

Rybczynski, W. (2002) "The Bilbao Effect." *Atlantic Monthly* (September), 95.

Salmon, F. (2013) "Why Privately-Financed Public Parks Are a Bad Idea." http://blogs.reuters.com/felix-salmon/2013/11/21/why-privately-financed-public-parks-are-a-bad-idea (accessed 14 March 2015).

Sander-Regier, R. (2009) "Bare Roots: Exploring Botanical Agency in the Personal Garden." *TOPIA: Canadian Journal of Cultural Studies* 21: 63–84.

Sandilands, C. (2002) "Lesbian Separatist Communities and the Experience of Nature: Toward a Queer Ecology." *Organization & Environment* 15(2): 131–163.

———. (2005) "Unnatural Passions? Notes toward a Queer Ecology." *Invisible Culture* 9. http://www.invisibleculture.rochester.edu/in_visible_culture/Issue_9/issue9_sandilands.pdf (accessed 22 February 2013).

———. (2008) "Queering Ecocultural Studies." *Cultural Studies* 22(3–4): 455–476.

———. (2014) "Queer Life: Ecocriticsm after the Fire." In *Oxford Companion to Ecocriticism*. Oxford: Oxford University Press, 305–319.

Sandilands, C., and B. Erickson (2010) "A Genealogy of Queer Ecologies." In C. Sandilands and B. Erickson (eds.), *Queer Ecologies: Sex, Nature, Politics, Desire*. Bloomington: Indiana University Press, 1–47.

Sandström, S. F. (2002) "Green Infrastructure Planning in Urban Sweden." *Planning Practice and Research* 17(4): 373–385.

Sarfatti, M. (1993) *Behind the Postmodern Façade: Architectural Change in Late-Twentieth Century America*. Berkeley: University of California Press.

Sassen, S. (2010) "A Savage Sorting of Winners and Losers: Contemporary Versions of Primitive Accumulation." *Globalizations* 7(1–2): 23–50.

Saul, M., and M. West (2013) "De Blasio Parks Stance Unsettles Some." *Wall Street Journal*, 13 October.

Scammell, M. (2000) "The Internet and Civic Engagement: The Age of the Citizen-Consumer." *Political Communication* 17: 351–355.

Scheer, B. (2011) "Metropolitan Form and Landscape Urbanism." In T. Banerjee and A. Loukaitou-Sideris (eds.), *Companion to Urban Design*. London: Routledge, 611–618.

Schoenberger, E. (2004) "The Spatial Fix Revisited." *Antipode* 36(3): 427–433.

Schumpeter, J. ([1942] 1994) *Capitalism, Socialism, and Democracy*. New York: Routledge.

Schweber, N. (2012) "Outpouring of Support for Parents of 2 Boys Killed." *New York Times*, 29 July, A17.

Scobey, D. (1992) "Anatomy of the Promenade: The Politics of Bourgeois Sociability in Nineteenth-Century New York." *Social History* 17(2): 203–227.

Scruggs, G. (2015) "Brazil May Be Getting Its Own High Line." *Next City*, 16 January. http://nextcity.org/daily/entry/brazil-may-be-getting-its-own-high-line (accessed 16 May 2016).

Shah, B. (1997) "The Checkered Career of *Ailanthus altissima*." *Arnoldia* 3: 21–27.

Shepard, B. (2012) "Occupy Wall Street, Social Movements, and Contested Public Space." In R. Shiffman et al. (eds.), *Beyond Zuccotti Park: Freedom of Assembly and the Occupation of Public Space*. Oakland, CA: New Village Press, 21–33.

Shepard, B., and G. Smithsimon (2011) *The Beach beneath the Streets: Contesting New York City's Public Spaces*. Albany, NY: SUNY Press.

Sicha, C. (2003) "The Hanging Garden of Babble-On." *New York Observer*, 17 November. http://observer.com/2003/11/hanging-garden-of-babbleon (accessed 21 May 2016).

Sinha, A. (2007) "Introduction: The Revolution Will Not Be Funded." In *INCITE! Women of Color against Violence: The Revolution Will Not Be Funded*. Cambridge, MA: South End Press, 1–20.

———. (2013) "Slow Landscapes of Elevated Linear Parks: Bloomingdale Trail in Chicago." *Studies in the History of Gardens and Designed Landscapes* 34(2): 113–122.

Smith, N. (1992) "Contours of a Spatialized Politics: Homeless Vehicles and the Production of Geographical Scale." *Social Text* 33: 54–81.

———. (1996) *The New Urban Frontier: Gentrification and the Revanchist City*. New York: Routledge.

———. (2000) "Gentrification." In R. J. Johnston, D. Gregory, G. Pratt, and M. Watts (eds.), *The Dictionary of Human Geography*. Malden, MA: Blackwell, 294–296.

———. (2002) "New Globalism, New Urbanism: Gentrification as Global Urban Strategy." *Antipode* 34(3): 427–450.

Smith, P. (1988) *Discerning the Subject*. Minneapolis: University of Minnesota Press.

Smithsimon, G. (2008) "Dispersing the Crowd: Bonus Plazas and the Creation of Public Space." *Urban Affairs Review* 43(3): 325–351.

Sorkin, M. (1992) *Variations on a Theme Park: The New American City and the End of Public Space*. New York: Hill and Wang.

Soskis, B. (2013) "Parks and Accumulation," *New Yorker*, 21 November.

Squadron, D. (2013) "Can a Tree Grow in the Bronx?" *New York Times*, 24 May.

———. (2014) "Testimony to New York City Council Committee on Parks and Recreation: Equity in Parks." New York: Pratt Center, April 23.

Stallabrass, J. (1999) *High Art Lite: British Art in the 1990s*. Verso: London.

Stalter, S. (2006) "Farewell to the El: Nostalgic Urban Visuality on the Third Avenue Elevated Train." *American Quarterly* 58(2): 869–890.

Sternfeld, J. (2001) *Walking the High Line*. New York: Steidl/Pace/MacGill Gallery.

Stone, C. (1989) *Regime Politics: Governing Atlanta, 1946–1988*. Lawrence: University Press of Kansas.

Stryker, S. (2008) *Transgender History*. Berkeley, CA: Seal Press.

Subramanian, M. (2006) "Blasts from the Past." *New York Times*, 5 February. http://www.nytimes.com/2006/02/05/nyregion/thecity/05high.html/partner/rssnyt (accessed 7 June 2011).

Swyngedouw, E. (2009) "The Antinomies of the Postpolitical City: In Search of a Democratic Politics of Environmental Production." *International Journal of Urban and Regional Research* 33(3): 601–620.

Swyngedouw, E., and N. Heynen (2003) "Urban Political Ecology, Justice, and the Politics of Scale." *Antipode* 35(5): 898–918.

Takahashi, A. (2015) "A luta de 40 anos pela implantação do Parque Augusta." *CartaCapital*, 27 January. http://www.cartacapital.com.br/sociedade/a-luta-de-40-anos-pela-implantacao-do-parque-augusta-1521.html (accessed 24 April 2016).

Tamir, K. (2011) Interview by T. Baker, 16 June.

Tarr, J. (1984) "The Evolution of Urban Infrastructure in the 19th and 20th Centuries." In R. Hanson (ed.), *Perspectives on Urban Infrastructure*. Washington DC: National Academy Press, 4–66.

Tate, A. (2015) *Great City Parks*. 2nd ed. New York: Routledge.

Taylor, D. E. (1999) "Urban Parks, Social Class and Leisure Behavior in Nineteenth-Century America." *Journal of Leisure Research* 31(4): 420–477.

———. (2010) "Equity, Influence, and Access: Central Park's Role in Historical and Contemporary Urban Park Financing." *Research in Social Problems and Public Policy* 18: 29–73.

Taylor, K. (2014) "After High Line's Success, Other Cities Look Up." *New York Times*, 24 July. http://www.nytimes.com/2010/07/15/arts/design/15highline.html?_r=0.

Terry, T. (2014) "Presentation of the QueensWay's Preliminary Plans." Queens College, 20 March.

Thrift, N. (1999) "Steps to an Ecology of Place." In D. Massey, J. Allen, and P. Sarre (eds.), *Human Geography Today*. Cambridge: Polity Press, 295–321.

———. (2005a) "But Malice Aforethought: Cities and the Natural History of Hatred." *Transactions of the Institute of British Geographers* 30(2): 133–150.

———. (2005b) *Knowing Capitalism*. London: Sage.

———. (2008) *Non-Representational Theory: Space | Politics | Affect*. London: Routledge.

Trebay, G. (2008) "The High Line Steps Out for a Night." *New York Times*, 8 September. http://www.nytimes.com/2008/09/09/fashion/shows/09DIARY.html?_r=0 (accessed 21 May 2016).

Tzoulas, K., et al. (2007) "Promoting Ecosystem and Human Health in Urban Areas Using Green Infrastructure: A Literature Review." *Landscape and Urban Planning* 81(3): 167–178.

Ulam, A. (2013) "The Murky Ethics and Uncertain Longevity of Privately Financed Public Parks." http://www.citylab.com/politics/2013/05/murky-ethics-and-uncertain-longevity-privately-financed-public-parks/5563 (accessed 5 November 2014).

United States Department of Agriculture (2015) "Plants Database." http://plants.usda.gov/java.

Vance, S. (2014) "New Development, Investment Anticipates Future Bloomingdale Trail." *StreetsBlog Chicago*. http://chi.streetsblog.org/2014/11/17/new-development-investment-anticipating-future-bloomingdale-trail/ (accessed 10 December 2015).

Vargas, J. C. (2014) "Black Disidentification: The 2013 Protests, Rolezinhos, and Racial Antagonism in Post-Lula Brazil." *Critical Sociology* 42(4–5): 1–15.

Veblen, T. ([1899] 2007) *The Theory of the Leisure Class*. New York: Oxford University Press.

Vergara, C. J. (1999) *American Ruins*. New York: Monacelli Press.

Vidler, A. (1994) *The Architectural Uncanny: Essays in the Modern Unhomely*. Cambridge, MA: MIT Press.

Virilio, P. (2001) "Speed-Space." In J. Armitage (ed.), *Virilio Live: Selected Interviews*. London: Sage, 69–80.

Vitale, A. (2008) *City of Disorder: How the Quality of Life Campaign Transformed New York Politics*. New York: New York University Press.

Waldheim, C. (ed.) (2006) *The Landscape Urbanism Reader*. New York: Princeton Architectural Press.

Ward, K. (1996) "Rereading Urban Regime Theory: A Sympathetic Critique." *Geoforum* 27(4): 427–438.

———. (2011) "Policies in Motion and in Place." In E. McCann and K. Ward (eds.), *Mobile Urbanism: Cities and Policymaking in the Global Age*. Minneapolis: University of Minnesota Press, 71–95.

Warren, C. (2007) "Perspectives on the 'Alien' versus 'Native' Species Debate: A Critique of Concepts, Language, and Practice." *Progress in Human Geography* 31(4): 427–446.

Washburn, A. (2008) "Civic Virtue by Design: The Meaning behind Mayor Bloomberg's Vision for New York City." Unpublished manuscript in the possession of Scott Larson.

———. (2013) *The Nature of Urban Design: A New York Perspective on Resilience*. Washington, DC: Island Press/Center for Resource Economics.

———. (2014) "Oculus Book Talk: New York's New Edge: Contemporary Art, the High Line, and Urban Megaprojects on the Far West Side." New York: Center for Architecture.

Wells, W. D. (1975) "Psychographics: A Critical Review." *Journal of Marketing Research*, 196–213.

Wesselman, D. (2013) "The High Line, 'The Balloon,' and Heterotopia." *Space and Culture* 16(1): 16–27.

Whatmore, S. (2002) *Hybrid Geographies*. London: Sage.

While, A., A.E.G. Jonas, and D. Gibbs (2004) "The Environment and the Entrepreneurial City: Searching for the 'Urban Sustainability Fix' in Manchester and Leeds." *International Journal of Urban and Regional Research* 28(3): 549–569.

Whitt, A. J. (1987) "Mozart in the Metropolis: The Arts Coalition and the Growth Machine." *Urban Affairs Review* 23(1): 15–36.

Whittaker, J. S. (2014) "Maluf, o Minhocão e a Gentrificacao." *Cidades Para Que(m)*, 22 August. http://cidadesparaquem.org/blog/2014/8/22/maluf-o-minhoco-e-a-gentrificao (accessed 20 May 2016).

Whitworth, M. (2009) "The New Central Park." *Telegraph*, 16 July. http://blogs.telegraph.co.uk/news/melissawhitworth/100003585/the-new-central-park (accessed 27 April 2015).

Whyte, W. (1980) "The Social Life of Small Urban Spaces." Conservation Foundation. https://vimeo.com/111488563.

Wilson, A. (1991) *The Culture of Nature: North American Landscape from Disney to the Exxon Valdez*. Toronto: Between the Lines.

Wilson, D., and R. Keil (2008) "The Real Creative Class." *Social & Cultural Geography* 9(8): 841–847.

Wilson, J., and G. Kelling (1982) "Broken Windows: The Police and Neighborhood Safety." *Atlantic* (March).

Wilson, M. (2011) "The Park Is Elevated: Its Crime Is Anything But." *New York Times*, 10 June. http://www.nytimes.com/2011/06/11/nyregion/the-high-line-park-is-elevated-its-crime-rate-is-not.html (accessed 18 August 2011).

Winston, A. (2014) "The Highline Is a 'Pulling Back from Architecture' Say Diller and Scofidio." *Dezeen Magazine*, 3 November.

Wolch, J. R., J. Byrne, and J. P. Newell (2014) "Urban Green Space, Public Health, and Environmental Justice: The Challenge of Making Cities 'Just Green Enough.'" *Landscape and Urban Planning* 125: 234–244.

Wolch, J., J. P. Wilson, and J. Fehrenbach (2005) "Parks and Park Funding in Los Angeles: An Equity-Mapping Analysis." *Urban Geography* 26(1): 4–35.

Woodhaven Residents Block Association (2012) "Rockaway Branch Rail Line Forum." http://events.woodhaven-nyc.org/2012/09/rockaway-branch-rail-line-forum.html (accessed 28 January 2014).

Wright, M. W. (2004) "From Protests to Politics: Sex Work, Women's Worth, and Ciudad Juárez Modernity." *Annals of the Association of American Geographers* 94(2): 369–386.

Wylie, J. (2007) *Landscape*. New York: Routledge.

Zukin, S. (1982) "Loft Living as 'Historic Compromise' in the Urban Core: The New York Experience." *International Journal of Urban and Regional Research* 6(2): 256–267.

———. (1989) *Loft Living: Culture and Capital in Urban Change*. New Brunswick, NJ: Rutgers University Press.

———. (1991) *Landscapes of Power: From Detroit to Disney World*. Berkeley: University of California Press.

———. (1995) *The Cultures of Cities*. Cambridge, MA: Wiley-Blackwell.

———. (2008) "Consuming Authenticity: From Outposts of Difference to Means of Exclusion." *Cultural Studies* 22(5): 724–748.

———. (2010) *Naked City: The Death and Life of Authentic Urban Places*. Oxford: Oxford University Press.

———. (2011) Interview with T. Baker, 17 June.

NOTES ON CONTRIBUTORS

TOM BAKER grew up in South East London. He holds a degree in geography from the University of Cambridge and a master's in urban studies from University College London. He works as a journalist and broadcaster, with interests in politics, culture, and urban change.

PHIL BIRGE-LIBERMAN is assistant professor in residence in the Urban and Community Studies program at the University of Connecticut. An urban-historical geographer, his teaching focuses on urban history, urban redevelopment, and issues associated with park restoration and gentrification. His research examines the changing social practices of urban park use, the privatization of public space, and the relationship between urban re-greening, sustainability, and political economy.

JULIAN BRASH is associate professor of anthropology at Montclair State University. He is the author of *Bloomberg's New York: Class and Governance in the Luxury City* (2011), and his work has appeared in *Social Text, Urban Anthropology, Critique of Anthropology, Journal of Cultural Anthropology, Antipode, Anthropology Now, Urban Geography, City Limits, The Brooklyn Rail,* and several edited volumes. His current research on the political-economic, cultural, and aesthetic aspects of the High Line and other new urban public spaces has been funded by the National Science Foundation and the National Endowment for the Humanities.

JAMES CORNER is a registered landscape architect and urban designer, and founder and director of James Corner Field Operations, where he oversees the production of all design projects in the office. He was chair of the Department of Landscape Architecture at the University of Pennsylvania School of Design from 2000 to 2012 and is currently a professor in the department. His practice, research, and teaching interests focus on developing innovative approaches toward landscape architectural design and urbanism.

SCOTT LARSON is lecturer and co-director of the Office of Community Studies in the Urban Studies Department at Queens College, City University of New York. He studies and writes about urban geography and the historical evolution of the built environment, as well as issues of inequality, gentrification, and marginalization. He is the author of *Building like Moses with Jacobs in Mind: Contemporary Planning in New York City* (2013).

CHRISTOPH LINDNER is professor and dean of the School of Architecture and Allied Arts at the University of Oregon and honorary research professor in cultural analysis at the University of Amsterdam. His recent books include *Imagining New York City: Literature, Urbanism, and the Visual Arts, 1890–1940* (2015), as well as the edited volumes *Global Garbage: Urban Imaginaries of Waste, Excess, and Abandonment* (2016), *Cities Interrupted: Visual Culture and Urban Space* (2016), *Inert Cities: Globalization, Mobility, and Suspension in Visual Culture* (2014), and *Paris-Amsterdam Underground* (2013).

KEVIN LOUGHRAN is a PhD candidate in sociology at Northwestern University. His work on cities, culture, and political economy has appeared in *City & Community, Du Bois Review,* and the *Routledge International Handbook of Memory Studies.* His current research examines issues of urbanization, racialization, nature, and culture in a cross-regional study of the use of and access to urban parks in the post–World War II United States.

NATE MILLINGTON is a researcher and writer currently based at the University of Cape Town. He is interested in the politics of urban environments, public space, and landscape design. He spent nearly two years in São Paulo as a Fulbright scholar and researcher, where he conducted research on water governance and flood prevention in the urban periphery. His work has appeared in the *International Journal of Urban and Regional Research* and *Environment and Planning A.*

DARREN J. PATRICK is a researcher, activist, and writer based in Toronto and Bologna. Patrick has published on queer theory and politics, urbanization and urban theory, and environment and ecology. His work has appeared in *Social and Cultural Geography, UnderCurrents: Journal of Critical Environmental Studies,* and in the edited collections *Urban Forests, Trees, and*

Greenspace (2015), *Vegetal Politics: Belonging, Practices, and Places* (2016), and *Rethinking Life at the Margins* (2016).

BRIAN ROSA is assistant professor of urban studies (Queens College) and earth and geography (The Graduate Center) at the City University of New York. An urban planner and human geographer by training, Rosa's academic interests are at the intersection of the built environment, the political economy of urban redevelopment, critical urban theory, heritage and memory studies, and experimental qualitative methodologies. His current research deals with the relationship between urban infrastructures, deindustrializing cities, and the reappropriation of "wastelands" in postindustrial cities, as well as the contested politics and practices of urban heritage in the United States, United Kingdom, and Spain.

DANYA SHERMAN is an urban planner specializing in cultural program development, community engagement, education, and business strategy. She was the founding director of the Public Programs, Education, and Community Engagement Department at Friends of the High Line (New York City) where she conceived, produced, and expanded community engagement initiatives, cultural events, and educational programs that have become cornerstones of the organization. She has consulted and managed projects with ArtPlace America, the San Francisco Public Utilities Commission, PolicyLink, Project Row Houses (Houston), the MIT Community Innovators Lab, the CREATE program (Durban, South Africa), and the MIT Center for Real Estate. Sherman holds a bachelor of arts in science in society from Wesleyan University and a master's in city planning from MIT.

ALAN SMART is an architect, researcher, and critic with interests in performance and other "non-object" art practices in relation to urban space, as well as issues of production and reproduction in the city. He has studied architecture at the University of California at Berkeley and at Princeton University and has taught at Syracuse University, Ohio State University, Hong Kong University, and in the design department at the Sandberg Institute. He has also been a researcher at the Jan van Eyck Academie and has worked for architectural practices, including Diller Scofidio + Renfro. Smart currently practices independently and as part of the design collective Other Forms, working between architecture, graphic design, and publishing.

DAAN WESSELMAN is lecturer in literary studies at the University of Amsterdam. As a researcher affiliated with the Amsterdam School for Cultural Analysis, his focus is on finding common ground between the humanities and urban studies, writing about concepts such as heterotopia, nonplace, and the posthuman. In 2012, he received his PhD from Leiden University with a dissertation titled "Reflections of/on the City: Literature, Space, and Postmodernity."

INDEX

Page numbers in italics indicate illustrations; a t denotes a table.